AMERICAN HISTORY
BY AMERICAN POETS

AMERICAN HISTORY
BY AMERICAN POETS

EDITED BY

NELLIE URNER WALLINGTON

AUTHOR OF "HISTORIC CHURCHES OF AMERICA"

**

NEW YORK
DUFFIELD & COMPANY
1911

COPYRIGHT, 1911, BY

DUFFIELD & COMPANY

THE TROW PRESS, NEW YORK

ACKNOWLEDGMENT

The publishers and compilers take pleasure in acknowledging courteous permissions to include copyrighted poems herein, as follows: to Mrs. Florence Earle Coates, for "Buffalo"; to the late Mrs. Julia Ward Howe, for "The Battle Hymn of the Republic"; to Mrs. Kate B. Sherwood, for "Ulric Dahlgren"; to Miss Helen Gray Cone and Mr. Richard G. Badger, for "Greencastle Jenny"; to Miss Caroline Duer, for "An International Episode"; to Miss Florence Holbrooke, on behalf of her father, the late Edmund S. Holbrooke, for an excerpt from "The Mexican War"; to Miss Harriet Monroe, for excerpts from "The Columbian Ode"; to Miss E. Boyle O'Reilly, on behalf of her father, the late John Boyle O'Reilly, for "At Fredericksburg," "Chicago," and "Midnight"; to Mr. Christopher Bannister, for "David Glasgow Farragut"; to Mr. Joel Benton, for "Grover Cleveland"; to Mr. Robert Bridges and Messrs. Charles Scribner's Sons, for "At the Farragut Statue"; to Mr. Francis Fisher Browne, for "Vanquished"; to Major S. H. M. Byers, for "Sherman's March to the Sea"; to Mr. Madison Cawein, for "Ku-Klux" and "Mosby at Hamilton"; to Mr. Robert W. Chambers, for "The Gray Horse Troop"; to Mr. John Vance Cheney, for "Lincoln" and "San Francisco"; to Mr. Charles De Kay, for "The Draft Riot"; to Messrs. the Funk & Wagnalls Company, for the late Ernest Crosby's "Rebels," and for the late Richard Realf's "The Defence of Lawrence"; to Mr. Hamlin Garland, for "Logan at Peach Tree Creek" and "The Gold Seekers"; to Mr. Arthur Guiterman, for "The Call to the Colours"; to Harper's Magazine, for the late Thomas Dunn English's "The Battle of the King's Mill"; to Mr. William Hamilton Hayne, on behalf of his father, the late Paul Hamilton Hayne, and to Messrs. the Lothrop, Lee & Shepard Company, for "Butler's Proclamation," "Charleston," "The Battle of Charleston Harbour," "Vicksburg," and "Yorktown's Centennial Lyric," as well as for Mr. Hamilton Hayne's own "The Charge at Santiago"; to Mr.

6074

John Jarvis Holden, for "A Solemn Jubilee"; to Messrs. the Houghton Mifflin Company, for the late Edmund Clarence Stedman's "Hymn of the West" and "The Old Admiral"; to Mr. Walter Learned, for "The Last Reservation"; to Messrs. the J. B. Lippincott Company, for the late George Henry Boker's "Dirge for a Soldier," "Elisha Kent Kane," "The Bay-Fight," "The River-Fight," "The Camp of November," "The Eagle of Corinth," and "Sumter"; to Mr. Ernest McGaffey and Messrs. Dodd, Mead & Company, for "Geronimo" and "Little Big Horn"; to Mr. Oliver Marble, for "Four Centuries: Hudson and Fulton"; to Mr. Freeman Edwin Miller, for "Kansas"; to Mr. Joaquin Miller and Messrs. the Whitaker & Ray Company, for "Alaska," "The Defence of the Alamo," "Forty-Nine," and "In Yosemite Valley"; to Doctor S. Weir Mitchell, for "The Kearsarge"; to Mr. Wilbur D. Nesbit, for "The Man Lincoln"; to Mr. Courtlandt E. Palmer, on behalf of his late father, John Williamson Palmer, for "Stonewall Jackson's Way" and "The Fight at San Jacinto"; to Mr. William A. Phelan, for "Paul Jones"; to Mr. James Whitcomb Riley and Messrs. the Bobbs-Merrill Company, for "Emerson"; to Mr. Charles G. D. Roberts and Messsrs. L. C. Page & Company, for "A Ballad of Manila Bay"; to Mr. Edwin A. Robinson, for "Klondike"; to Mr. Charles E. Russell, for "Benjamin Harrison" and "Our Fleet at Santiago"; to Mr. Clinton Scollard, for "Ad Patriam," "The Ballad of Paco Town," "Colonel Liscum of the Ninth," "The Daughter of the Regiment," "The Deed of Lieutenant Miles," "Deeds of Valour at Santiago," "The Men of the Maine," "The Men of the Merrimac," "A Rhyme of the Rough Riders," "Riding with Kilpatrick," and "The Valour of Ben Milam"; to Mr. Frank L. Stanton, for "One Country"; to Mr. Will H. Thompson, and the Century Magazine, for "High Tide at Gettysburg"; to Mr. Culver Van Slycke, for "Doniphan's Men"; to the late Robert Burns Wilson, for "'Cut the Cables'!"; and to Mr. Clement V. Zane, for "Zest for Invasion."

AMERICAN HISTORY
BY AMERICAN POETS

A SOLEMN JUBILEE

HARK to the solemn notes of Jubilee
That ring to mark the birth of Liberty!

God lifts a gleaming altar in the hearts
Of godlike men through every age. 'T is there
The glory of His image he imparts
To light man toward the skies. For e'er
As the Shekinah vividly it glows,
Its various aspects three, its essence, one.
Some look and call it Love, the kindling rose
Of life; some see it as a flaming sword,
And name it Justice; and there still are those
To whom it blazes as a very sun
In noonday splendour and the enduring word
Of God Himself: Liberty. Yet man knows
There is no Justice without Love, nor Love
When Justice fails, nor Liberty above
In the azure save when Love and Justice hold
The heavens at her side with hands of gold.
These three are one, as God's Divinity
Is one, and they are in and of His law.
Gaze on them, then, in reverence, aye, in awe;
For by them God is bound—no tyrant He.

In this firm faith was our Republic founded
And through that faith has come our Jubilee.
Love, Liberty, and Justice! all unbounded
Stretches a future sacred to these three.
To Him who holds these attributes in scope
We offer thanks, and send our fervent prayer
That we may live and die therefor, our hope
Undimmed, still glowing in the ambient air.
Let us rejoice! and, joying, dedicate
Ourselves anew to service of the State!

So dawned our Jubilee. Ere day was done,
As if to sanctify it to all time,
Our mightiest, Adams and Jefferson,
Had passed away; and every merry chime
Was hushed, and the bells' deep and solemn tolling
From the two shrines where they had lived went rolling
Far to the outmost regions of the land
To which, just fifty years before, their lives,
Their fortunes, and their sacred honour had
So solemnly been pledged. To understand
As they have understood, their faith revives
In us anew, and leaves us chastened, glad
That they have lived, nor sorry that they died—
Since they must die—to mark this day of pride.

Adams! To him was given prescient vision
In days of storm and quick transition
To hold hard fast to Justice, Liberty,
And Love. To him was brought these precious gifts
Whereby the Nation's soul to Heaven uplifts
Itself; and at his feet the people laid
Their highest honours, generously repaid
By the bright ægis that this great man threw
Before the hemisphere of this New World.
Above two continents has he unfurled
The standard at which Europe stands afraid,
So powerful in the right, not might, are we.
Thus shall America for ever be
Confirmed in Justice, Love and Liberty.

Jefferson! From his pen has flowed the word
Of independence, and the nations heard
The solemn doctrine that is death to kings—
That government all its just power derives
Not from the skies but from the governed, thrives

Only in their consent; that all men are
Equal before the law, with equal right
To liberty, to life, and the pursuit
Of happiness. The doctrines that were moot
Before, he made self-evident, in sight
Of all. Give thanks for this, our guiding star!

Toll, bells! but ring out our thanksgiving, too,
For this our year of blesséd Jubilee!
Toll, bells! but let a hymn of gladness through
For these two lives that shall for ever be
A hope and inspiration unto every one
Who loves the Justice, Love, and Liberty
That spoke in Adams and in Jefferson!
                              —*John Jarvis Holden.*

"OLD IRONSIDES"

AYE, tear her tattered ensign down,
    Long has it waved on high,
And many an eye has danced to see
    That banner in the sky;
Beneath it rung the battle shout,
    And burst the cannon's roar;
The meteor of the ocean air
    Shall sweep the clouds no more!

Her deck, once red with heroes' blood,
    Where knelt the vanquished foe,
When winds were hurrying o'er the flood,
    And waves were white below,
No more shall feel the victor's tread,
    Or know the conquered knee;
The harpies of the shore shall pluck
    The eagle of the sea!

5

Oh, better that her shattered hulk
  Should sink beneath the wave;
Her thunders shook the mighty deep,
  And there should be her grave:
Nail to the mast her holy flag,
  Set every threadbare sail;
And give her to the god of storms,
  The lightning and the gale!

—Oliver Wendell Holmes.

LA FAYETTE

BORN, nurtured, wedded, prized, within the pale
  Of peers and princes, high in camp—at court—
  He hears, in joyous youth, a wild report,
Swelling the murmurs of the western gale,
Of a young people struggling to be free!
  Straight, quitting all, across the wave he flies,
  Aids with his sword, wealth, blood, the high emprize!
And shares the glory of its victory.

Then comes for fifty years a high romance
Of toils, reverses, sufferings, in the cause
  Of man and justice, liberty and France,
Crowned, at the last, with hope and wide applause.
Champion of Freedom! Well thy race was run!
All time shall hail thee, *Europe's noblest Son!*

—Dolly Madison.

THE VALOUR OF BEN MILAM

OH, *who will follow old Ben Milam into San Antonio?*
    Such was the thrilling word we heard in the chill
        December glow;
Such was the thrilling word we heard, and a ringing, an-
        swering cry

Went up from the dun adobé walls to the cloudless Texan
    sky.

He had won from the reek of a Mexique jail back without
    map or chart,
With his mother-wit and his hero-grit and his staunch Ken-
    tucky heart;
He had trudged by vale and by mountain trail, and by
    thorny and thirsty plain,
And now, with joy on his grizzled brow, he had come to his
    own again.

They 're the spawn of hell! we heard him tell; they will
    knife and lie and cheat;
At the board of none of the swarthy horde would I deign
    to sit at meat;
They hold it naught that I bled and fought when Spain was
    their ruthless foe;
Oh, who will follow old Ben Milam into San Antonio?

It was four to one, not gun for gun, but never a curse cared
    we,
Three hundred faithful and fearless men who had sworn to
    make Texas free.
It was mighty odds, by all the gods, this brood of the Mexi-
    que dam,
But it was not much for heroes such as followed old Ben
    Milam!

With rifle-crack and sabre-hack we drove them back in the
    street;
From house to house in the red carouse we hastened their
    flying feet;
And ever that shout kept pealing out with a swift and sure
    death-blow:
Oh, who will follow old Ben Milam into San Antonio?

Behind the walls from the hurtling balls Cos cowered and
    swore in his beard,
While we slashed and slew from dawn till dew, and, Bexar,
    how we cheered!
But ere failed each ruse, and the white truce on the failing
    day was thrown,
Our fearless soul had gone to the goal in the Land of the
    Great Unknown.

Death brought the darksome boon too soon to this truest
    one of the true,
Or, men of the fated Alamo, Milam had died with you!
So when their names that now are Fame's—the scorner of
    braggart Sham;—
In song be praised, let a rouse be raised for the name of
    Ben Milam!

—Clinton Scollard.

DEFENCE OF THE ALAMO

SANTA ANA came storming, as a storm might come;
    There was rumble of cannon; there was rattle of blade;
There was cavalry, infantry, bugle and drum,—
    Full seven thousand in pomp and parade,
The chivalry, flower of Mexico;
    And a gaunt two hundred in the Alamo.

And thirty lay sick, and some were shot through;
    For the siege had been bitter and bloody and long.
"Surrender, or die!"—"Men, what will you do?"
    And Travis, great Travis, drew sword, quick and strong;
Drew a line at his feet. "Will you come? Will you go?
    I die with my wounded, in the Alamo."

The Bowie gasped, "Lead me over that line!"
    Then Crockett, one hand on the sick, one hand on his gun,

8

Crossed with him; then never a word nor a sign,
  Till all, sick or well—all, all save but one,
One man. Then a woman stepped, praying, and slow
  Across; to die at her post in the Alamo.

Then that one coward fled, in the night, in that night
  When all men silently prayed and thought
Of home; of to-morrow; of God and the right,
  Till dawn: and with dawn came Travis's cannon-shot,
In answer to insolent Mexico,
From the old bell-tower of the Alamo.

Then came Santa Ana; a crescent of flame!
  Then the red escalade; then the fight hand to hand;
Such an unequal fight as never had name
  Since the Persian hordes butchered that doomed Spartan
      band.
All day—all day and all night, and the morning? so slow,
  Through the battle smoke mantling the Alamo.

Now silence! Such silence! Two thousand lay dead
  In a crescent outside! And within? Not a breath
Save the gasp of a woman, with gory gashed head,
  All alone, all alone there, waiting for death;
And she but a nurse. Yet when shall we know
  Another like this of the Alamo?

Shout "Victory, victory, victory ho!"
  I say 't is not always to the hosts that win!
I say that the victory, high or low,
  Is given the hero who grapples with sin,
Or legion or single; just asking to know,
  When duty fronts death in his Alamo.
                              —*Joaquin Miller.*

9

THE FIGHT AT SAN JACINTO

"NOW for a brisk and cheerful fight!"
    Said Harman, big and droll,
As he coaxed his flint and steel for a light,
    And puffed at his cold clay bowl;
"For we are a skulking lot," says he,
    "Of land-thieves hereabout,
And the bold señoras, two to one,
    Have come to smoke us out."

Santa Ana and Castrillon,
    Almontê brave and gay,
Portilla red from Goliad,
    And Cos with his smart array.
Dulces and cigaritos,
    And the light guitar, ting-tum!
Sant' Ana courts siesta—
    And Sam Houston taps his drum.

The buck stands still in the timber—
    "Is 't patter of nuts that fall?"
The foal of the wild mare whinnies—
    "Did he hear the Comanche call?"
In the brake by the crawling bayou
    The slinking she-wolves howl,
And the mustang's snort in the river sedge
    Has startled the paddling fowl.

A soft low tap, and a muffled tap,
    And a roll not loud nor long—
We would not break Sant' Ana's nap,
    Nor spoil Almontê's song.
Saddles and knives and rifles!
    Lord! but the men were glad
When Deaf Smith muttered "Alamo!"
    And Karnes hissed "Goliad!"

The drummer tucked his sticks in his belt,
  And the fifer gripped his gun.
Oh, for one free, wild Texan yell,
  And we took the slope in a run!
But never a shout nor a shot we spent,
  Nor an oath nor a prayer that day,
Till we faced the bravos, eye to eye,
  And then we blazed away.

Then we knew the rapture of Ben Milam,
  And the glory that Travis made,
With Bowie's lunge and Crockett's shot,
  And Fannin's dancing blade;
And the heart of the fighter, bounding free
  In his joy so hot and mad—
When Millard charged for Alamo,
  Lamar for Goliad.

Deaf Smith rode straight, with reeking spur,
  Into the shock and rout:
"I've hacked and burned the bayou bridge,
  There's no sneak's back-way out!"
Muzzle or butt for Goliad,
  Pistol and blade and fist!
Oh, for the knife that never glanced,
  And the gun that never missed!

Dulces and cigaritos,
  Song and the mandolin!
That gory swamp was a gruesome grove
  To dance fandangos in.
We bridged the bog with the sprawling herd
  That fell in that frantic rout;
We slew and slew till the sun set red,
  And the Texan star flashed out.

—John Williamson Palmer.

SONG OF TEXAS

MAKE room on our banner bright
　　That flaps in the lifting gale,
For the orb that lit the fight
　　In Jacinto's storied vale.
Through clouds, all dark of hue,
　　It arose with radiant face;
Oh, grant to a sister true,
　　Ye stars, in your train a place!

The blood of the Saxon flows
　　In the veins of the men who cry,—
"Give ear, give ear unto those
　　Who pine for their native sky!
We call on our Motherland
　　For a home in Freedom's hall,—
While stretching forth the hand,
　　Oh, build no dividing wall!

"The Mexican vaunteth no more;
　　In strife we have tamed his pride;
The coward raps not at your door,
　　Speak out! shall it open wide?
Oh, the wish of our hearts is strong,
　　That the star of Jacinto's fight
Have place in the flashing throng
　　That spangle your banner bright."
　　　　　　　—*William Henry Cuyler Hosmer.*

CONCORD HYMN

BY the rude bridge that arched the flood,
　　Their flag to April's breeze unfurled,
Here once the embattled farmers stood,
　　And fired the shot heard round the world.

The foe long since in silence slept;
  Alike the conqueror silent sleeps;
And Time the ruined bridge has swept
  Down the dark stream which seaward creeps.

On this green bank, by this soft stream,
  We set to-day a votive stone;
That memory may their deed redeem,
  When, like our sires, our sons are gone.

Spirit that made those heroes dare
  To die, and leave their children free,
Bid Time and Nature gently spare
  The shaft we raise to them and thee.
                    —*Ralph Waldo Emerson.*

DEATH OF HARRISON

WHAT! soared the old eagle to die at the sun!
  Lies he stiff with spread wings at the goal he had won!
Are there spirits more blest than the "Planet of Even,"
Who mount to their zenith, then melt into Heaven—
No waning of fire, no quenching of ray,
But rising, still rising, when passing away?
Farewell, gallant eagle! thou'rt buried in light!
God-speed into Heaven, lost star of our night!

Death! Death in the White House! Ah, never before,
Trod his skeleton foot on the President's floor!
He is looked for in hovel, and dreaded in hall—
The king in his closet keeps hatchment and pall—
The youth in his birthplace, the old man at home,
Make clean from the door-stone the path to the tomb;—

13

But the lord of this mansion was cradled not here—
In a churchyard far off stands his beckoning bier!
He is here as the wave-crest heaves flashing on high—
As the arrow is stopped by its prize in the sky—
The arrow to earth, and the foam to the shore—
Death finds them when swiftness and sparkle are o'er—
But Harrison's death fills the climax of story—
He went with his old stride—from glory to glory!

Lay his sword on his breast! There 's no spot on its blade
In whose cankering breath his bright laurels will fade!
'T was the first to lead on at humanity's call—
It was stayed with sweet mercy when " glory " was all!
As calm in the council as gallant in war,
He fought for its country and not its " hurrah!"
In the path of the hero with pity he trod—
Let him pass—with his sword—to the presence of God!

What more? Shall we on with his ashes? Yet, stay!
He hath ruled the wide realm of a king in his day!
At his word, like a monarch's, went treasure and land—
The bright gold of thousands has pass'd through his hand.
Is there nothing to show of his glittering hoard?
No jewel to deck the rude hilt of his sword—
No trappings—no horses?—what had he, but now?
On!—on with his ashes!—HE LEFT BUT HIS PLOUGH!

Follow now, as ye list! The first mourner to-day
Is the nation—whose father is taken away!
Wife, children, and neighbour, may moan on his knell—
He was " lover and friend " to his country, as well!
For the stars on our banner, grown suddenly dim,
Let us weep, in our darkness—but weep not for him!
Not for him—who, departing, leaves millions in tears!

14

Not for him—who has died full of honour and years!
Not for him—who ascended Fame's ladder so high
From the round at the top he has stepped to the sky!
                                —*Nathaniel Parker Willis.*

TO MASSACHUSETTS

WHAT though around thee blazes
    No fiery rallying sign?
From all thy own high places,
    Give heaven the light of thine!
What though unthrilled, unmoving,
    The statemen stand apart,
And comes no warm approving
    From Mammon's crowded mart?

Still let the land be shaken
    By a summons of thine own!
By all save truth forsaken,
    Stand fast with that alone!
Shrink not from strife unequal!
    With the best is always hope;
And ever in the sequel
    God holds the right side up!

But when, with thine uniting,
    Come voices long and loud,
And far-off hills are writing
    Thy fire-words on the cloud;
When from Penobscot's fountains
    A deep response is heard,
And across the Western mountains
    Rolls back thy rallying word;

Shall thy line of battle falter,
    With its allies just in view?

Oh, by hearth and holy altar,
　My fatherland, be true!
Fling abroad thy scrolls of Freedom!
　Speed them onward far and fast!
Over hill and valley speed them,
　Like the sibyl's on the blast!

Lo! the Empire State is shaking,
　The shackles from her hands;
With the rugged North is waking
　The level sunset land!
On they come, the free battalions!
　East and West and North they come,
And the heart-beat of the millions
　Is the beat of Freedom's drum.

"To the tyrant's plot no favour!
　No heed to place-fed knaves!
Bar and bolt the door forever
　Against the land of slaves!"
Hear it, mother Earth, and hear it
　The heavens above us spread!
The land is roused,—its spirit
　Was sleeping, but not dead!
　　　　　　—*John Greenleaf Whittier.*

THE GUNS IN THE GRASS

A S hang two mighty thunderclouds
　　Ere lightnings link the twain,
So lie we and the Mexican
　On Palo Alto plain;
And silence, solemn, dread, profound,
Broods o'er the waiting battle-ground.

16

We see the foeman's musketeers
    Deployed upon his right,
And on his left the cavalry
    Stand, hungry for the fight;
But that blank centre—what?   Alas,
'T is hidden by the prairie grass!

Old Rough and Ready scans the foe;
    "I would I knew," says he,
"Whether or no that lofty grass
    Conceals artillery.
Could I but bring that spot in ken,
'T were worth to me five thousand men!"

Then forward steps Lieutenant Blake,
    Touches his hat, and says,
"I wait command to ride and see
    What 'neath that prairie lays."
We stand amazed: no cowards, we:
But this is more than bravery!

"'Command'!" cries Taylor; "nay, I ne'er
    To such a deed 'command'!"
Then bends he o'er his horse's neck
    And takes as brave a hand
As e'er a loyal sabre bore:
"God bless you, Blake!" he says—no more.

The soldier to his saddle springs
    And gayly waves good bye,
Determination on his lips,
    A proud light in his eye:
And then, as pity holds our breath,
We see him dare that road of death.

To utmost pace his steed he spurs.
  Save that his sword hangs free,
It were as though a madman charged
  A nation's chivalry!
On, on, he flies, his steed unreined
Till yonder hillock's crest is gained.

And now he checks his horse, dismounts,
  And coolly through his glass
Surveys the phalanx of his foe
  That lies beyond the grass.
A musket-flash! They move! Advance!
Halt—'t was the sunlight on a lance!

He turns, remounts, and speeds him back.
  Hark! what is that we hear?
Across the rolling prairie rings—
  A gun? Ah, no—a cheer!
A noble tribute sweeps the plain;
A thousand throats take up the strain.

Safe! But the secret to unveil
  Taylor no longer seeks;
For with a roar that shakes the earth
  That unmasked centre speaks!
'Gainst fearful odds, till set of sun,
We battle—and the field is won!

—*Thomas Frost.*

MONTEREY

WE were not many—we who stood
    Before the iron sleet that day;
Yet many a gallant spirit would
Give half his years if but he could
  Have been with us at Monterey.

Now here, now there, the shot it hailed
    In deadly drifts of fiery spray,
Yet not a single soldier quailed
When wounded comrades round them wailed
    Their dying shout at Monterey.

And on—still on our column kept,
    Through walls of flame, its withering way;
Where fell the dead, the living stepped
Still charging on the guns which swept
    The slippery streets of Monterey.

The foe himself recoiled aghast
    When, striking where he strongest lay,
We swooped his flanking batteries past,
And braving full their murderous blast,
    Stormed home the towers of Monterey.

Our banners on those turrets wave,
    And there our evening bugles play:
Where orange-boughs above their grave
Keep green the memory of the brave
    Who fought and fell at Monterey.

We are not many—we who pressed
    Beside the brave who fell that day;
But who of us has not confessed
He'd rather share their warrior rest
    Than not have been at Monterey.
                    —*Charles Fenno Hoffman.*

BUENA VISTA

FROM the Rio Grande's waters to the icy lakes of
    Maine,
Let all exult! for we have met the enemy again;

Beneath their stern old mountains we have met them in their
      pride,
And rolled from Buena Vista back the battle's bloody tide;
Where the enemy came surging swift, like the Mississippi's
      flood,
And the reaper, Death, with strong arms swung his sickle
      red with blood.

Santa Ana boasted loudly that, before two hours were past,
His Lancers through Saltillo should pursue us fierce and
      fast:—
On comes his solid infantry, line marching after line;
Lo! their great standards in the sun like sheets of silver
      shine:
With thousands upon thousands,—yea, with more than three
      to one,—
Their forests of bright bayonets fierce-flashing in the sun.

Lo! Guanajuato's regiment; Morelos' boasted corps,
And Guadalajara's chosen troops!—all veterans tried be-
      fore.
Lo! galloping upon the right four thousand lances gleam,
Where, floating in the morning wind, their blood-red pen-
      nons stream;
And here his stern artillery climbs up the broad plateau:
To-day he means to strike at us an overwhelming blow.

Now, Wool, hold strongly to the heights! for lo! the mighty
      tide
Comes, thundering like an avalanche, deep, terrible, and
      wide.
Now, Illinois, stand steady! Now, Kentucky, to their aid!
For a portion of our line, alas! is broken and dismayed:
Great bands of shameless fugitives are fleeing from the field,
And the day is lost, if Illinois and brave Kentucky yield.

One of O'Brien's guns is gone!—On, on their masses drift,
Till their cavalry and infantry outflank us on the left;
Our light troops, driven from the hills, retreat in wild dis-
  may
And round us gather, thick and dark, the Mexican array.
Santa Ana thinks the day is gained; for now, approaching
  near,
Miñon's dark cloud of Lancers sternly menaces our rear.

Now, Lincoln, gallant gentleman, lies dead upon the field,
Who strove to stay those cravens, when before the storm
  they reeled.
Fire, Washington, fire fast and true! Fire, Sherman, fast
  and far!
Lo! Bragg comes thundering to the front, to breast the ad-
  verse war!
Santa Ana thinks the day is gained! On, on, his masses
  crowd,
And the roar of battle swells again more terrible and loud.

Not yet! our brave old General comes to regain the day;
Kentucky, to the rescue. Mississippi, to the fray!
Again our line advances! Gallant Davis fronts the foe,
And back before his rifles, in red waves, the Lancers flow.
Upon them yet once more, ye braves! The avalanche is
  stayed!
Back roll the Aztec multitudes, all broken and dismayed.

Ride, May!—To Buena Vista! for the Lancers gain our
  rear,
And we have few troops there to check their vehement
  career.
Charge, Arkansas! Kentucky, charge! Yell, Porter,
  Vaughan, are slain,
But the shattered troops cling desperately unto the crimsoned
  plain;

Till, with the Lancers intermixed, pursuing and pursued,
Westward, in combat hot and close, drifts off the multitude.

And May comes charging from the hills with his ranks of
    flaming steel,
While, shattered with a sudden fire, the foe already reel;
They flee amain!—Now to the left, to stay the torrent
    there,
Or else the day is surely lost, in horror and despair!
For their hosts pour swiftly onward, like a river in the
    spring,
Our flank is turned, and on our left their cannon thundering.

Now, good Artillery! bold Dragoons! Steady, brave hearts,
    be calm!
Through rain, cold hail, and thunder, now nerve each
    gallant arm!
What though their shot fall round us here, yet thicker than
    the hail?
We 'll stand against them, as the rock stands firm against
    the gale.
Lo! their battery is silenced! but our iron sleet still showers:
They falter, halt, retreat!—Hurrah! the glorious day is
    ours!

In front, too, has the fight gone well, where upon gallant
    Lane,
And on stout Mississippi, the thick Lancers charged in
    vain:
Ah! brave Third Indiana! you have nobly wiped away
The reproach that through another corps befell your State
    to-day;
For back, all broken and dismayed, before your storm of fire,
Santa Ana's boasted chivalry, a shattered wreck, retire.

Now charge again, Santa Ana! or the day is surely lost,—
For back, like broken waves, along our left your hordes
    are tossed.
Still faster roar his batteries,—his whole reserve moves on;
More work remains for us to do, ere the good fight is won.
Now for your wives and children, men! Stand steady yet
    once more!
Fight for your lives and honours! Fight as you never fought
    before!

Ho! Hardin breasts it bravely! and heroic Bissell there
Stands firm before the storm of balls that fill the astonished
    air:
The Lancers dash upon them, too! The foe swarm ten
    to one:
Hardin is slain; McKee and Clay the last time see the sun;
And many another gallant heart, in that last desperate fray,
Grew cold, its last thought turning to its loved ones far
    away.

Speed, speed, Artillery! to the front! for the hurricane of
    fire
Crushes those noble regiments, reluctant to retire!
Speed swiftly! Gallop! Ah, they come! Again Bragg
    climbs the ridge,
And his grape sweeps down the swarming foe, as a strong
    man moweth sedge;
Thus baffled in their last attack, compelled perforce to yield,
Still menacing in firm array, their columns leave the field.

The guns still roared at intervals; but silence fell at last,
And on the dead and dying came the evening shadows fast.
And then above the mountains rose the cold moon's silver
    shield,
And patiently and pityingly she looked upon the field.

While careless of his wounded, and neglectful of his dead,
Despairingly and sullenly by night Santa Ana fled.

And thus on Buena Vista's heights a long day's work was
    done
And thus our brave old general another battle won.
Still, still our glorious banner waves, unstained by flight
    or shame,
And the Mexicans among the hills still tremble at our name.
So honour unto those that stood! Disgrace to those that fled!
And everlasting glory unto Buena Vista's dead!

                                        —*Albert Pike.*

DONIPHAN'S MEN

O'ER the bitter and beautiful desert, in the dust and heat
    and haze,
Through mornings of ruby and topaz and evenings of chry-
    soprase,
The golden noon of a pitiless June, and the heat of a fierce
    July,
We tramped and limped till the August flame lit up the merci-
    less sky,
All the thirsty way to Santa Fé, and there, without a blow,
We take in a day to keep for ay the land of New Mexico.

It is the Army of the West goes forth to glorious war:
Kearny for California; and a thousand men and more
Of Missouri's best are on the quest, bold mounted volun-
    teers
Who can shoot and ride with a proper pride in the blood
    of pioneers,
With Alexander Doniphan to lead us against the foe:
He is ordered to Chihuahua, and to Chihuahua he shall go.

October's high in the glaring sky when Doniphan sets forth
To carry south to old Mexico the standard of the North.
We taste the breath of the Journey of Death, and come on
    Christmas Day
To Brazito on the Norte in our ragged, neglected way;
For we never drew one cent or two, an accoutrement, or
    store
From the day we left Missouri till the fighting all was o'er.

With booming drums De Leon comes, and his thirteen hun-
    dred braves,
"No Quarter" on the battle-flag that black above them
    waves;
His bugles sound, and o'er the ground the Dragoons from
    Vera Cruz
Come thundering down in their renown, and a pretty fight
    ensues;
But in half an hour we 've proved our power, and their
    wounded and their dead
Are all the Mexicans in sight, so quickly have they fled.

Eight months and a thousand miles from home, foemen be-
    hind and before,
And February's final day sees us at Chihuahua's door.
There, safe and sound on their own ground, in the Sacra-
    mento fort
The Mexicans wait, our bull to bait, and have their bit
    of sport.
Across the pass their cannon they mass in fortifications
    tall
To guard Chihuahua from our might with bayonet and ball.

"Surrender, or we charge!" they cried, sure of easy vic-
    tory.

But Doniphan laughed at their confident craft: "Charge and
    be damned!" said he.
So on they came in a wall of flame; and if they were not
    damned
Three hours of hell they have to tell, with death and fury
    crammed.
They were bound for Buena Vista, General Taylor to beset;
But for all that Santa Ana 'll see they 're going the wrong
    way yet.

A ragged band of scouts were we; but Doniphan gave the
    word,
And our horse and foot with a yell and a hoot over their
    breastworks poured;
Our cannon dashed and their thunder crashed, and at fifty
    yards, aghast,
They hurled their ire in murderous fire, a withering, billow-
    ing blast.
We swept their host like an idle boast away from their bold
    redoubts,
And the Greasers went with a shriek hell-bent from our
    ragged band of scouts.

In all the books that ever were writ there never was such
    charge
As old Missouri made that day our histories to enlarge:
Horse, foot, and gun, four to our one, sword, grape, and
    bayonet,
A thousand against four thousand in firm entrenchments set:
But we blew them and we slew them, and when the morning
    came
We marched into Chihuahua as the prize of our desperate
    game.

This is the tale of Doniphan and the men Missouri sent,
This the little story of a great accomplishment.

Ready to feel the Mexican steel, they laughed their foe to
    scorn,
With his pirate flag and his Spanish brag, and left his hope
    forlorn;
So when you indite your histories and need to name a man
Who won his odds from the battle gods, remember
    DONIPHAN.

                  —Culver Van Slycke.

BATTLE OF THE KING'S MILL

SAID my landlord, white-headed Gil Gomez,
    With newspaper held in his hand—
"So they 've built from El Paso a railway
    That Yankees may visit our land.
As guests let them come and be welcome,
    But not as they came here before;
They are rather rough fellows to handle
    In the rush of the battle and roar.

"They took Vera Cruz and its castle;
    In triumph they marched through the land;
We fought them with desperate daring,
    But lacked the right man to command.
They stormed, at a loss, Cerro Gordo—
    Every mile in their movement it cost;
And when they arrived at Puebla,
    Some thousands of men they had lost.

"Ere our capital fell, and the city
    By foreign invaders was won,
We called out among its defenders
    Each man who could handle a gun.
Chapultepec stood in their pathway;
    Churubusco they had to attack;
The mill of the King—well, I fought there,
    And they were a hard nut to crack.

"While their right was assailing the ramparts,
  Our force struck their left on the field,
Where our colonel, in language that stirred us,
  To love of our country appealed.
And we swore that we never would falter
  Before either sabre or ball;
We would beat back the foeman before us,
  Or dead on the battle-field fall.

"Fine words, you may say, but we meant them;
  And so when they came up the hill,
We poured on them volley on volley,
  And riddled their ranks with a will.
Their line in a moment was broken;
  They closed it, and came with a cheer;
But still we fired quickly and deadly,
  And felt neither pity nor fear.

"We smote the blue column with grape-shot,
  But it rushed as the wild torrent runs;
At the pieces they slew our best gunners,
  And took in the struggle our guns.
We sprang in a rage to retake them,
  And lost nearly half of our men;
Then, baffled and beaten, retreated,
  And gained our position again.

"Ceased their yell, and in spite of our firing
  They dressed like an arrow in line,
Then, standing there moveless a moment,
  Their eyes flashed with purpose malign,
All still as the twilight in summer,
  No cloud on the sky to deform,
Like the lull in the voices of nature
  Ere wakens the whirlwind and storm.

"We had fought them with death-daring spirit,
   And courage unyielding till then;
No man could have forced us to falter,
   But these were more demons than men.
Our ranks had been torn by their bullets,
   We filled all the gaps they had made;
But the pall of that terrible silence
   The hearts of our boldest dismayed.

"Before us no roaring of cannon,
   Rifle-rattle, or musketry peal;
But there on the ocean of battle
   Surged steady the billow of steel.
Fierce we opened our fire on the column,
   We pierced it with ball here and there;
But it swept on in pitiless sternness
   Till we faltered and fled in despair.

"After that all their movements were easy;
   At their storming Chapultepec fell,
And that ended the war—we were beaten:
   No story is left me to tell.
And now they come back to invade us,
   Though not with the bullet and blade;
They are here with their goods on a railway,
   To conquer the country by trade."
                              —*Thomas Dunn English.*

THE SIEGE OF CHAPULTEPEC

WIDE o'er the valley the pennons are fluttering,
   War's sullen story the deep guns are muttering,
Forward! blue-jackets, in good steady order,
Strike for the fame of your good northern border;
Forever shall history tell of the bloody check
Waiting the foe at the siege of Chapultepec.

Let the proud deeds of your fathers inspire ye still,
Think ye of Monmouth, and Princeton, and Bunker Hill,
Come from your hallowed graves, famous in story,
Shades of our heroes and lead us to glory.
Side by side, son and father with hoary head
Struggle for triumph, or death on a gory bed.

Hark! to the charge! the war-hail is pattering,
The foe through our ranks red rain is scattering;
Huzza! forward! no halting or flagging till
Proudly the red stripes float o'er yon rocky hill.
Northern and Southerner, let your feuds smoulder
Charge! for our banner's fame, shoulder to shoulder!

Flash the fort guns, and thunders their stunning swell
Far o'er the valley to white Popocatapetl.
Death revels high in the midst of the bloody sport,
Bursting in flame from each black-throated castle-port.
Press on the line with keen sabres dripping wet,
Cheer, as ye smite with the death-dealing bayonet!

Our bold Northern eagle, king of the firmament,
Shares with no rival the skies of the continent.
Yields the fierce foeman! down let his flag be hurled
Shout, as our own from the turret is wide unfurled!
Shout! for long shall Mexico mourn the wreck
Of her proud state at the siege of Chapultepec.

—William Haines Lytle.

ILLUMINATION FOR VICTORIES IN MEXICO

LIGHT up your homes, Columbia,
    For those chivalric men
Who bear to scenes of warlike strife
    Thy conquering arms again.

Where glorious victories, flash on flash,
   Reveal their stormy way,—
Resaca's, Palo Alto's fields,
   The heights of Monterey!

They pile with thousands of thy foes,
   Buena Vista's plain;
With maids and wives, at Vera Cruz,
   Swell high the list of slain!
They paint upon the Southern skies
   The blaze of burning domes,—
Their laurels drew with blood of babes!
   Light up, light up, thy homes!

Light up your homes, O fathers!
   For these young hero bands,
Whose march is still through vanquished towns,
   And over conquered lands!
Whose valour, wild, impetuous,
   In all its fiery glow,
Pours onward, like a lava-tide,
   And sweeps away the foe!

For those whose dead brows glory crowns,
   On crimson couches sleeping,
And for home faces wan with grief,
   And fond eyes dim with weeping,
And for the soldier, poor, unknown,
   Who battled, madly brave,
Beneath a stranger soil to share,
   A shallow, unmarked grave.

Light up your home, young mother!
   Then gaze in pride and joy
Upon those fair and gentle girls,
   That eagle-eyed young boy;

And clasp thy darling little one
    Yet closer to thy breast,
And be thy kisses on its lips
    In yearning love impressed.

In yon beleaguered city
    Were homes as sweet as thine;
Where trembling mothers felt loved arms
    In fear about them twine,—
The lad with brow of olive hue,
    The babe like lily fair,
The maiden with her midnight eyes,
    And wealth of raven hair.

The booming shot, the murderous shell,
    Crashed through the crumbling walls,
And filled with agony and death
    Those sacred household halls!
Then, bleeding, crushed, and blackened, lay
    The sister by the brother,
And the torn infant gasped and writhed
    On the bosom of the mother!

O sisters, if ye have no tears
    For fearful tales like these,
If the banners of the victors veil
    The victim's agonies,
If ye lose the babe's and mother's cry
    In the noisy roll of drums,
If your hearts with martial pride throb high,
    Light up, light up your homes.

                    —*Grace Greenwood.*

THE VOLUNTEERS

THE Volunteers! the Volunteers!
    I dream, as in the by-gone years,
I hear again their stirring cheers,
        And see their banners shine,
What time the yet unconquered North
Pours to the wars her legions forth,
For many a wrong to strike a blow
With mailed hand at Mexico.

The Volunteers! Ah, where are they
Who bade the hostile surges stay
When the black forts of Monterey
        Frowned on their dauntless line?
When, undismayed amid the shock
Of war, like Cerro Gordo's rock,
They stood, or rushed more madly on
Than tropic tempest o'er San Juan.

On Angostura's crowded field
Their shattered columns scorned to yield,
And wildly yet defiance pealed
        Their flashing batteries' throats;
And echoed then the rifle's crack,
As deadly as when on the track
Of flying foe, of yore, its voice
Bade Orleans' dark-eyed girls rejoice.

Blent with the roar of guns and bombs,
How grandly from the dim past comes
The roll of their victorious drums,
        Their bugles' joyous notes,
When over Mexico's proud towers,
And the fair valley's storied bowers,

Fit recompense of toil and scars,
In triumph waved their flag of stars.

Ah, comrades of your own tried troop,
Whose honour ne'er to shame might stoop,
Of lion heart and eagle swoop,
    But you alone remain;
On all the rest has fallen the hush
Of death; the men whose battle-rush
Was wild as sun-loosed torrent's flow
On Orizaba's crest of snow.

The Volunteers! the Volunteers!
God send us peace through all our years,
But if the cloud of war appears,
    We 'll see them once again.
From broad Ohio's peaceful side,
From where the Maumee pours its tide,
From storm-lashed Erie's wintry shore,
Shall spring the Volunteers once more.
                    —*William Haines Lytle.*

FROM "THE MEXICAN WAR"

'T WAS first at Palo Alto the Invader's guns were heard;
    How quick and deep and strong within the Nation's
    heart was stirred.
The call rings out through all the land: "Send forth the
    volunteers!"
The thousands rally everywhere with shouts and songs and
    cheers.
A victory fans the rising flame; what though a Ringgold
    falls,
The shining path of Glory leads to Montezuma's halls,
We leave the party forum where our words run high and
    strong;

This patriot thought our union seals: "Our country, right
  or wrong."

Our sad "Farewells" are spoken, and the columns march
  away;—
Anon the sound of clashing arms is heard at Monterey;
Sweet, beautiful, and fair she sits amidst the peaceful hills,
Yet now dread War's shrill clarion her heart with terror
  thrills.
Would that some better Arbiter might vanquish civil strife,
Than swords and slaughtering engines for the waste of
  human life:
How strange that man, with fierce revenge and thoughts of
  death, awaits
The Beauty of the mountains and the loved within her gates!

The Vale of Angostura, with her serried mountain walls,—
How heavy on her trembling hills the shock of battle falls!
Sant' Ana, with her well-trained hosts, the nation's strength
  and pride,
Will surely crush our little band, in skill of arms untried.
We know th' unequal contest, but we will not, cannot fly;
We throw our souls into the fight, and resolve to wine or die;
We think of Home and Country; we "Remember Washing-
  ton";
The field is ours, and Victory by the morrow's setting sun.

San Juan d'Uloa and Vera Cruz, sweet smiling o'er the sea,

In blind security of place, read not Fate's harsh decree.
Our grand Flotilla warns them, as it marches o'er the wave,
I vain they 'll trust their native strength, or warrior's skill
    to save.
To soldier's eye, surpassing grand, and beautiful the sight,
Those streaming meteors of death, each day and through the
    night!
Earth trembles, and the Ocean foams at War's destructive
    powers;
Our flags, unfurling o'er the walls, proclaim that they are
    ours.

At Cerro Gordo next the foe essayed to make defense,
Appealing first to Nature's aid,—her grand Omnipotence,—
To mountain, hill, and rock, and stream, and these by labour
    crowned
With cannon, mortar, bayonet, lance, till every feature
    frowned.
Yet, fearful as the fortress flames, we rush into the fire!
The combat rages fiercer yet, our steps ascend yet higher!
At last we reach the central tower, it falls, our flag ascends;
Our foes address themselves to flight, and Fear her pinion
    lends.

Our course is now straight onward, to the city and the vale,
The Home-land of the Aztecs, where sweet airs and flowers
    regale:
But see Contreras, as we march, that rises to our view,
And Churubusco, full of strength, and San Antonio, too.

Again our cannons shake the hills, th' assault and charge
again!
The breaking hosts before us flee and scatter o'er the plain!
Old Harney's cavalry, let loose, pursues them as they fly!—
At eve, we celebrate at once a threefold victory. . . .
Chapultepec, the sentry of the city at her feet,
How grand and fixed in sweet repose, in armour how com-
plete!
Our last great work shall be our best, to lay her wondrous
power,
And float "the Red, the White, the Blue" above her highest
tower.
To say it, was the act itself—the scalers volunteer!
The cannons roar, the troops ascend yet nearer and more
near!
A conflict hand-to-hand ensues, the stormers mount the
walls!—
A moment more of life and death—the grand old fortress
falls!

Our standard crowns the Capitol,—a Nation prostrate lies;
The music aids our swelling pride, but not for sacrifice.
Victors in every battle (they 're a score or more I 'm told),
Our hands are free from violence, our hearts unstained by
gold.
The tidings reach our Country and she gives us words of
praise;
The fallen brave are mourned and crowned with memorable
bays;
Peace with our triumphs gives us lands that stretch from
shore to shore;

We strike our tents, we bear our flags, and are at home
    once more. . . .

Ill-starred, distracted Mexico, all at her fate must weep!
Should we have bound her to our car and drawn her up the
    steep?
Then Freedom, Learning, Labour, Law, had given her peace
    and rest,
And she had mounted to her place and sat among the Blest.
We pray and hope her happier hour will some time come;
    but then,
As now, we turn from her, we think, as wiser, better men,
And give to our America, her glorious name and ways,
Our lives, our hearts, our works, our thoughts, our noblest
    words of praise.

—Edmund S. Holbrook.

THE BIVOUAC OF THE DEAD

THE muffled drum's sad roll has beat
    The soldier's last tattoo;
No more on Life's parade shall meet
    That brave and fallen few.
On Fame's eternal camping ground
    Their silent tents are spread,
And Glory guards, with solemn round,
    The bivouac of the dead.

No rumour of the foe's advance
    Now swells upon the wind;
No troubled thought at midnight haunts
    Of loved ones left behind;
No vision of the morrow's strife
    The warrior's dream alarms;

No braying horn, nor screaming fife,
  At dawn shall call to arms.

Their shivered swords are red with rust,
  Their plumèd heads are bowed;
Their haughty banner, trailed in dust,
  Is now their martial shroud.
And plenteous funeral tears have washed
  The red stains from each brow,
And the proud forms, by battle gashed,
  Are free from anguish now.

The neighing troop, the flashing blade,
  The bugle's stirring blast,
The charge, the dreadful cannonade,
  The din and shout are past;
Nor war's wild note, nor glory's peal
  Shall thrill with fierce delight
Those breasts that never more may feel
  The rapture of the fight.

Like the fierce northern hurricane,
  That sweeps the great plateau,
Flushed with the triumph yet to gain,
  Came down the serried foe.
Who heard the thunder of the fray
  Break o'er the field beneath,
Knew well the watchword of that day
  Was " Victory or Death."

Long had the doubtful conflict raged
  O'er all that stricken plain,
For never fiercer fight had waged
  The vengeful blood of Spain;
And still the storm of battle blew,
  Still swelled the gory tide;

Not long, our stout old chieftain knew,
  Such odds his strength could bide.

'T was in that hour his stern command
  Called to a martyr's grave
The flower of his belovèd land,
  The nation's flag to save.
By rivers of their fathers' gore
  His first-born laurels grew,
And well he deemed the sons would pour
  Their lives for glory too.

Full many a norther's breath has swept
  O'er Angostura's plain—
And long the pitying sky has wept
  Above its mouldering slain.
The raven's scream, or eagle's flight,
  Or shepherd's pensive lay,
Alone awakes each sullen height
  That frowned o'er that dread fray.

Sons of the Dark and Bloody Ground,
  Ye must not slumber there,
Where stranger steps and tongues resound
  Along the heedless air;
Your own proud land's heroic soil
  Shall be your fitter grave;
She claims from war his richest spoil—
  The ashes of her brave.

Thus, 'neath their parent turf they rest,
  Far from the gory field,
Borne to a Spartan mother's breast,
  On many a bloody shield;
The sunshine of their native sky
  Smiles sadly on them here,

And kindred eyes and hearts watch by
   The heroes' sepulchre.

Rest on, embalmed and sainted dead,
   Dear as the blood ye gave;
No impious footstep here shall tread
   The herbage of your grave;
Nor shall your glory be forgot
   While Fame her record keeps,
Or Honour points the hallowed spot
   Where Valour proudly sleeps.

Yon marble minstrel's voiceless stone,
   In deathless song shall tell,
When many a vanished age hath flown,
   The story how ye fell;
Nor wreck, nor change, nor winter's blight,
   Nor Time's remorseless doom,
Shall dim one ray of glory's light
   That gilds your deathless tomb.
                              —*Theodore O'Hara.*

'FORTY-NINE

WE have worked our claims,
   We have spent our gold,
Our barks are a-strand on the bars;
We are battered and old,
Yet at night we behold
Outcroppings of gold in the stars.

When the rabbits play,
Where the quail all day
Pipe on the chaparral hill;
A few more days,

41

And the last of us lays
His pick aside and all is still.

We are wreck and stray,
We are cast away,
Poor battered old hulks and spars;
But we hope and pray
On the judgement day,
We shall strike it up in the stars.

Though battered and old,
Our hearts are bold;
Yet oft do we repine
For the days of old,
For the days of gold,
For the days of 'Forty-Nine.

—*Joaquin Miller.*

THE GOLD SEEKERS

I SAW these dreamers of dreams go by,
   I trod in their footsteps a space;
Each marched with his eyes on the sky,
   Each passed with a light on his face.

They came from the hopeless and sad,
   They faced the future and gold;
Some the tooth of want's wolf had made mad,
   And some at the forge had grown old.

Behind them these serfs of the tool
   The rags of their service had flung;
No longer of fortune the fool,
   This word from each bearded lip rung:

" Once more I 'm a man, I am free!
   No man is my master, I say;

To-morrow I fail, it may be,—
  No matter, I 'm freeman to-day."

They go to a toil that is sure,
  To despair and hunger and cold;
Their sickness no warning can cure,
  They are mad with a longing for gold.

The light will fade from each eye,
  The smile from each face;
They will curse the impassable sky,
  And the earth when the snow torrents race.

Some will sink by the way and be laid
  In the frost of the desolate earth;
And some will return to a maid,
  Empty of hand as at birth.

But this out of all will remain,
  They have lived and have tossed;
So much in the game will be gain,
  Though the gold of the dice has been lost.
                                —*Hamlin Garland.*

ON THE DEATH OF GENERAL ZACHARY TAYLOR

WEEP not for him! The Thracians wisely gave
  Tears to the birth-couch, triumph to the grave.
Weep not for him! Go, mark his high career;
It knew no shame, no folly, and no fear.
Nurtured to peril, lo! the peril came,
To lead him on, from field to field, to fame.
Weep not for him whose lustrous life has known
No field of fame he has not made his own!
In many a fainting clime, in many a war,
Still bright-browed Victory drew the patriot's car.

Whether he met the dusk and prowling foe
By oceanic Mississippi's flow;
Or where the Southern swamps, with steamy breath,
Smite the worn warrior with no warrior's death!
Or where, like surges on the rolling main,
Squadron on squadron sweep the prairie plain,—
Dawn—and the field the haughty foe o'erspread;
Sunset—and Rio Grandé's waves ran red!
Or where, from rock-ribbed safety, Monterey
Frowns death, and dares him to the unequal fray;
Till crashing walls and slippery streets bespeak
How frail the fortress where the heart is weak;
How vainly numbers menace, rocks defy,
Men sternly knit, and firm to do or die;—
Or where on thousands thousands crowding rush
(Rome knew not such a day) his ranks to crush,
The long day paused on Buena Vista's height,
Above the cloud with flashing volleys bright,
Till angry Freedom, hovering o'er the fray,
Swooped down, and made a new Thermopylæ;——
In every scene of peril and of pain,
His were the toils, his country's was the gain.
From field to field—and all were nobly won—
He bore, with eagle flight, her standard on;
New stars rose there—but never star grew dim
While in his patriot grasp. Weep not for him!
His was a spirit simple, grand and pure;
Great to conceive, to do, and to endure;
Yet the rough warrior was, in heart, a child,
Rich in love's affluence, merciful and mild.
His sterner traits, majestic and antique,
Rivalled the stoic Roman or the Greek;
Excelling both, he adds the Christian name,
And Christian virtues make it more than fame.
To country, youth, age, love, life—all were given!
In death, she lingered between him and Heaven;

Thus spake the patriot, in his latest sigh,—
"MY DUTY DONE—I DO NOT FEAR TO DIE!"

—*Robert Taylor Conrad.*

CALIFORNIA

THE Grecian Muse, to earth who bore
　　Her goblet filled with mine of gold,
Dispersed the frown that Ages wore
　　Upon their foreheads grim and cold,
　　What time the lyric thunders rolled.

O'er this new Eden of the West
　　The mightier Muse enkindles now:
Her joy-lyre fashions in my breast,
　　And wreathes the song-crown for my brow,
　　Ere yet her loftier powers avow.

Though like Tithonus old and gray,
　　I serve her 'mid the swords and shields;
Her being opens for my way,
　　And there I find Elysian fields;
　　And there I dwell while Nature yields.

My Dian of the sparkling West,
　　My lady of the silver bow!
Here, where the savage man made quest
　　For golden spoils in earth that grow,
　　She leads the Golden Age below.

Beneath her feet the maiden May
　　Sits crowned with roses where I sing.
My brows with frosted age are gray,
　　But all my being glows for spring:
　　A golden youth 'tis hers to bring.

So in her, for her, I abide,
  And taste the goblets of her bliss;
Upon the hills with morning dyed,
  All as a new acropolis,
  Her shrine shall yet arise, iwis.

And here shall greater Hellas burn,
  Irradiant for the Solar Powers;
And men the love of strife unlearn,
  Tasting from lips that breathe of flowers,
  Made young by joys that live from ours.
                      —*Thomas Lake Harris.*

IN YOSEMITE VALLEY

SOUND! sound! sound!
  O colossal walls and crowned
In one eternal thunder!
Sound! sound! sound!
O ye oceans overhead,
While we walk, subdued in wonder,
In the ferns and grasses, under
And beside the swift Merced!

Fret! fret! fret!
Streaming, sounding banners, set
On the giant granite castles
In the clouds and in the snow!
But the foe he comes not yet,—
We are loyal, valiant vassals,
And we touch the trailing tassels
Of the banners far below.

Surge! surge! surge!
From the white Sierra's verge,
To the very valley blossom.
Surge! surge! surge!

Yet the song-bird builds a home,
And the mossy branches cross them,
And the tasselled tree-tops toss them,
In the clouds of falling foam.

Sweep! sweep! sweep!
O ye heaven-born and deep,
In one dread, unbroken chorus!
We may wonder or may weep,—
We may wait on God before us;
We may shout or lift a hand,—
We may bow down and deplore us,
But may never understand.

Beat! beat! beat!
We advance, but would retreat
From this restless, broken breast
Of the earth in a convulsion.
We would rest, but dare not rest,
For the angel of expulsion
From this Paradise below
Waves us onward and . . . we go.

—Joaquin Miller.

THE GALLANT FIFTY-ONE

FREEDOM called them—up they rose,
   Grasped their swords and showered blows
On the heads of Freedom's foes—
   And Freedom's foes alone.
Fate decreed that they should die;
Pitying angels breathed a sigh;
Freedom wildly wept on high,
   For the gallant Fifty-One!

There they stood in proud array;
None for mercy there would pray;
None would coward looks betray—
　All stood forth with fearless eye,
Showing by their dauntless air,
What their noble souls could dare;
Showing to the tyrants there,
　How Freedom's sons could die.
　None there strove their fate to shun—
　Gallant band of Fifty-One!

Then a voice the stillness broke,
'T was their gallant leader spoke,
Scorning to receive Death's stroke,
　Kneeling humbly on the sod!
Gazing calmly on the dead,
Whose life-blood had just been shed,
Proudly then the words he said:
　"Americans kneel but to God!"
　Perished thus Kentucky's son—
　Leader of the Fifty-One.

Rejoice! sons of Thermopylæ!
Kindred spirits join with thee,
Who fell in fight for Liberty,
　For Freedom's sacred name.
Future days their deeds shall tell,
How they nobly fought and fell,
Youthful bosoms proudly swell
　At mention of their fame—
　Rays of light from Freedom's sun,
　Gallant band of Fifty-One!

Honour's rays will ever shed
Glory round their hallowed bed,
Though their hearts are cold and dead.

Though their sands of life have run,
Still their names revered will be,
Among the noble and the free—
Glorious sons of Liberty—
    Gallant band of Fifty-One!
                    —*Henry Lynden Flash.*

DANIEL WEBSTER

THE great are falling from us—to the dust
    Our flag droops midway full of many sighs;
A nation's glory and a people's trust
    Lie in the ample pall where Webster lies.

The great are falling from us—one by one
    As fall the patriarchs of the forest trees,
The winds shall seek them vainly, and the sun
    Gaze on each vacant space for centuries.

Lo, Carolina mourns her steadfast pine
    Which towered sublimely o'er the Southern realm,
And Ashland hears no more the voice divine
    From out the branches of its stately elm:—

And Marshfield's giant oak, whose stormy brow
    Oft turned the ocean tempest from the West
Lies on the shore he guarded—and now
    Our startled eagle knows not where to rest!
                    —*Thomas Buchanan Read.*

THE KANSAS EMIGRANTS

WE cross the prairie as of old
    The pilgrims crossed the sea,
To make the West, as they the East,
    The homestead of the free!

49

We go to rear a wall of men
  On Freedom's southern line,
And plant beside the cotton-tree
  The rugged Northern pine!

We're flowing from our native hills
  As our free rivers flow;
The blessing of our Mother-land
  Is on us as we go.

We go to plant her common schools
  On distant prairie swells,
And give the Sabbaths of the wild
  The music of her bells.

Upbearing, like the Ark of old
  The Bible in our van,
We go to test the truth of God
  Against the fraud of man.

No pause, nor rest, save where the streams
  That feed the Kansas run,
Save where our Pilgrim gonfalon
  Shall flout the setting sun!

We 'll tread the prairie as of old
  Our fathers sailed the sea,
And make the West, as they the East,
  The homestead of the free!
                    —*John Greenleaf Whittier.*

THE FLAG

I NEVER have got the bearings quite,
  Though I 've followed the course for many a year,

If he was crazy, clean outright,
  Or only what you might say was " queer."

He was just a simple sailor man.
  I mind it as well as yesterday,
When we messed abroad of the old *Cyane*.
  Lord! how the time does slip away!
That was five and thirty year ago,
  And I never expect such times again,
For sailors was n't afraid to stow
  Themselves on a Yankee vessel then.
He was only a sort of bos'n's mate,
  But every inch of him taut and trim;
Stars and anchors and togs of state
  Tailors don't build for the like of him.
He flew a no-account sort of name,
  A reg'lar fo'castle " Jim " or " Jack,"
With a plain " McGinnis " abaft the same,
  Giner'ly reefed to simple " Mack."
Mack, we allowed, was sorter queer,—
  Ballast or compass was n't right.
Till he licked four Juicers one day, a fear
  Prevailed that he had n't larned to fight.
But I reckon the Captain knowed his man,
  When he put the flag in his hand the day
That we went ashore from the old *Cyane*.
  On a madman's cruise for Darien Bay.
Forty days in the wilderness
  We toiled and suffered and starved with Strain,
Losing the number of many a mess
  In the Devil's swamps of the Spanish Main.
All of us starved, and many died,
  One laid down, in his dull despair;
His stronger messmate went to his side—
  We left them both in the jungle there.
It was hard to part with shipmates so;

But standing by would have done no good.
We heard them moaning all day, so slow
  We dragged along through the weary wood.
McGinnis, he suffered the worst of all;
  Not that he ever piped his eye
 Or would n't have answered to the call
  If they 'd sounded it for " All hands to die."
I guess 't would have sounded for him before,
  But the grit inside of him kept him strong,
Till we met relief on the river shore;
  And we all broke down when it came along.

All but McGinnis. Gaunt and tall,
  Touching his hat, and standing square:
" Captain, the Flag."—And that was all;
  He just keeled over and foundered there.
" The Flag? " We thought he had lost his head—
  It might 'nt be much to lose at best—
Till we came, by and by, to dig his bed,
  And we found it folded around his breast.
He laid so calm and smiling there,
  With the flag wrapped tight about his heart;
Maybe he saw his course all fair,
  Only—*we* could n't read the chart.
                                    —*James Jeffrey Roche.*

THE CAMP OF NOVEMBER

FAST o'er the desert rode Frémont,
    O'er the broad and burning plain—
By the Bitter Lake, and the frozen font
  In wild Nevada's chain.
The wolf howled long round his lonely camp,
The mist of morning was cold and damp,
And the dark Platte foamed o'er his charger's neck
Ere he stood on the grand Sierra's Peak.

There 's a blacker tide to stem, my boys!
　　There 's a rougher hill to climb!
We shall camp 'mid faction's snarling noise,
　　And the howl of startled crime.
There 's work to do ere we gain the goal—
There are logs and lumps from our track to roll—
There are mules to spur—there are wolves to scare
From the prey they gorge in their bloody lair.
　　　　　　　　　—*Henry Howard Brownell.*

THE DEFENSE OF LAWRENCE

A LL night upon the guarded hill,
　　Until the stars were low,
Wrapped round as with Jehovah's will,
　　We waited for the foe;
All night the silent sentinels
　　Moved by like gliding ghosts;
All night the fancied warning bells
　　Held all men to their posts.

We heard the sleeping prairies breathe,
　　The forest's human moans,
The hungry gnashing of the teeth
　　Of wolves on bleaching bones;
We marked the roar of rushing fires,
　　The neigh of frightened steeds,
The voices as of far-off lyres
　　Among the river reeds.

We were but thirty-nine who lay
　　Beside our rifles then;
We were but thirty-nine, and they
　　Were twenty hundred men.
Our lean limbs shook and reeled about,
　　Our feet were gashed and bare,

53

And all the breezes shredded out
  Our garments in the air.

    .   .   .   .

They came: the blessed Sabbath day,
  That soothed our swollen veins,
Like God's sweet benediction, lay
  On all the singing plains;
The valleys shouted to the sun,
  The great woods clapped their hands,
And joy and glory seemed to run
  Like rivers through the lands.

And then our daughters and our wives,
  And men whose heads were white,
Rose sudden into kingly lives
  And walked forth to the fight;
And we drew aim along our guns
  And calmed our quickening breath,
Then, as is meet for Freedom's sons,
  Shook loving hands with Death.

And when three hundred of the foe
  Rode up in scorn and pride,
Whoso had watched us then might know
  That God was on our side;
For all at once a mighty thrill
  Of grandeur through us swept,
And strong and swiftly down the hill,
  Like Gideons we leaped.

And all throughout that Sabbath day
  A wall of fire we stood,
And held the baffled foe at bay,
  And streaked the ground with blood.
And when the sun was very low
  They wheeled their stricken flanks,

54

And passed on, wearily and slow,
  Beyond the river banks.

Beneath the everlasting stars
  We bended childlike knees,
And thanked God for the shining scars
  Of His large victories.
And some, who lingered, said they heard
  Such wondrous music pass
As though a seraph's voice had stirred
  The pulses of the grass.

—*Richard Realf.*

ELISHA KENT KANE

O MOTHER EARTH, thy task is done
    With him who slumbers here below;
From thy cold Arctic brow he won
  A glory purer than thy snow.

Thy warmer bosom gently nursed
  The dying hero; for his eye
The tropic Spring's splendors burst,—
  "In vain!" a thousand voices cry.

"In vain, in vain!" The poet's art
  Forsook me when the people cried;
Naught but the grief that fills my heart,
  And memories of my friend, abide.

We parted in the midnight street,
  Beneath a cold autumnal rain;
He wrung my hand, he stayed my feet
  With "Friend, we shall not meet again."

I laughed; I would not then believe;
  He smiled; he left me; all was o'er.
How much for my poor laugh I 'd give!—
  How much to see him smile once more!

I know my lay bemeans the dead
  That sorrow is an humble thing,
That I should sing his praise instead,
  And strike it on a higher string.

Let stronger minstrels raise their lay,
  And follow where his fame has flown;
To the whole world belongs his praise,
  His friendship was to me alone.

So close against my heart he lay,
  That I should make his glory dim,
And hear a bashful whisper say,
  "I praise myself in praising him."

O, gentle mother, following nigh
  His long, long funeral march, resign
To me the right to lift this cry,
  And part the sorrow that is thine.

O, father, mourning by his bier,
  Forgive this song of little worth!
My eloquence is but a tear,
  I cannot, would not rise from earth.

O, stricken brothers, broken band,—
  The link that held the jewel lost,—
I pray you give me leave to stand
  Amid you, from the sorrowing host.

We 'll give his honours to the world,
  We 'll hark for echoes from afar;
Where'er our country's flag 's unfurled
  His name shall shine in every star.

We feel no fear that time shall keep
  Our hero's memory. Let us move
A little from the world to weep,
  And for our portion take his love.
                    —*George Henry Boker.*

ODE

O TENDERLY the haughty day
    Fills his blue urn with fire;
One morn is in the mighty heaven,
    And one in our desire.

The cannon booms from town to town,
    Our pulses beat not less,
The joy-bells chime their tidings down,
    Which children's voices bless.

For He that flung the broad blue fold
    O'er-mantling land and sea,
One third part of the sky unrolled
    For the banner of the free.

The men are ripe of Saxon kind
    To build an equal state,—
To take the statute from the mind
    And make of duty fate.

United States! the ages plead,—
    Present and Past in under-song,—

Go put your creed into your deed,
  Nor speak with double tongue.

For sea and land don't understand,
  Nor skies without a frown
See rights for which the one hand fights
  By the other cloven down.

Be just at home; then write your scroll
  Of honour o'er the sea,
And bid the broad Atlantic roll
  A ferry of the free.

And henceforth there shall be no chain,
  Save underneath the sea
The wires shall murmur through the main
  Sweet songs of liberty.

The conscious stars accord above,
  The waters wild below,
And under, through the cable wove,
  Her fiery errands go.
                    —*Ralph Waldo Emerson.*

BLOOD IS THICKER THAN WATER

E BBED and flowed the muddy Pei-Ho by the gulf of
    Pechili,
  Near its waters swung the yellow dragon-flag;
Past the batteries of China, looking westward we could see
  Lazy junks along the lazy river lag;
Villagers in near-by Ta-Kou toiled beneath their humble
    star,
  On the flats the ugly mud fort lay and dreamed;
While the *Powhatan* swung slowly at her station by the bar,
  While the *Toey-Wan* with Tattnall onward steamed.

Lazy East and lazy river, fort of mud in lazy June,
  English gunboats through the waters slowly fare,
With the dragon-flag scarce moving in the lazy afternoon
  O'er the mud-heap storing venom in the glare.
We were on our way to Peking, to the Son of Heaven's
    throne,
  White with peace was all our mission to his court;
Peaceful, too, the English vessels on the turbid stream be-
    strown,
  Seeking passage up the Pei-Ho past the fort.

By the bar lay half the English, while the rest, with gallant
    Hope,
  Wrestled with the slipping ebb-tide up the stream;
They had cleared the Chinese irons, reached the double
    chain and rope,
  Where the ugly mud fort scowled upon their beam;—
Boom! the heavens split asunder with the thunder of the
    fight
  As the hateful dragon made its faith a mock;
Every cannon spat its perfidy, each casemate blazed its spite,
  Crashing down upon the English, shock on shock.

In his courage Rason perished, brave McKenna fought and
    fell;
  Scores were dying as they 'd lived, like valiant men;
And the meteor flag that upward prayed to Heaven from
    that hell,
  Wept below for those who ne'er should weep again.
Far away the English launches near the *Powhatan* swung
    slow,
  All despairing, useless, out of reach of war,
Knew their comrades in the battle, saw them reel beneath the
    blow,
  Lying helpless 'gainst the ebb-tide by the bar.

On the *Toey-Wan* stood Tattnall, Stephen Trenchard at his
    side—

"Old Man" Tattnall, he who dared at Vera Cruz,—
Saw here, crippled by the cannon; saw there, throttled by the
     tide,
  Men of English blood and speech—could he refuse?
*I 'll be damned, says he to Trenchard, if Old Tattnall 's stand-
     ing by*
  Seeing white men butchered here by such a foe!
*Where 's my barge? No side-arms, mind you! See those
     English fight and die—*
  Blood is thicker, sir, than water. Let us go!

Quick we man the boat, and quicker plunge into that devil's
     brew—
  "An official call," and Tattnall went in state.
Trenchard 's hurt, our flag in ribbons and the rocking barge
     shot through,
  Hart, our coxswain, dies beneath the Chinese hate;
But the cheers those English give us as we gain their Ad-
     miral's ship
  Make the shattered boat and weary arms seem light—
Then the rare smile from "Old" Tattnall, and Hope's hearty
     word and grip,
  Lying wounded, bleeding, brave in hell's despite.

Tattnall nods, and we go forward, find a gun no longer
     fought—
  What is peace to us when all its crew lie dead?
One bright English lad brings powder and a wounded man
     the shot,
  And we scotch that Chinese dragon, tail and head.
Hands are shaken, faith is plighted, sounds our Captain's
     cheery call,
  In a British boat we speed us fast and far;
And the *Toey-Wan* and Tattnall down the ebb-tide slide
     and fall
  To the launches lying moaning by the bar.

Eager for an English vengeance, battle-light on every face,
  See the Clustered Stars lead on the Triple Cross!
Cheering, swinging into action, valiant Hope takes heart of
    grace
  From the cannons' cloudy roar, the lanyards' toss.
How they fought, those fighting English! How they cheered
    the *Toey-Wan,*
  Cheered our sailors, cheered "Old" Tattnall, grim and
    gray!
And their cheers ring down the ages as they rang beneath
    the sun
  O'er those bubbling, troubled waters far away.

Ebbs and flows the muddy Pei-Ho by the gulf of Pechili,
  Idly floats beside the stream the dragon-flag;
Past the batteries of China, looking westward still you see
  Lazy junks along the lazy river lag.
Let the long, long years drip slowly on that lost and
    ancient land,
  Ever dear one scene to hearts of gallant men;
There 's a hand-clasp and a heart-throb, there 's a word we
    understand;
  Blood is thicker, sir, than water, now as then.
                                    —*Wallace Rice.*

HOW OLD BROWN TOOK HARPER'S FERRY

JOHN BROWN in Kansas settled, like a steadfast Yankee
    farmer,
  Brave and godly, with four sons, all stalwart men of might.
There he spoke aloud for freedom, and the Border-strife
    grew warmer,
  Till the Rangers fired his dwelling, in his absence, in the
    night;
    And Old Brown.

61

Ossawatomie Brown,
Came homeward in the morning—to find his house burned
down.

Then he grasped his trusty rifle and boldly fought for free-
dom;
Smote from border unto border the fierce, invading band;
And he and his brave boys vowed—so might Heaven help
and speed 'em!—
They would save those grand old prairies from the curse
that blights the land;
And Old Brown,
Ossawatomie Brown,
Said, " Boys, the Lord will aid us! " and he shoved his ram-
rod down.

And the Lord *did* aid these men and they laboured day and
even,
Saving Kansas from its peril; and their very lives seemed
charmed,
Till the ruffians killed one son, in the blessed light of
Heaven,—
In cold blood the fellows slew him, as he journeyed all
unarmed;
Then Old Brown,
Ossawatomie Brown,
Shed not a tear, but shut his teeth and frowned a terrible
frown!

Then they seized another brave boy,—not amid the heat of
battle,
But in peace, behind his ploughshare,—and they loaded him
with chains,
And with pikes, before their horses, even as they goad their
cattle,

Drove him cruelly, for their sport, and at last blew out his
　　brains;
　　　Then Old Brown,
　　　Ossawatomie Brown,
Raised his right hand up to Heaven, calling Heaven's ven-
　　geance down.

And he swore a fearful oath, by the name of the Almighty,
　He would hunt this ravening evil that had scathed and
　　torn him so;
He would seize it by the vitals; he would crush it day and
　　night; he
　Would so pursue its footsteps, so return it blow for blow,
　　　That Old Brown,
　　　Ossawatomie Brown,
Should be a name to swear by, in backwoods or in town!

Then his beard became more grizzled, and his wild blue eye
　　grew wilder,
　And more sharply curved his hawk's-nose, snuffing battle
　　from afar;
And he and the two boys left, though the Kansas strife
　　waxed milder,
　Grew more sullen, till was over the bloody Border War,
　　　And Old Brown,
　　　Ossawatomie Brown,
Had gone crazy, as they reckoned by his fearful glare and
　　frown.

So he left the plains of Kansas and their bitter woes behind
　　him.
　Slipt off into Virginia, where the statesmen all are born.
Hired a farm by Harper's Ferry, and no one knew where
　　to find him,
　Or whether he 'd turned parson, or was jacketed and shorn;
　　　For Old Brown,

Ossawatomie Brown,
Mad as he was, knew texts enough to wear a parson's gown.

He bought no ploughs and harrows, spades and shovels, and
    such trifles;
  But quietly to his rancho there came, by every train,
Boxes full of pikes and pistols, and his well-beloved Sharp's
    rifles;
  And eighteen other madmen joined their leader there
    again.
      Says Old Brown,
      Ossawatomie Brown,
" Boys, we 've got an army large enough to march and take
    the town!

" Take the town, and seize the muskets, free the negroes and
    then arm them;
  Carry the County and the State, aye, and all the potent
    South.
On their own heads be the slaughter, if their victims rise to
    harm them—
  These Virginians! who believed not, nor would heed the
    warning mouth."
      Says Old Brown,
      Ossawatomie Brown,
" The world shall see a Republic, or my name is not John
    Brown."

'T was the sixteenth of October, on the evening of a Sunday:
  " This good work," declared the captain, " shall be on a
    holy night!"
It was on a Sunday evening, and before the noon of Monday,
  With two sons and Captain Stephens, fifteen privates—
    black and white,
      Captain Brown,

Ossawatomie Brown,
Marched across the bridge Potomac, and knocked the sentry
down;
Took the guarded armoury-building, and the muskets and the
cannon;
Captured all the county majors and the colonels, one by one;
Scared to death each gallant scion of Virginia they ran on,
And before the noon of Monday, I say, the deed was done.
Mad Old Brown,
Ossawatomie Brown,
With his eighteen other crazy men, went in and took the
town.

Very little noise and bluster, little smell of powder made he;
It was all done in the midnight, like the Emperor's *coup
d'état.*
"Cut the wires! Stop the rail-cars! Hold the streets and
bridges," said he
Then declared the new Republic, with himself for guiding
star,—
This Old Brown,
Ossawatomie Brown;
And the bold two thousand citizens ran off and left the town.

There was riding and railroading and expressing here and
thither;
And the Martinsburg Sharpshooters and the Charlestown
Volunteers,
And the Shepherdstown and Winchester militia hastened
whither
Old Brown was said to muster his ten thousand grenadiers.
General Brown!
Ossawatomie Brown!
Behind whose rampart banner all the North was pouring
down.

But at last, 't is said, some prisoners escaped from Old
    Brown's durance,
  And the effervescent valour of the Chivalry broke out,
When they learned that nineteen madmen had the marvelous
    assurance—
  Only nineteen—thus to seize the place and drive them
    straight about:
        And Old Brown,
        Ossawatomie Brown,
Found an army come to take him, encamped around the town.

But to storm, with all the forces I have mentioned, was too
    risky;
  So they hurried off to Richmond for the Government
    Marines,
Tore them from their weeping matrons, fired their souls with
    Bourbon whisky,
  Till they battered down Brown's castle with their ladders
    and machines;
        And Old Brown,
        Ossawatomie Brown,
Received three bayonet stabs, and a cut on his brave old
    crown.

Tallyho! the old Virginia gentry gather to the baying!
  In they rushed and killed the game, shooting lustily away;
And whene'er they slew a rebel, those who came too late for
    slaying,
  Not to lose a share of glory, fired their bullets in his clay;
        And Old Brown,
        Ossawatomie Brown,
Saw his sons fall dead beside him, and between them laid
    him down.

How the conquerors wore their laurels; how they hastened
    on the trial;

How Old Brown was placed, half dying, on the Charles-
town court-house floor;
How he spoke his grand oration, in the scorn of all denial;
What the brave old madman told them—these are known
the country o'er.
"Hang Old Brown,
Ossawatomie Brown,"
Said the judge, "and all such rebels!" with his most judicial
frown.

But, Virginians, don't do it! for I tell you that the flagon,
Filled with blood of old Brown's offspring, was first poured
by Southern hands,
And each drop from old Brown's life-veins, like the red gore
of the dragon,
May spring up a vengeful Fury, hissing through your
slave-worn lands!
And Old Brown,
Ossawatomie Brown,
May trouble you more than ever, when you've nailed his
coffin down!

—*Edmund Clarence Stedman.*

JOHN BROWN

MEN silenced on his faithful lips
Words of resistless truth and power;
Those words re-echoing now, have made
The gathering war-cry of the hour.

They thought to darken down in blood
The light of freedom's burning rays;
The beacon-fires we tend to-day
Where lit in that undying blaze.

They took the earthly prop and staff
    Out of an unresisting hand;
God came, and led him safely on,
    By ways they could not understand.

They knew not, when from his old eyes
    They shut the world for evermore,
The ladder by which angels come
    Rests firmly on the dungeon's door.

They deemed no vision bright could cheer
    His stony couch and prison ward;
He slept to dream of Heaven, and rose
    To build a Bethel to the Lord!

They showed to his unshrinking gaze
    The "sentence" men have paled to see;
He read God's writing of "reprieve,"
    And grant of endless liberty.

They tried to conquer and subdue
    By marshalled power and bitter hate;
The simple manhood of the man
    Was braver than the armèd state.

They hoped at last to make him feel
    The felon's shame, and felon's dread;
And lo! the martyr's crown of joy
    Settled for ever on his head!

                  —Phœbe Cary.

BROTHER JONATHAN'S LAMENT FOR SISTER CAROLINE

SHE has gone—she has left us in passion and pride,—
    Our stormy-browed sister, so long at our side!

She has torn her own star from our firmament's glow,
And turned on her brother the face of a foe!

O Caroline, Caroline, child of the sun,
We can never forget that our hearts had been one,—
Our foreheads both sprinkled in Liberty's name,
From the fountain of blood with the finger of flame!

You were always too ready to fire at a touch;
But we said " She is hasty—she does not mean much."
We have scowled when you uttered some turbulent threat;
But Friendship still whispered, " Forgive and forget! "

Has our love all died out? Have its altars grown cold?
Has the curse come at last which the fathers foretold?
Then Nature must teach us the strength of the chain
That her petulant children would sever in vain.

They may fight till the buzzards are gorged with their spoil,
Till the harvest grows black as it rots in the soil,
Till the wolves and the catamounts troop from their caves,
And the shark tracks the pirate, the lord of the waves:

In vain is the strife! When its fury is past,
Their fortunes must flow in one channel at last,
As the torrents that rush from the mountains of snow
Roll mingled in peace through the valleys below.

Our Union is river, lake, ocean, and sky;
Man breaks not the medal when God cuts the die!
Though darkened with sulphur, though cloven with steel,
The blue arch will brighten, the waters will heal!

O Caroline, Caroline, child of the sun,
There are battles with fate that can never be won!

The star-flowering banner must never be furled,
For its blossoms of light are the hope of the world!

Go, then, our rash sister, afar and aloof,—
Run wild in the sunshine away from our roof;
But when your heart aches, and your feet have grown sore,
Remember the pathway that leads to our door!

—*Oliver Wendell Holmes.*

ANNUS MEMORABILIS

STAND strong and calm as Fate! not a breath of scorn
  or hate—
  Of taunt for the base, or of menace for the strong—
Since our fortunes must be sealed on that old and famous
    Field
  Where the Right is set in battle with the Wrong.
'T is coming with the loom of Khamsin or Simoom,
  The tempest that shall try if we are of God or no—
Its roar is in the sky,—and they there be which cry,
  "Let us cower, and the storm may over-blow."

Now, nay! stand firm and fast! (that was a spiteful blast!)
  This is not a war of men, but of Angels Good and Ill—
'T is hell that storms at heaven—'t is the black and deadly
    Seven,
  Sworn 'gainst the Shining Ones to work their damnéd
    will!
How the Ether glooms and burns, as the tide of combat
    turns,
  And the smoke and dust above it whirl and float!
It eddies and it streams—and, certes, oft it seems
  As the Sins had the Seraphs fairly by the throat.

But we all have read (in that Legend grand and dread),
  How Michael and his host met the Serpent and his crew—
Naught has reached us of the Fight—but, if I have dreamed
    aright,

'T was a loud one and a long, as ever thundered through!

Right stiffly, past a doubt, the Dragon fought it out,
 And his Angels, each and all, did for Tophet their de-
  voir—
There was creak of iron wings, and whirl of scorpion stings,
 Hiss of bifid tongues, and the Pit in full uproar!
But, naught thereof enscrolled, in one brief line 't is told
 (Calm as dew the Apocalyptic Pen).
That on the Infinite Shore their place was found no more.
 God send the like on this our earth! Amen.
     —Henry Howard Brownell.

KANSAS ADMITTED TO THE UNION

SHE felt, they say,
 The battle-storms of earth,
The cannons cradled her,
The war-drums beat fierce lullabies
 At her wild birth;
Yet she in danger found a paradise,
 And bowed,—its worshipper!

'T was thus she roused
 The multitudes to arms,
And made the nations feel
The precepts they had taught and talked
 Of hurts and harms;
Until God came and led her, and she walked
 The child of sword and steel.

What though she loves
 The Novel and the New?
What though she sometimes fall
When scaling heights of sky and star
 To find the True?

For him that strives, God's angels shall unbar
   The gates of all in all!

    What though her wounds
      Be many and severe?
What though her shoulder bend
Beneath the crushing loads
    She does not fear?
Travel is easy in the beaten roads,—
   Ease has no worthy end.

    Though bruises come,
    The brave pursue the quest;
Though failure and defeat
Their harsh, ignoble measures sing,
    To strive is best;
To sloth the Fates no crowns of laurel bring,
   And conquering is sweet.

    Who never strives
    For ever falls and fails
  Where Terror sways her hosts
And Force with all the fraud of greeds
    Makes fierce assails;
  'T is only he that battles on and bleeds
  Deserves his boasts.

    She seeks the New,—
    She loves its laughing youth;
  She leaves the Old, as fear
Forsakes the ways of pestilence;
    And for the truth,
Warm in the heart of high Omnipotence,
  She struggles year by year.

Her heart, her hope,
  Is boundless as her plains;
 She walks the starry ways,
She leaps the vale and mountain-side,
    For endless gains;
Her faith haunts all the far horizons wide
  With voice of prayer and praise!

    And so to thee,
    O Kansas, unto thee,
  Proud child of tale and song,
Whom brave men filled with hope and health,
    Let blessings be!
Thou hast the soul of empires, commonwealth
  Whose infancy was strong!

    Free blood fast bounds
    Along the sleepy veins
  At mention of thy name;
Thine eyes are on the future, great
    With wondrous gains;
Such be thy glory, and the years elate
  Shall justify thy fame!
                    —*Freeman Edwin Miller.*

THIRTY-FOUR

FLING out the banner on the breeze;
    Shake out each starry fold;
Summon the stalwart soldiers forth,
    The mighty, and the bold—
The bell of Freedom from its tower
    Its solemn call has tolled.

The sound sweeps wildly o'er the land,
    Sweeps o'er the bounding sea;

It echoes, from each mountain-top,
  The anthem of the free;
t snaps the chain which sin has forged
  It sings for liberty.

Marshal the legions for the fight,
  The youthful and the brave,
Stand for the noble and the right,
  The glorious Union save:
Stand for the cause for which their blood
  Our patriot fathers gave.

Dread not the angry foeman's rage;
  Dread not the tempest's crash;
Dread not the billows, though the cliffs
  Along the shore they lash;
Dread not the awful thunder's roar,
  Nor lightnings' piercing flash.

Above the cloud, the brilliant sky
  Shines in immortal blue;
And light, like Heaven's approving smile,
  Streams, in its glory, through;
Be patient, till the strife is o'er;
  Have faith to dare and do.

With willing heart Heaven's high behest
  Fulfil without alarm;
The foe has planted for our hand,
  And nursed the conqueror's palm;
And He that bade the sea " Be still,"
  The stormy waves will calm.

Then fling the banner to the wind—
  The emblem of the free;
Strike the sweet harp-tones that proclaim

The reign of Liberty;
And bid the melody rebound
  From every trembling key.

And count each star that studs the blue,
  Whate'er the past has been,
A wayward wanderer, welcomed back,
  To fill its place again;—
A loving band of sister-lights,
  Just like the Old Thirteen.

Strike not one jewel from the crest
  The loving mother wore;
Reset the gems upon her breast,
  Each where it stood before.
Clasp in the glorious cynosure,
  The whole dear Thirty-Four.
                    —*Samuel Francis Smith.*

SUMTER

SO, they will have it!
    The Black witch (curse on her)
  Always had won her
Greediest demand—for we gave it—
  All but our honour!

Thirty hours thundered
  Siege-guns and mortars—
  (Flames in the quarters!)
One to a hundred
  Stood our brave Forters!

No more of parties!—
  Let them all moulder—
  Here's work that's bolder!

Forward, my hearties!
  Shoulder to shoulder.

Sight o'er the trunnion—
  Send home the rammer—
  Linstock and hammer!
Speak for the Union!
  Tones that won't stammer!

Men of Columbia,
  Leal hearts from Annan,
  Brave lads of Shannon!
We are all one to-day—
  On with the cannon!
            —*Henry Howard Brownell.*

MEN OF THE NORTH AND WEST

MEN of the North and West,
    Wake in your might,
Prepare, as the rebels have done,
  For the fight!
You cannot shrink from the test;
Rise! Men of the North and West!

They have torn down your banner of stars;
  They have trampled the laws;
They have stifled the freedom they hate,
  For no cause.
Do you love it or slavery best?
Speak! Men of the North and West.

They strike at the life of the State;
  Shall the murder be done?
They cry: "We are two!" And you:
  "We are one!"

76

You must meet them, then, breast to breast,
On! Men of the North and West!

Not with words; they laugh them to scorn,
  And tears they despise;
But with swords in your hands, and death
  In your eyes!
Strike home! Leave to God all the rest;
Strike! Men of the North and West.
                    —*Richard Henry Stoddard.*

THE SOUTHERN PLEIADES

WHEN first our Southern flag arose,
      Beside the heaving sea,
It bore upon its silken folds
  A green Palmetto tree.
All honour to that banner brave,
  It roused the blood of yore,
And nerved the arm of Southern men
  For valiant deeds once more.

When storm clouds darkened o'er our sky,
  That star, the first of seven,
Shone out amid the mist and gloom,
  To light our country's heaven.
The glorious seven! long may their flag
  Wave proudly on the breeze;
Long may they burn on fame's broad sky—
  The Southern Pleiades!
                    —*Laura Lorrimer.*

WE COME! WE COME!

WE come! we come, for death or life,
      For the grave or victory!

We come to the broad Red Sea of strife,
    Where the black flag waveth free!
We come, as men, to do or die,
    Nor feel that the lot is hard,
When our Hero calls—and our battle-cry
    Is "On to Beauregard!"

Up, craven up! 't is no time for ease,
    When the crimson war-tide rolls
To our very doors—up, up, for these
    Are times to try men's souls!
The purple gore calls from the sod
    Of our martyred brothers' graves,
And raises a red right hand to God
    To guard our avenging braves.

And unto the last bright drop that thrills
    The depths of the Southern heart,
We must battle for our sunny hills,
    For the freedom of our mart—
For all that Honour claims, or Right—
    For country, love, and Home!
Shout to the trampling steeds of Might
    Our cry—"We come! we come!"

And let our path through their serried ranks
    Be the fierce tornado's track,
That bursts from the torrid's fervid banks
    And scatters destruction black!
For the hot life leaping in the veins
    Of our young Confederacy,
Must break for ay the galling chains
    Of dark-browed Treachery.

On! on! 't is our gallant chieftain calls
    (He must not call in vain),

For aid to guard his homestead walls—
  Our Hero of the Plain!
We come! we come, to do or die,
  Nor feel that the lot is hard;
" God and our Rights! " be our battle-cry,
  And " On to Beauregard! "

—Millie Mayfield.

A CRY TO ARMS

HO, woodsmen of the mountain-side!
    Ho, dwellers in the vales!
Ho, ye who by the chafing tide
  Have roughened in the gales!
Leave barn and byre, leave kin and cot,
  Lay by the bloodless spade;
Let desk and case and counter rot,
  And burn your books of trade!

The despot roves your fairest lands;
  And, till he flies or fears,
Your fields must grow but arméd bands,
  Your sheaves be sheaves of spears!
Give up to mildew and to rust
  The useless tools of gain,
And feed your country's sacred dust
  With floods of crimson rain!

Come, with the weapons at your call—
  With musket, pike, or knife:
He wields the deadliest blade of all
  Who lightest holds his life.
The arm that drives its unbought blows
  With all a patriot's scorn,
Might brain a tyrant with a rose,
  Or stab him with a thorn!

79

Does any falter? Let him turn
    To some brave maiden's eyes,
And catch the holy fires that burn
    In those sublunar skies.
Oh, could you like your women feel,
    And in their spirit march,
A day might see your lines of steel
    Beneath the victor's arch!

What hope, O God! would not grow warm
    When thoughts like these give cheer?
The lily calmly braves the storm,
    And shall the palm tree fear?
No! rather let its branches court
    The rack that sweeps the plain,
And from the lily's regal port
    Learn how to breast the strain!

Ho! woodsmen of the mountain-side!
    Ho! dwellers in the vales!
Ho! ye who by the roaring tide
    Have roughened in the gales!
Come! flocking gaily to the fight,
    From forest, hill, and lake;
We battle for our country's right,
    And for the lily's sake!

—*Henry Timrod.*

OUR COUNTRY'S CALL

LAY down the ax; fling down the spade;
    Leave in its track the toiling plough;
The rifle and the bayonet-blade
    For arms like yours were fitter now;
And let the hands that ply the pen
    Quit the light task, and learn to wield

The horseman's crooked brand, and rein
   The charger on the battle-field.

Our country calls; away! away!
   To where the blood-stream blots the green.
Strike to defend the gentlest sway
   That Time in all his course has seen.
See, from a thousand coverts, see,
   Spring the armed foes that haunt her track;
They rush to smite her down, and we
   Must beat the banded traitors back.

Ho! sturdy as the oaks ye cleave,
   And moved as soon to fear and flight,
Men of the glade and forest! leave
   Your woodcraft for the field of fight.
The arms that wield the ax must pour
   An iron tempest on the foe;
His serried ranks shall reel before
   The arm that lays the panther low.

And ye, who breast the mountain-storm
   By grassy steep or highland lake,
Come, for the land ye love, to form
   A bulwark that no foe can break.
Stand, like your own grey cliffs that mock
   The whirlwind, stand in her defence;
The blast as soon shall move the rock
   As rushing squadrons bear ye thence.

And ye, whose homes are by her grand
   Swift rivers, rising far away,
Come from the depth of her green land,
   As mighty in your march as they;
As terrible as when the rains
   Have swelled them over bank and borne,

With sudden floods to drown the plains
  And sweep along the woods uptorn.

And ye, who throng, beside the deep,
  Her ports and hamlets of the strand,
In number like the waves that leap
  On his long-murmuring marge of sand—
Come like that deep, when, o'er his brim
  He rises, all his floods to pour,
And flings the proudest barks that swim,
  A helpless wreck, against the shore!

Few, few were they whose swords of old
  Won the fair land in which we dwell,
But we are many, we who hold
  The grim resolve to guard it well.
Strike, for that broad and goodly land,
  Blow after blow, till men shall see
That Might and Right move hand in hand,
  And glorious must their triumph be!
                    —*William Cullen Bryant.*

THE REVEILLE

HARK! I hear the tramp of thousands,
    And of arméd men the hum;
Lo! a nation's hosts have gathered
  Round the quick-alarming drum,—
      Saying, "Come,
      Freemen, come!
Ere your heritage be wasted," said the quick-
  alarming drum.

"Let me of my heart take counsel:
  War is not of life the sum;
Who shall stay and reap the harvest
  When the autumn days shall come?"

But the drum
Echoed: "Come.
Death shall reap the braver harvest," said the
solemn-sounding drum.

"But when won, the coming battle,
What of profit springs therefrom?
What if conquest, subjugation,
Even greater ills become?"
But the drum
Answered, "Come!
You must do the sum to prove it," said the
Yankee-answering drum.

"What, if 'mid the cannons' thunder,
Whistling shot and bursting bomb,
When my brothers fall around me,
Should my heart grow cold and numb?"
But the drum
Answered, "Come!
Better there in death united than in life a
recreant,—Come!"

Thus they answered—hoping, fearing,
Some in faith, and doubting some—
Till a triumph-voice proclaiming,
Said: "My chosen people, come!"
Then the drum
Lo! was dumb;
For the great heart of the nation, throbbing,
answered, "Lord, we come!"

—*Francis Bret Harte.*

83

BATTLE HYMN OF THE REPUBLIC

MINE eyes have seen the glory of the coming of the Lord:
    He is trampling out the vintage where the grapes of
    wrath are stored;
He hath loosed the fateful lightning of his terrible swift
    sword:
        His truth is marching on.

I have seen Him in the watch-fires of a hundred circling
    camps;
They have builded Him an altar in the evening's dews and
    damps;
I can read His righteous sentence by the dim and flaring
    lamps.
        His day is marching on.

I have read a fiery gospel, writ in burnished rows of steel:
"As ye deal with my contemners, so with you my grace shall
    deal;
Let the hero, born of woman, crush the serpent with his heel,
        Since God is marching on."

He has sounded forth the trumpet that shall never call re-
    treat;
He is sifting out the hearts of men before His judgement-
    seat;
Oh, be swift, my soul, to answer Him! be jubilant, my feet!
        Our God is marching on.

In the beauty of the lilies, Christ was born across the sea,
With a glory in His bosom that transfigures you and me:
As He died to make men holy, let us die to make them free,
        While God is marching on.

                —Julia Ward Howe.

LATE BUT SURE

THE foe has hemmed us round: we stand at bay,
  Here we will perish, or be free to-day!
  To drum and bugle sternly sounding,
  The Southern soldier's heart is bounding;
But stay—oh stay! Virginia is not here!
  Hush your strains of martial cheer;
    O bugle, peace!
    O war-drum, cease!
  Virginia is not here!

Suspend, O chief, your word of fight!
She will be soon in sight!
  Her children never called in vain!
    She comes not—comes not: the disgrace
Were bitterer than the tyrant's chain!
    Oh, death! we dare thee face to face!

A gun! the foe's defiant shot—be still!
Hurrah! an answering gun behind the hill;
  And o'er its summit wildly streaming
  The squadrons of Virginia gleaming!
Hurrah! hurrah! the Old Dominion comes!
  Blow your bugles! beat your drums!
    O doubt accursed!
    The last is first—
  The Old Dominion comes!
She grasps her thunderbolts of war;
Hurrah! hurrah! hurrah!

  Now loose, O chief! your battle storm!
    We hang impatient on your breath;
  Here in the flashing front we form!
    Virginia!—victory or death!
                —*William Henry Holcombe.*

85

THROUGH BALTIMORE

'T WAS Friday morn: the train drew near
        The city and the shore.
Far through the sunshine, soft and clear,
We saw the dear old flag appear,
And in our hearts arose a cheer
    For Baltimore.

Across the broad Patapsco's wave,
    Old Fort McHenry bore
The starry banner of the brave,
As when our fathers went to save,
Or in the trenches find a grave
    At Baltimore.

Before us, pillared in the sky,
    We saw the statue soar
Of Washington, serene and high:—
Could traitors view that form, nor fly?
Could patriots see, nor gladly die
    For Baltimore?

"O city of our country's song!
    By that swift aid we bore
When sorely pressed, receive the throng
Who go to shield our flag from wrong,
And give us welcome, warm and strong,
    In Baltimore!"

We had no arms; as friends we came,
    As brothers evermore,
To rally round one sacred name—
The charter of our power and fame:
We never dreamed of guilt and shame
    In Baltimore.

The coward mob upon us fell:
  McHenry's flag they tore:
Surprised, borne backward by the swell,
Beat down with mad, inhuman yell,
Before us yawned, a traitorous hell
  In Baltimore!

The streets our soldier-fathers trod
  Blushed with their children's gore:
We saw the craven rulers nod,
And dip in blood the civic rod—
Shall such things be, O righteous God,
  In Baltimore?

No, never! By that outrage black,
  A solemn oath we swore,
To bring the Keystone's thousands back,
Strike down the dastards who attack,
And leave a red and fiery track
  Through Baltimore!

Bow down, in haste, thy guilty head!
  God's wrath is swift and sore:
The sky with gathering bolts is red—
Cleanse from thy skirts the slaughter shed,
Or make thyself an ashen bed,
  O Baltimore!

              —*Bayard Taylor.*

MY MARYLAND

THE despot's heel is on thy shore,
    Maryland!
His torch is at thy temple door,
    Maryland!
Avenge the patriotic gore

That flecked the streets of Baltimore
And be the battle queen of yore,
    Maryland, my Maryland!

Hark to an exiled son's appeal,
    Maryland!
My mother State, to thee I kneel,
    Maryland!
For life or death, for woe or weal,
Thy peerless chivalry reveal,
And gird thy beauteous limbs with steel,
    Maryland, my Maryland!

Thou wilt not cower in the dust,
    Maryland!
Thy beaming sword shall never rust,
    Maryland!
Remember Carroll's sacred trust,
Remember Howard's warlike thrust,
And all thy slumberers with the just,
    Maryland, my Maryland!

Come! 't is the red dawn of the day,
    Maryland!
Come with thy panoplied array,
    Maryland!
With Ringgold's spirit for the fray,
With Watson's blood at Monterey,
With fearless Lowe and dashing May,
    Maryland, my Maryland!

Dear Mother, burst the tyrant's chain,
    Maryland!
Virginia shall not call in vain,
    Maryland!
She meets her sisters on the plain,

" Sic semper! " 't is the proud refrain
That baffles minions back amain,
>> Maryland!
Arise in majesty again,
>> Maryland, my Maryland!

Come! for thy shield is bright and strong,
>> Maryland!
Come! for thy dalliance does thee wrong,
>> Maryland!
Come to thy own heroic throng
Stalking with Liberty along,
And chant thy dauntless slogan-song,
>> Maryland, my Maryland!

I see the blush upon thy cheek,
>> Maryland!
But thou wast ever bravely meek,
>> Maryland!
But lo! there surges forth a shriek,
From hill to hill, from creek to creek,
Potomac calls to Chesapeake,
>> Maryland, my Maryland!

Thou wilt not yield to Vandal toll,
>> Maryland!
Thou wilt not crook to his control,
>> Maryland!
Better the fire upon thee roll,
Better the shot, the blade, the bowl,
Than crucifixion of the soul,
>> Maryland, my Maryland!

I hear the distant thunder-hum,
>> Maryland!

The " Old Line's " bugle, fife, and drum;
　　　　Maryland!
She is not dead, nor deaf, nor dumb;
Huzza! she spurns the Northern scum—
She breathes! She burns! She 'll come!
　　　She 'll come!
　　　　Maryland, my Maryland!
　　　　　　　　—*James Ryder Randall.*

THE BONNIE BLUE FLAG

WE are a band of brothers, and natives of the soil,
　　Fighting for the property we gained by honest toil;
And when our rights were threatened, the cry rose near and
　　　far—
Hurrah for the bonnie Blue Flag that bears a single star!

As long as the Union was faithful to her trust,
Like friends and like brothers, kind were we and just;
But now when Northern treachery attempts our rights to
　　　mar,
We hoist on high the bonnie Blue Flag that bears a single
　　　star.

First, gallant South Carolina nobly made the stand;
Then came Alabama, who took her by the hand;
Next, quickly, Mississippi, Georgia, and Florida—
All raised the flag, the bonnie Blue Flag that bears a single
　　　star.

Ye men of valour, gather round the banner of the Right;
Texas and fair Louisiana join us in the fight.
Davis, our loved President and Stephens, statesmen are—
Now rally round the bonnie Blue Flag that bears a single
　　　star.

And here 's to brave Virginia! the Old Dominion State,
With the young Confederacy at length has linked her fate.
Impelled by her example, now other states prepare
To hoist on high the bonnie Blue Flag that bears a single
    star.

Then here 's to our Confederacy; strong we are and brave,
Like patriots we 'll fight, our heritage to save;
And rather than submit to shame, to die we would prefer;
So cheer for the bonnie Blue Flag that bears a single star.

Then cheer, boys, cheer, raise the joyous shout—
For Arkansas and North Carolina now have both gone out;
And let another rousing cheer for Tennessee be given,
The single star of the bonnie Blue Flag has grown to be
    eleven!

—Harry McCarthy.

"HOW ARE YOU, SANITARY?"

DOWN the picket-guarded lane,
  Rolled the comfort-laden wain,
Cheered by shouts that shook the plain,
  Soldier-like and merry;
Phrases such as camps may teach,
Sabre-cuts of Saxon speech,
Such as " Bully! " " Them 's the peach! "
  " Wade in, Sanitary! "

Right and left the caissons drew
As the car went lumbering through,
Quick succeeding in review
  Squadrons military;
Sunburnt men with beards like frieze,
Smooth-faced boys, and cries like these,—

91

"U. S. San. Com." "That 's the cheese!"
"Pass in, Sanitary!"

In such cheer it struggled on
Till the battle front was won,
Then the car, its journey done,
  Lo! was stationary;
And where bullets whistling fly,
Came the sadder, fainter cry,
"Help us, brothers, ere we die,—
  Save us, Sanitary!"

Such the work. The phantom flies,
Wrapped in battle clouds that rise;
But the brave—whose dying eyes,
  Veiled and visionary,
See the jasper gates swung wide,
See the parted throng outside—
Hears the voice to those who ride:
  "Pass in, Sanitary!"

                    —*Francis Bret Harte.*

DIXIE

SOUTHRONS, hear your country call you!
Up! lest worse than death befall you!
  To arms! to arms! to arms, in Dixie!
Lo! all the beacon fires are lighted,
Let all hearts be now united!
  To arms! to arms! to arms, in Dixie!
    Advance the flag of Dixie!
      Hurrah! Hurrah!
For Dixie's land we take our stand,
  And live and die for Dixie!
    To arms! to arms!

And conquer peace for Dixie!
To arms! to arms!
And conquer peace for Dixie!

Hear the Northern thunders mutter!
Northern flags in South winds flutter!
    To arms! to arms! to arms! in Dixie!
Send them back your fierce defiance!
Stamp upon the accursed alliance!

Fear no danger! Shun no labour!
Lift up rifle, pike, and sabre!
    To arms! to arms! to arms, in Dixie!
Shoulder pressing close to shoulder!
Let the odds make each heart bolder!

How the South's great heart rejoices
At your cannons' ringing voices!
    To arms! to arms! to arms, in Dixie!
For faith betrayed, and pledges broken,
Wrongs inflicted, insults spoken.

Strong as lions, swift as eagles,
Back to their kennels hunt these beagles!
    To arms! to arms! to arms! in Dixie!
Cut the unequal bonds asunder!
Let them hence each other plunder!

Swear upon your country's altar
Never to submit or falter!
    To arms! to arms! to arms, in Dixie!
Till the spoilers are defeated,
Till the Lord's work is completed.

Halt not till our Federation
Secures among earth's powers its station!

To arms! to arms! to arms, in Dixie!
Then at peace, and crowned with glory,
Hear your children tell the story!

If the loved ones weep in sadness,
Victory soon will bring them gladness;
    To arms! to arms! to arms, in Dixie!
Exultant pride soon banish sorrow;
Smiles chase tears away to-morrow.
    To arms! to arms! to arms, in Dixie!
        Advance the flag of Dixie!
            Hurrah! Hurrah!
For Dixie's land we take our stand,
    And live and die for Dixie!
        To arms! to arms!
        And conquer peace for Dixie!

—Albert Pike.

DIXIE'S LAND

I WISH I was in de land ob cotton,
    Cimmon seed an' sandy bottom—

In Dixie's Land whar I was born in,
Early on one frosty mornin.

Look away—look away—Dixie Land.
Den I wish I was in Dixie, Hooray—Hooray!

In Dixie's Land we 'll take our stand
To lib and die in Dixie.

Old Missus marry Will de weaber,
William was a gay deceaber.

94

When he put his arms around 'er,
He look as fierce as a forty pounder.

His face was sharp like butcher's cleaber,
But dat did n't seem to grieb her;

Will run away—Missus took a decline, oh,
Her face was de color ob bacon rine—oh.

How could she act such a foolish part
As marry a man dat break her heart?

Here 's a health to de next old Missus,
And all de gals dat wants to kiss us.

Now if you want to dribe away sorrow,
Come and hear dis song to-morrow!

Sugar in de gourd and stonny batter,
De whites grow fat an' de niggers fatter!

Den hoe it down and scratch your grabble,
To Dixie's Land I am bound to trabble.

Look away—Look away—Dixie Land.
Den I wish I was in Dixie. Hooray! Hooray!

COLONEL ELLSWORTH

IT fell upon us like a crushing woe,
Sudden and terrible. "Can it be?" we said,
"That he from whom we hoped so much, is dead.
Most foully murdered ere he met the foe?"
Why not? The men that would disrupt the State
By such base plots as theirs—frauds, thefts, and lies—
What code of honour do they recognise?

They thirst for blood to satisfy their hate,
Our blood: so be it; but for every blow
Woe shall befall them; not in their wild way,
But stern and pitiless, we will repay,
Until, like swollen streams, *their* blood shall flow:
And should we pause; the thought of Ellsworth slain,
Will steel our aching hearts to strike again!

—Richard Henry Stoddard.

STEPHEN ARNOLD DOUGLAS

HERE behold a son of the great Republic!
  To the land he loved, through fierce years of conflict,
Never faltering in his duty, Douglas
        Died at her altar.

Simply bred was he; widowed, poor his mother;
With his hands he worked in his straitened boyhood;
Yet loved learning well, gleaning golden grain from
        Life's fields of wisdom.

Here to Illinois, to the virgin prairie
Youthful feet he turned; in her schools a master,
Till within her courts winning rank and station;
        Thence to the forum.

By clean wit and strength gaining thousands to him,
To the Nation's halls in aspiring manhood
Went he, finding there broader reputation,
        Scope for the statesman.

Eager for the right, never had a people,
Never had the country a servant more unselfish;
Nor was one reproach breathed upon his honour,
        Tried and found steadfast.

96

'Gainst the swelling tide that was rising southward
Threatening all with wreck, rushing on to ruin,
To the Constitution he rallied all his
        Friends and supporters.

When the Nation's rulers would leave her shameless,
Douglas raised his voice in a fiery protest,
Thrust aside ambition and mean alliance
        Plotting against her.

So the South refused him and left him, beaten,
Though a million men to his standard rallied;
Lincoln, who had lost to him lesser office,
        Rose to the highest;

Then awoke in wrath the slaveholders' forces,
By the gods made mad. As against Buchanan
Douglas once had warred, now in Lincoln's vanguard
        Stood he for battle,

Brought to lip his bugle to blare the warning
Out to waiting myriads through the Northland,
Calling to the Flag his loyal following,
        Legions of freemen.

Lost the Southern wish for a Northern treason;
As one man marched forth Freedom's host to triumph;
Perished all the hope for the great secession,
        Blasted for ever!

To his country's cause when in desperation
Thus were consecrated the weeks remaining;
Loud and clear his note, though death's seal was on him,
        To save the Union!

Be it not forgot! Let a land united,
Sure that for her sake Illinois gave nobly,
Know that near the shrines where rest Grant and Lincoln,
    Proudly sleeps Douglas.

—Wallace Rice.

MANASSAS

THEY have met at last—as storm-clouds
    Meet in heaven,
And the Northmen back and bleeding
    Have been driven;
And their thunders have been stilled,
And their leaders crushed or killed,
And their ranks with terror thrilled,
    Rent and riven.

Like the leaves of Vallambrosa
    They are lying;
In the moonlight, in the midnight,
    Dead and dying;
Like those leaves before the gale,
Swept their legions, wild and pale;
While the host that made them quail
    Stood, defying.

When aloft in morning sunlight
    Flags were flaunted,
And " swift vengeance on the rebel "
    Proudly vaunted:
Little did they think that night
Should close upon their shameful flight.
And rebels, victors in the fight,
    Stand undaunted.

But peace to those who perished
    In our passes!
Light be the earth above them;
    Green the grasses!
Long shall Northmen rue the day
When they met our stern array,
And shrunk from battle's wild affray
    At Manassas.
           —*Caroline Anne Warfield.*

TO JOHN C. FREMONT

THY error, Frémont, simply was to act
  A brave man's part, without the statesman's tact,
And, taking counsel but of common sense,
To strike at cause as well as consequence.
Oh, never yet since Roland wound his horn
At Roncesvalles, has a blast been blown
Far-heard, wide-echoed, startling as thine own,
Heard from the van of freedom's hope forlorn!
It had been safer, doubtless, for the time,
To flatter treason, and avoid offence
To that Dark Power whose underlying crime
Heaves upward its perpetual turbulence.
But if thine be the fate of all who break
The ground for truth's seed, or forerun their years
Till lost in distance, or with stout hearts make
A lane for freedom through the level spears,
Still take thou courage! God has spoken through thee,
Irrevocable, the mighty words, Be free!
The land shakes with them, and the slave's dull ear
Turns from the rice-swamp stealthily to hear.
Who would recall them now must first arrest
The winds that blow down from the free Northwest,
Ruffling the Gulf; or like a scroll roll back
The Mississippi to its upper springs.

Such words fulfil their prophecy, and lack
But the full time to harden into things.
                              —*John Greenleaf Whittier.*

BALL'S BLUFF

ONE noonday at my window in the town,
    I saw a sight—the saddest that eyes can see—
  Young soldiers marching lustily
      Unto the wars,
With fifes, and flags in mottoed pageantry;
  While all the porches, walks and doors
Were rich with ladies cheering loyally.

They moved like June morning on the wave,
    Their hearts were fresh as clover in its prime
    (It was a breezy summer-time),
      Life throbbed so strong,
How should they dream that Death, in a rosy clime
  Would come to thin their shining throng?
Youth feels immortal, like the gods sublime.

Weeks passed; and at my window, leaving bed,
    By night I mused, of easeful sleep bereft,
    On those brave boys (Ah War! thy theft);
      Some marching feet
Found pause at last by the cliffs Potomac cleft;
  Wakeful I mused, while in the street
Far footfalls died away till none were left.
                              —*Herman Melville.*

READY

LOADED with gallant soldiers,
  A boat shot in to the land,

And lay at the right of Rodman's Point,
   With her keel upon the sand.

Lightly, gaily, they came to shore,
   And never a man afraid;
When sudden the enemy opened fire
   From his deadly ambuscade.

Each man fell flat on the bottom
   Of the boat; and the captain said:
"If we lie here, we all are captured,
   And the first who moves is dead!"

Then out spoke a negro sailor,
   No slavish soul had he;
"Somebody's got to die, boys,
   And it might as well be me!"

Firmly he rose, and fearlessly
   Stepped out into the tide;
He pushed the vessel safely off,
   Then fell across her side;

Fell, pierced by a dozen bullets,
   As the boat swung clear and free;—
There was n't a man of them that day
   Who was fitter to die than he!
               —*Phœbe Cary.*

THE PICKET-GUARD

"ALL quiet along the Potomac," they say,
   "Except now and then a stray pickèt
Is shot as he walks on his beat to and fro,
   By a rifleman hid in the thicket.

'T is nothing: a private or two, now and then
  Will not count in the news of the battle;
Not an officer lost—only one of the men,
  Moaning out, all alone, the death rattle."

All quiet along the Potomac to-night,
  Where the soldiers lie peacefully dreaming;
Their tents in the rays of the clear autumn moon,
  Or the light of the watch-fires, are gleaming.
A tremulous sigh, as the gentle night-wind
  Through the forest leaves softly is creeping;
While stars up above, with their glittering eyes,
  Keep guard, for the army is sleeping.

There 's only the sound of the lone sentry's tread,
  As he tramps from the rock to the fountain,
And thinks of the two in the low trundle-bed
  Far away in the cot on the mountain.
His musket falls slack; his face, dark and grim,
  Grows gentle with memories tender,
As he mutters a prayer for the children asleep—
  For their mother—may Heaven defend her!

The moon seems to shine just as brightly as then,
  That night, when the love yet unspoken
Leaped up to his lips—when low-murmured vows
  Were pledged to be ever unbroken.
Then drawing his sleeve roughly over his eyes,
  He dashes off tears that are welling,
And gathers his gun closer up to its place
  As if to keep down the heart-swelling.

He passes the fountain, the blasted pine tree;
  The footstep is lagging and weary;
Yet onward he goes, through the broad belt of light,
  Towards the shades of the forest so dreary.

Hark! was it the night-wind that rustled the leaves?
  Was it moonlight so wondrously flashing?
It looked like a rifle—" Ha! Mary, good bye! "
  And the life-blood is ebbing and plashing.

All quiet along the Potomac to-night,
  No sound save the rush of the river;
While soft falls the dew on the face of the dead—
  The picket 's off duty for ever!
                              —*Ethel Lynn Beers.*

ZOLLICOFFER

FIRST in the fight, and first in the arms
    Of the white-winged angels of glory,
With the heart of the South at the feet of God,
    And his wounds to tell the story.

For the blood that flowed from his hero heart,
    On the spot where he nobly perished,
Was drunk by the earth as a sacrament
    In the holy cause he cherished.

In Heaven a home with the brave and blessed,
    And for his soul's sustaining
The apocalyptic eyes of Christ—
    And nothing on earth remaining,

But a handful of dust in the land of his choice,
    A name in song and story,
And fame to shout with immortal voice,
    Dead on the field of glory.
                              —*Henry Lynden Flash.*

BOY BRITTAN—only a lad—a fair-haired boy—six-
    teen,
        In his uniform!
Into the storm—into the roaring jaws of grim Fort Henry—
  Boldly bears the Federal flotilla—
        Into the battle storm!

Boy Brittan is master's mate aboard of the *Essex*—
  There he stands, buoyant and eager-eyed,
        By the brave Captain's side;
Ready to do and dare. Aye, aye, sir! always ready—
        In his country's uniform!
Boom! boom! and now the flag-boat sweeps, and now the
    Essex,
        Into the battle storm!

Boom! boom! till river and fort and field are overclouded
  By battle's breath; then from the fort a gleam
And a crashing gun, and the *Essex* is wrapped and shrouded
        In a scalding cloud of steam!

        But victory! victory!
Unto God all praise be ever rendered,
  Unto God all praise and glory be!
  See, Boy Brittan, see, boy, see!
They strike! Hurrah! the fort has just surrendered!
  Shout! shout! my boy, my warrior-boy!
And wave your cap and clap your hands for joy!
  Cheer answer cheer and bear the cheer about—
Hurrah! hurrah! for the fiery fort is ours;
  And "Victory!" "Victory!" "Victory!"
        Is the shout.
Shout—for the fiery fort, and the field, and the day are
    ours—

The day is ours—thanks to the brave endeavour
      Of heroes, boy, like thee!
The day is ours—the day is ours—
Glory and deathless love to all who shared with thee,
And bravely endured and dared with thee—
    The day is ours—the day is ours—
        For ever!
Glory and love for one and all; but—but—for thee—
  Home! home! a happy "Welcome! welcome home!" for
    thee!
       And kisses of love for thee—
And a mother's happy, happy tears, and a virgin's bridal
    wreath of flowers—
        For thee!

        Victory! victory!
But suddenly wrecked and wrapped in seething steam, the
    Essex
  Slowly drifted out of the battle's storm;
Slowly, slowly down—laden with the dead and the dying;
And there, at the Captain's feet, among the dead and the
    dying,
The shot-marred form of a beautiful boy is lying—
      There in his uniform!

Laurels and tears for thee, boy,
      Laurels and tears for thee!
Laurels of light moist with the precious dew
  Of the inmost heart of the nation's loving heart,
And blessed by the balmy breath of the beautiful and the
    true;
  Moist—moist with the luminous breath of the singing
    spheres
      And the nation's starry tears!
And tremble-touched by the pulse-like gush and start

Of the universal music of the heart,
                And all deep sympathy!
Laurels and tears for thee, boy,
                Laurels and tears for thee—
Laurels of light and tears of love, for evermore—
                For thee!

And laurels of light and tears of truth,
                And the mantle of immortality;
And the flowers of love and of immortal youth,
And the tender heart-tokens of all true ruth—
                And the everlasting victory!
    And the breath and bliss of liberty,
    And the loving kiss of liberty;
And the welcoming light of Heavenly eyes,
    And the over-calm of God's canopy;
And the infinite love-span of the skies
That cover the valleys of Paradise—
    For all of the brave who rest with thee;
    And for one and all who died with thee,
    And now sleep side by side with thee;
And for every one who lives and dies
    On the solid land or the heaving sea,
                Dear warrior-boy—like thee!

                Oh! the victory—the victory
                Belongs to thee!
God ever keeps the brightest crown for such as thou—
                He gives it now to thee!
O young and brave, and early and thrice blessed—
                Thrice, thrice, thrice blessed!
The country turns once more to kiss thy youthful brow,
    And takes thee—gently—gently to her breast;
And whispers lovingly: "God bless thee—bless thee now—
                My darling, thou shalt rest!"
                                —*Forceythe Willson.*

THE "CUMBERLAND"

A T anchor in Hampton Roads we lay,
   On board of the *Cumberland*, sloop-of-war;
And at times from the fortress across the bay
   The alarum of drums swept past,
   Or a bugle blast
From the camp on the shore.

Then far away to the south uprose
   A little feather of snow-white smoke,
And we knew that the iron ship of our foes
   Was steadily steering its course
   To try the force
Of our ribs of oak.

Down upon us heavily runs,
   Silent and sullen, the floating fort;
Then comes a puff of smoke from her guns,
   And leaps the terrible death,
   With fiery breath,
From each open port.

We are not idle, but send her straight
   Defiance back in a full broadside!
As hail rebounds from a roof of slate,
   Rebounds our heavier hail
   From each iron scale
Of the monster's hide.

" Strike your flag!" the rebel cries,
   In his arrogant old plantation strain.
"Never!" our gallant Morris replies;
   "It is better to sink than to yield!"
   And the whole air pealed
With the cheers of our men.

Then, like a kraken huge and black,
  She crushed our ribs in her iron grasp!
Down went the *Cumberland* all a wrack,
    With a sudden shudder of death,
    And the cannon's breath
  For her dying gasp.

Next morn, as the sun rose over the bay,
  Still floated our flag at the mainmast head.
Lord, how beautiful was Thy day!
    Every waft of the air
    Was a whisper of prayer,
  Or a dirge for the dead.

Ho! brave hearts that went down in the seas!
  Ye are at peace in the troubled stream;
Ho! brave land! with hearts like these,
    Thy flag, that is rent in twain,
    Shall be one again,
  And without a seam!
            —*Henry Wadsworth Longfellow.*

THE CRUISE OF THE "MONITOR"

OUT of a Northern city's bay,
  'Neath lowering clouds, one bleak March day,
Glided a craft—the like, I ween,
On ocean's crest was never seen
Since Noah's float, that ancient boat,
Could o'er a conquered deluge gloat.

No raking masts, with clouds of sail,
Bent to the breeze, or braved the gale;
No towering chimney's wreaths of smoke
Betrayed the mighty engine's stroke;

But low and dark, like the crafty shark,
Moved in the waters this novel bark.

The fishers stared as the flitting sprite
Passed their huts in the misty light,
Bearing a turret huge and black,
And said, " The old sea-serpent 's back,
Carting away by light of day,
Uncle Sam's fort from New York Bay."

Forth from a Southern city's dock
Our frigates' strong blockade to mock,
Crept a monster of rugged build,
The work of crafty hands, well skilled—
Old *Merrimac,* with an iron back
Wooden ships would find hard to crack.

Straight to where the *Cumberland* lay,
The mail-clad monster made its way;
Its deadly prow struck deep and sure,
And the hero's fighting days were o'er.
Ah! many the braves who found their graves,
With that good ship, beneath the waves!

But with their fate is glory wrought,
Those hearts of oak like heroes fought
With desperate hope to win the day,
And crush the foe that 'fore them lay.
Our flag up run, the last-fired gun,
Tokens how bravely duty was done.

Flushed with success, the victor flew,
Furious, the startled squadron through:
Sinking, burning, driving ashore,
Until that Sabbath day was o'er,

Resting at night to renew the fight
With vengeful ire by morning's light.

Out of its den it burst anew,
When the gray mist the sun broke through,
Steaming to where, in clinging sands,
The frigate *Minnesota* stands,
A sturdy foe to overthrow,
But in woful plight to receive a blow.

But see! Beneath her bow appears
A champion no danger fears;
A pigmy craft, that seems to be
To this new lord who rules the sea,
Like David of old to Goliath bold—
Youth and giant, by Scripture told.

Round the roaring despot playing,
With willing spirit, helm obeying,
Spurning the iron against it hurled,
While belching turret rapid whirled,
And swift shot's seethe, with smoky wreath,
Told that the shark was showing his teeth.

The *Monitor* fought. In grim amaze
The *Merrimacs* upon it gaze,
Cowering beneath the iron hail,
Crashing into their coat of mail;
They swore " this craft, the devil's shaft,
Looked like a cheese-box on a raft."

Hurrah! little giant of '62!
Bold Worden with his gallant crew
Forces the fight; the day is won;
Back to his den the monster 's gone,

With crippled claws and broken jaws,
Defeated in a reckless cause.

Hurrah for the master mind that wrought,
With iron hand, this iron thought!
Strength and safety, with speed combined,
Ericsson's gift to all mankind;
To curb abuse, and chains to loose,
Hurrah for the *Monitor's* famous cruise!
—*George Henry Boker.*

THE DAUGHTER OF THE REGIMENT

WHO with the soldiers was staunch danger-sharer,—
  Marched in the ranks through the shriek of the shell?
Who was their comrade, their brave colour-bearer?
  Who but the resolute Kady Brownell!

Over the marshland and over the highland,
  Where'er the columns wound, meadow or dell,
Fared she, this daughter of little Rhode Island,—
  She, the intrepid one, Kady Brownell!

While the mad rout at Manassas was surging,
  When those around her fled wildly, or fell,
And the bold Beauregard onward was urging,
  Who so undaunted as Kady Brownell!

When gallant Burnside made dash upon Newberne,
  Sailing the *Neuse* 'gainst the sweep of the swell,
Watching the flag on the heaven's broad blue burn,
  Who higher hearted than Kady Brownell?

In the deep slough of the springtide debarking,
  Toiling o'er leagues that are weary to tell,

Time with the sturdiest soldiery marking
　　Forward, straight forward, strode Kady Brownell.

Reaching the lines where the army was forming,
　　Forming to charge on those ramparts of hell,
When from the wood came her regiment swarming,
　　Nay, but this woman would—Kady Brownell!

See! why she saw that their friends thought them foemen;
　　Muskets were levelled, and cannon as well!
Save them from direful destruction would no men?
　　Nay, but this woman would,—Kady Brownell!

Waving her banner she raced for the clearing;
　　Fronted them all, with her flag as a spell;
Ah, what a volley—a volley of cheering—
　　Greeted the heroine, Kady Brownell!

Gone (and thank God!) are those red days of slaughter!
　　Brethren again we in amity dwell;
Just one more cheer for the Regiment's Daughter!—
　　Just one more cheer for her, Kady Brownell!
　　　　　　　　　　　　—Clinton Scollard.

JOHNSTON AT SHILOH

'MID dim and solemn forests, in the dawning chill and
　　gray,
Over dank, unrustling leaves, or through stiff and sodden
　　clay,
With never a fife or bugle, or mutter of rumbling drum,
With shivering forms and solemn souls the Southern soldiers
　　come;
Their long lines vanishing in mist as onward they are
　　sweeping,

With step as silent as the dawn's, to where the foe is sleeping.
A challenge!—"Halt!"—The expected shot,—and then a
dozen more,
Like pebbles pattering down the steep the avalanche before;
And then a rush, and then a yell, and then a blinding glare,
And then a crash to lift the feet resounding everywhere!
Now vanish chill and solemn thoughts, now burns the fren-
zied blood;
The tottering tents toss to and fro upon the driving flood,
And the campfires flash and darken fast beneath the masses'
tread—
Now smoke behind in scattered brands 'mid wounded men and
dead.
And forward crowd the fugitives in panic-driven race;
In vain in bush, ravine, and brake they hunt a hiding-
place;
For still that long line onward sweeps unbroken far and
near,
As War, himself, with pinions bowed, were screaming in
their rear.
But far beyond the panic's reach the foe is forming fast,
And in our path stands rank on rank of long battalions
massed.
Now, Southern soldiers, nerve your hearts and gather up your
strength,
The time of trial waited for is come to you at length!
A hundred pieces open, and their shrieking missiles pour,
While full ten thousand muskets flash and mingle with the
roar,
Till the cannon's boom is swallowed in the din of musketry,
As the booming of the ocean when the thunders crash on
high.
But momently our labouring lines are charging o'er the
field,
And forcing back the stubborn ranks that only inches yield;

For at every fence they rally and oppose our surging flood,
Till their dead lie heaped before us wherever they have
    stood.
A Southern regiment there is matched against a full brigade,
And not a hundred yards apart in open field arrayed;
A brook half way between us, through a copse of willows
    glides—
There 's not a rock, fence, log, or tree to shelter ours
    besides;
But stubbornly, undauntedly, with ne'er a cheer nor shout,
With hands too busy for their lips they deal their volleys
    out.

Again the battle gathers strength on yonder wooded hill,
Behind whose awful batteries fresh ranks are forming
    still;
A reeking veil of undergrowth divides the hostile lines,
But lurid through its tangled web the vivid lightning
    shines!
And so affrighted Death appears behind that dreadful pall,
The stoutest spirit hesitates and flinches from his call.
Now who will pierce that curtain dire and meet the battle's
    brunt,
Before their armies gather there and burst upon our front?
Again the stern portentous cry of "Bayonets" is heard,
But not again the serried line springs forward at the word.
Behind the trees as skirmishers the cowering soldiers hide,
And from afar the harmless trade of musket balls is plied,
In vain, in vain, their leaders shout, they cannot make them
    stir,
But perish singly in the lead with scarce a follower!

But hark, a sound of hoofs behind, a clang of sabres loud!
I see a squad of mighty men go by me like a cloud!

As the immortals rode to war when Hector fought for Troy,
These ride, as if immortals, too, inspired with awful joy.
Before them spurs their leader with a form that fills the air,
So does his bearing fill their eyes, as if a god were there!
See how he goes to battle with a glory on his brow,
As if prophetic Victory held laurels o'er it now—
They 're racing to the rescue: it is Johnston rides before;
God grant they be in time to turn the battle's tide once
    more!

I hear their shoutings in the din; I hear the cries to " form! "
I see a stiffening battle line take shape within the swarm;
And again the rank advances with an impetus of wrath,
Their chieftain's rage in every heart impels them on the
    path.
A thousand rifles levelled low, but every rifle dumb,
The beating of a thousand feet as on a monster drum.
A surging of the war cloud as they disappear beneath,
A sickening of the spirit and a gasping of the breath;
Redoubled din—a lull—a cheer; I would the smoke would go!
Oh, see our sweeping battle flags! Oh, see the fleeing foe!
Now glory to those gallant men! and Father, to Thy hand
To-morrow shall our praises ring throughout our stricken
    land!

But where is he who rallied them? I miss his charger
    there;
I see him now 'midst yonder three whose saddles all are
    bare;
And two men staggering with a load this side of them I
    see;
Oh, who is it they carry in their arms so tenderly?
They lay him gently on the leaves. Ah, well I know him
    now!
I know that lordly figure and that grand imperial brow!

'T is he; but oh, how prostrate is that form which filled the
    air!
And his the pallid face; but look, the glory still is there!

Oh, ye daughters of Kentucky, ere your pæans are begun,
Your lips shall falter when they tell how Shiloh's fight was
    won!
Your hands shall weave the victor crown of laurels, but in
    vain;
His marble brow shall never feel, nor pulse beat quick again.
Oh, South, be sure a heart so pure had never loved so well!
A country which had wronged him sore he pardoned ere he
    fell.

—Fleming James.

BEAUREGARD

OUR trust is now in thee,
    Beauregard!
In thy hand the God of Hosts
    Hath placed the sword;
And the glory of thy fame
Has set the world aflame—
Hearts kindle at thy name,
    Beauregard!

The way that lies before
    Is cold and hard;
We are led across the desert
    By the Lord!
But the cloud that shines by night
To guide our steps aright,
Is the pillar of thy might,
    Beauregard!

Thou hast watched the southern heavens
    Evening starred,
And chosen thence thine emblems,
    Beauregard;
And upon thy banner's fold
Is that starry cross enrolled,
Which no Northman shall behold
    Shamed or scarred.

In the blood that crieth loudly
    From the sword,
We have sworn to keep around it
    Watch and ward.
And the standard of thine hand
Yet shall shine above a land,
Like its leader, free and grand,
    Beauregard!

                    —*Caroline Anne Warfield.*

ASTRÆA AT THE CAPITOL

WHEN first I saw our banner wave
    Above the nation's council-hall,
I heard beneath its marble wall
The clanking fetters of the slave!

In the foul market-place I stood,
    And saw the Christian mother sold,
    And childhood with its locks of gold,
Blue-eyed and fair with Saxon blood.

I shut my eyes, I held my breath,
    And smothering down the wrath and shame
    That set my Northern blood aflame,
Stood silent,—where to speak was death.

Beside me gloomed the prison-cell
  Where wasted one in slow decline
  For uttering simple words of mine,
And loving freedom all too well.

The flags that floated from the dome
  Flapped menace in the morning air;
  I stood a perilled stranger where
The human broker made his home.

For crime was virtue; Gown and Sword
  And Law their threefold sanction gave,
  And to the quarry of the slave
Went hawking with our symbol-bird.

On the oppressor's side was power;
  And yet I knew that every wrong,
  However old, however strong,
But waited God's avenging hour.

I knew that truth would crush the lie,—
  Somehow, sometime, the end would be;
  Yet scarcely dared I hope to see
The triumph with my mortal eye.

But now I see it! In the sun
  A free flag floats from yonder dome,
  And at the nation's hearth and home
A justice long delayed is done.

Not as we hoped, in calm of prayer,
  The message of deliverance comes,
  But heralded by roll of drums
On waves of battle-troubled air!

Midst sounds that madden and appal,
    The song that Bethlehem's shepherds knew!
    The harp of David melting through
The demon-agonies of Saul!

Not as we hoped; but what are we?
    Above our broken dreams and plans
    God lays with wiser hand than man's,
The corner-stones of liberty.

I cavil not with Him: the voice
    That Freedom's blessed gospel tells
    Is sweet to me as silver bells,
Rejoicing! yea, I will rejoice!

Dear friends still toiling in the sun;
    Ye dearer ones who, gone before,
    Are watching from the eternal shore
The slow work by your hands begun,

Rejoice with me! The chastening rod
    Blossoms with love; the furnace heat
    Grows cool beneath His blessed feet
Whose form is as the Son of God!

Rejoice! Our Marah's bitter springs
    Are sweetened; on our ground of grief
    Rise day by day in strong relief
The prophecies of better things.

Rejoice in hope! The day and night
    Are one with God, and one with them
    Who see by faith the cloudy hem
Of Judgement fringed with Mercy's light!
                    —*John Greenleaf Whittier.*

THE RIVER-FIGHT

DO you know of the dreary land,
   If land such region may seem,
Where 't is neither sea nor strand,
Ocean nor good dry land,
But the nightmare marsh of a dream—
Where the Mighty River his death-road takes,
'Mid pools and windings that coil like snakes,
A hundred leagues of bayous and lakes,
   To die in the great Gulf Stream?

No coast-line clear and true,
Granite and deep-sea blue,
On that dismal shore you pass,
Surf-worn boulder or sandy beach,
But ooze-flats as far as the eye can reach,
With shallows of water-grass;
Reedy savannahs, vast and dun,
Lying dead in the dim March sun;
Huge rotting trunks and roots that lie
Like the blackened bones of shapes gone by,
   And miles of sunken morass.

No lovely, delicate thing
Of life o'er the waste is seen,
But the cayman couched by his weedy spring,
And the pelican, bird unclean,
Or the buzzard, flapping with heavy wing,
Like an evil ghost o'er the desolate scene.
Ah, many a weary day
With our Leader there we lay,
In the sultry haze and smoke,
Tugging our ships o'er the bar,
Till the spring was wasted far,
Till his brave heart almost broke.

For the sullen river seemed
As if our intent he dreamed—
  All his shallow mouths did spew and choke.

But, ere April fully passed,
All ground over at last,
And we knew the die was cast—
Knew the day drew nigh
To dare to the end one stormy deed,
Might save the land at her sorest need,
  Or on the old deck to die!

Anchored we lay,—and a morn the more,
To his captains and all his men
Thus wrote our stout old Commodore
(He was n't an Admiral then) :—

GENERAL ORDERS

" Send your to'gallant masts down,
Rig in each flying jib-boom!
Clear all ahead for the loom
Of traitor fortress and town,
Or traitor fleet bearing down.

" In with your canvas high;
We shall want no sail to fly!
Topsail, foresail, spanker and jib,
(With the heart of oak in the oaken rib),
Shall serve us to win or die!
Trim every sail by the head
(So shall you spare the lead),
Lest, if she ground, your ship swing round,
Bows in-shore, for a wreck.
See your grapnels all clear, with pains,

And a solid kedge in your port main-chains,
With a whip to the main-yard:
Drop it, heavy and hard,
   When you grapple a traitor deck!

" On forecastle and on poop
Mount guns, as best you may deem.
If possible, rouse them up,
(For still you must bow the stream),
Also hoist and secure with stops
Howitzers firmly in your tops,
   To fire on the foe abeam.

" Look well to your pumps and hose;
Have water-tubs, fore and aft,
For quenching flame in your craft,
And the gun crew's fiery thirst,
See planks with felt fitted close,
To plug every shot-hole tight.
Stand ready to meet the worst!
For, if I have reckoned aright,
They will serve us shot,
Both cold and hot,
   Freely enough to-night.

" Mark well each signal I make
(Our life-long service at stake,
And honour that must not lag!)
Whate'er the peril and awe,
In the battle's fieriest flaw,
Let never one ship withdraw
   Till orders come from the flag! "

Would you hear of the river fight?
It was two, of a soft spring night;

God's stars looked down on all;
And all was clear and bright
But the low fog's clinging breath;
Up the River of Death
   Sailed the great Admiral.

On our high poop-deck he stood,
And around him ranged the men
Who have made their birthright good
Of manhood, once and again—
Lords of helm and of sail,
Tried in tempest and gale,
Bronzed in battle and wreck—
Bell and Bailey grandly led
Each his line of the Blue and Red;
Wainwright stood by our starboard rail,
Thornton fought the deck.
And I mind me of more than they,
Of the youthful, steadfast ones,
That have shown them worthy sons,
Of the seamen passed away.
Tyson conned our helm that day,
   Watson stood by his guns.

What thought our Admiral then,
Looking down on his men?
Since the terrible day
(Day of renown and tears!),
When at anchor the *Essex* lay,
Holding her foes at bay,
When a boy by Porter's side he stood,
Till deck and plank-sheer were dyed with blood,
'T is a half a hundred years—
   Half a hundred years to a day!

Who could fail with him?
Who reckon of life or limb?
Not a pulse but beat the higher!
There had you seen, by the star-light dim,
Five hundred faces strong and grim:
The Flag is going under fire!
Right up by the fort,
With her helm hard aport,
The *Hartford* is going under fire!

The way to our work was plain.
Caldwell had broken the chain
(Two hulks swung down amain
   Soon as 't was sundered).
Under the night's dark blue,
Steering steady and true,
Ship after ship went through—
Till, as we hove in view,
Jackson out-thundered!

Back echoed Philip! ah, then
Could you have seen our men,
How they sprung, in the dim night haze,
To their work of toil and of clamour!
How the boarders, with sponge and rammer,
And their captains, with cord and hammer,
Kept every muzzle ablaze.
How the guns, as with cheer and shout—
Our tackle-men hurled them out—
   Brought up on the water-ways!

First, as we fired at their flash,
'T was lightning and black eclipse,
With a bellowing roll and crash.
But soon, upon either bow,
What with forts and fire-rafts and ships
(The whole fleet was hard at it now),

All pounding away!—and Porter
Still thundering with shell and mortar—
'T was the mighty sound and form
Of an equatorial storm!
(Such you see in the far South,
After long heat and drought,
As day draws nigh to even—
Arching from north to south,
Blinding the tropic sun,
The great black bow comes on,
Till the thunder-veil is riven,
When all is crash and levin,
And the cannonade from heaven
   Rolls down the Amazon!)

But, as we worked along higher,
Just where the river enlarges,
Down came a pyramid of fire,—
It was one of your long coal barges,
(We had often had the like before.)
'T was coming down on us to larboard,
Well in with the eastern shore;
And our pilot, to let it pass round
(You may guess we never stopped to sound),
Giving us a rank sheer to starboard,
   Ran the Flag hard and fast aground!

'T was night abreast of the Upper Fort,
And straightway a rascal ram
(She was shaped like the devil's dam)
Puffed away from us with a snort,
And shoved it with spiteful strength,
Right alongside of us to port.
It was all of our ship's length,
A huge crackling Cradle of the Pit!
Pitch-pine knots to the brim,

Belching flame red and grim,
What a roar came up from it!

Well, for a little it looked bad:
But these things are, somehow, shorter
In the acting than in the telling;
There was no singing-out nor yelling,
Or any fussing and fretting,
No stampede, in short;
But there we were, my lad,
All afire on our port quarter,
Hammocks ablaze in the netting,
Flames spouting in at every port,
Our fourth cutter burning at the davit
(No chance to lower away and save it).

In a twinkling, the flames had risen
Halfway to maintop and mizzen,
Darting up the shrouds like snakes!
Ah, how we clanked at the brakes,
And the deep steaming pumps throbbed under,
Sending a ceaseless flow—
Our topmen, a dauntless crowd,
Swarmed in rigging and shroud:
There ('t was a wonder!)
The burning ratlines and strands
They quenched with their bare, hard hands;
But the great guns below
Never silenced their thunder!

At last, by backing and sounding,
When we were clear of grounding,
And under headway once more,
The whole rebel fleet came rounding
The point. If we had it hot before,
'T was now, from shore to shore,

One long, loud, thundering roar—
Such crashing, splintering, and pounding,
And smashing as you never heard before!

But that we fought foul wrong to wreck,
And to save the land we loved so well,
You might have deemed our long gun-deck
Two hundred feet of hell!
For all above was battle,
Broadside, and blaze, and rattle,
Smoke and thunder alone—
(But, down in the sick-bay,
Where our wounded and dying lay,
There was scarce a sob or a moan).

And at last, when the dim day broke,
And the sullen sun awoke,
Drearily blinking
O'er the haze and the cannon smoke,
That ever such morning dulls—
There were thirteen traitor hulls
On fire and sinking!

Now, up the river!—though mad Chalmette
Sputters a vain resistance yet,
Small helm we gave her, our course to steer—
'T was nicer work than you well would dream,
With cant and sheer to keep her clear
    Of the burning wrecks that cumbered the stream.

The *Louisiana,* hurled on high,
Mounts in thunder to meet the sky!
Then down to the depths of the turbid flood,
Fifty fathom of rebel mud!
The *Mississippi* comes floating down,
A mighty bonfire, from off the town;

And along the river, on stocks and ways,
A half-hatched devil's brood is ablaze—
The great Anglo-Norman is all in flames,
(Hark to the roar of her trembling frames!)
And the smaller fry that Treason would spawn
Are lighting Algiers like an angry dawn!

From stem to stern, how the pirates burn,
Fired by the furious hands that built!
So to ashes for ever turn
The suicide wrecks of wrong and guilt!

But as we neared the city,
By field and vast plantation,
(Ah, millstone of our nation!)
With wonder and with pity,
What crowds we there espied
Of dark and wistful faces,
Mute in their toiling places,
Strangely and sadly eyed
Haply 'mid doubt and fear,
Deeming deliverance near
(One gave the ghost of a cheer!)

And on that dolorous strand,
To greet the victor brave
One flag did welcome wave—
Raised, ah me! by a wretched hand,
All outworn on our cruel land,—
The withered hand of a slave!

But all along the levee,
In a dark and drenching rain
(By this, 't was pouring heavy),
Stood a fierce and sullen train,
A strange and frenzied time!
There were scowling rage and pain,

Curses, howls, and hisses,
Out of hate's black abysses—
Their courage and their crime
All in vain—all in vain!

For from the hour that the Rebel Stream,
With the Crescent City lying abeam,
Shuddered under our keel,
Smit to the heart with self-struck sting,
Slavery died in her scorpion-ring,
  And Murder fell on his steel.

'T is well to do and dare;
But ever may grateful prayer
Follow, as ay it ought,
When the good fight is fought,
When the true deed is done.
Aloft in heaven's pure light
(Deep azure crossed on white),
Our fair Church pennant waves
O'er a thousand thankful braves,
  Bareheaded in God's bright sun.

Lord of mercy and frown,
Ruling o'er sea and shore,
Send us such scene once more!
All in line of battle
When the black ships bear down
On tyrant fort and town,
'Mid cannon cloud and rattle;
And the great guns once more
Thunder back the roar
Of the traitor walls ashore,
And the traitor flags come down.
                    —*Henry Howard Brownell.*

BUTLER'S PROCLAMATION

AYE! drop the treacherous mask! throw by
  The cloak that veiled thine instincts fell,
Stand forth, thou base, incarnate Lie,
  Stamped with the signet brand of hell!
At last we view thee as thou art,
A trickster with a demon's heart.

Off with disguise! no quarter now
  To rebel honour! thou wouldst strike
Hot blushes up the anguished brow,
  And murder Fame and Strength alike.
Beware! ten million hearts aflame
Will burn with hate thou canst not tame!

We know thee now! we know thy race!
  Thy dreadful purpose stands revealed
Naked, before the nation's face!
  Comrades! let Mercy's font be sealed,
While the black banner courts the wind,
And cursed be he who lags behind!

O soldiers, husbands, brothers, sires!
  Think that each stalwart blow ye give
Shall quench the rage of lustful fires,
  And bid your glorious women live
Pure from a wrong whose tainted breath
Were fouler than the foulest death.

O soldiers, lovers, Christians, men!
  Think that each breeze that floats and dies
O'er the red field, from mount or glen,
  Is burdened with a maiden's sighs—
And each false soul that turns to flee,
Consigns his love to infamy!

Think! and strike home! the fabled might
  Of Titans were a feeble power
To that with which your arms should smite
  In the next awful battle-hour!
And deadlier than the bolts of heaven
Should flash your fury's fatal leven!

No pity! let your thirsty bands
  Drink their warm fill at caitiff veins;
Dip deep in blood your wrathful hands,
  Nor pause to wipe those crimson stains.
Slay! slay! with ruthless sword and will—
The God of vengeance bids you "kill!"

Yes! but there's *one who shall not die
  In battle harness!* One for whom
Lurks in the darkness silently
  Another and a sterner doom!
A warrior's end should crown the brave—
For *him,* swift cord! and felon grave!

As loathsome, charnel vapours melt,
  Swept by invisible winds to naught,
So, may this fiend of lust and guilt
  Die like nightmare's hideous thought!
Naught left to mark the mother's name,
Save—immortality of shame!
                        —*Paul Hamilton Hayne.*

KEARNY AT SEVEN PINES

SO that soldierly legend is still on its journey,—
    That story of Kearny who knew not to yield!
'T was the day when with Jameson, fierce Berry, and Birney,
  Against twenty thousand he rallied the field,
Where the red volleys poured, where the clamour rose
    highest,

131

Where the dead lay in clumps through the dwarf oak and
    pine,
Where the aim from the thicket was surest and nighest,—
No charge like Phil Kearny's along the whole line.

When the battle went ill, and the bravest were solemn,
    Near the dark Seven Pines, where we still held our ground,
He rode down the length of the withering column,
    And his heart at our war-cry leapt up with a bound;
He snuffed, like his charger, the wind of our powder,—
    His sword waved us on and we answered the sign;
Loud our cheer as we rushed, but his laugh rang the louder,
    "There 's the devil's own fun, boys, along the whole line!"

How he strode his brown steed! How we saw his blade
    brighten
    In the one hand still left,—and the reins in his teeth!
He laughed like a boy when the holidays heighten,
    But a soldier's glance shot from his visor beneath.
Up came the reserves to the mellay infernal,
    Asking where to go in,—through the clearing or pine?
"O, anywhere! Forward! 'T is all the same, Colonel:
    You 'll find lovely fighting along the whole line!"

Oh, evil the black shroud of night at Chantilly,
    That hid him from sight of his brave men and tried!
Foul, foul sped the bullet that clipped the white lily,
    The flower of our knighthood, the whole army's pride!
Yet we dream that he still,—in that shadowy region
    Where the dead form their ranks at the wan drummer's
        sign—
Rides on, as of old, down the length of his legion,
    And the word still is "Forward!" along the whole line.
                              —*Edmund Clarence Stedman.*

ASHBY

TO the brave all homage render;
  Weep, ye skies of June!
With a radiance pure and tender,
  Shine, O saddened moon!
"Dead upon the field of glory!"—
Hero fit for song and story—
  Lies our bold dragoon!

Well they learned, whose hands have slain him,
  Braver, knightlier foe
Never fought 'gainst Moor or Paynim—
  Rode at Templestowe:
With a mien how high and joyous,
'Gainst the hordes that would destroy us
  Went he forth, we know.

Nevermore, alas! shall sabre
  Gleam around his crest—
Fought his fight, fulfilled his labour,
  Stilled his manly breast—
All unheard sweet nature's cadence,
Trump of fame and voice of maidens;
  Now he takes his rest.

Earth, that all too soon hath bound him,
  Gently wrap his clay!
Linger lovingly around him,
  Light of dying day!
Softly fall, ye summer showers;
Birds and bees, among the flowers
  Make the gloom seem gay.

Then, throughout the coming ages,
  When his sword is rust,

And his deeds in classic pages—
    Mindful of her trust—
Shall Virginia, bending lowly,
Still a ceaseless vigil holy
    Keep above his dust!
             —*John Randolph Thompson.*

MALVERN HILL

YE elms that wave on Malvern Hill
    In prime of morn and May,
Recall ye how McClellan's men
    Here stood at bay?
While deep within yon forest dim
    Our rigid comrades lay—
Some with the cartridge in their mouth,
Others with fixed arms lifted south—
    Invoking so
The cypress glades? Ah, wilds of woe!

The spires of Richmond, late beheld
    Through rifts of musket-haze,
Were closed from view in clouds of dust
    On leaf-walled ways,
Where streamed our wagons in caravan;
    And the Seven Nights and Days
Of march and fast, retreat and flight,
Pinched our grimed faces to ghastly plight—
    Does the elm wood
Recall the haggard beards of blood?

The battle-smoked flag, with stars eclipsed,
    We followed (it never fell!)—
In silence husbanded our strength—
    Received their yell;

Till on this slope we patient turned
  With cannon ordered well;
Reverse we proved was not defeat;
But ah, the sod what thousands meet!—
  Does Malvern Wood
Bethink itself, and muse and brood?

We elms of Malvern Hill
  Remember everything;
But sap the twig will fill;
Wag the world how it will,
  Leaves must be green in Spring.
                    —*Herman Melville.*

THREE HUNDRED THOUSAND MORE

WE are coming, Father Abraham, three hundred thou-
      sand more,
From Mississippi's winding stream and from New Eng-
    land's shore;
We leave our ploughs and workshops, our wives and children
    dear,
With hearts too full for utterance, with but a silent tear;
We dare not look behind us, but steadfastly before:
We are coming, Father Abraham, three hundred thousand
    more!

If you look across the hill-tops that meet the northern sky,
Long moving lines of rising dust your vision may descry;
And now, the wind, an instant, tears the cloudy veil aside,
And floats aloft our spangled flag in glory and in pride,
And bayonets in the sunlight gleam, and bands brave music
    pour:
We are coming, Father Abraham, three hundred thousand
    more!

If you look all up our valleys where the growing harvests
shine,
You may see our sturdy farmer boys fast forming into line;
And children from their mothers' knees are pulling at the
weeds,
And learning how to reap and sow against their country's
needs;
And a farewell group stands weeping at every cottage door;
We are coming, Father Abraham, three hundred thousand
more!

You have called us, and we 're coming, by Richmond's bloody
tide
To lay us down, for Freedom's sake, our brothers' bones be-
side,
Or from foul treason's savage grasp to wrench the murderous
blade,
And in the face of foreign foes its fragments to parade.
Six hundred thousand loyal men and true have gone before:
We are coming, Father Abraham, three hundred thousand
more!

—James Sloane Gibbons.

"OUR LEFT"

FROM dawn to dark they stood
That long midsummer day,
While fierce and fast
The battle blast
Swept rank on rank away.

From dawn to dark they fought,
With legions torn and cleft;
And still the wide
Black battle tide
Poured deadlier on " Our Left."

136

They closed each ghastly gap;
  They dressed each shattered rank;
    They knew—how well—
    That freedom fell
  With that exhausted flank.

"Oh, for a thousand men
  Like these that melt away!"
    And down they came,
    With steel and flame,
  Four thousand to the fray!

Right through the blackest cloud
  Their lightning path they cleft;
    And triumph came
    With deathless fame
  To our unconquered "Left."

Ye of your sons secure,
  Ye of your dead bereft—
    Honour the brave
    Who died to save
  Your all upon "Our Left."
          —*Francis Orrery Ticknor.*

DIRGE FOR A SOLDIER

CLOSE his eyes, his work is done!
    What to him is friend or foeman,
Rise of moon, or set of sun,
  Hand of man, or kiss of woman?
    Lay him low, lay him low,
    In the clover or the snow!
    What cares he? he cannot know:
        Lay him low!

As man may, he fought his fight,
　　Proved his truth by his endeavour,
Let him sleep in solemn night,
　　Sleep for ever and for ever.
　　　Lay him low, lay him low,
　　　In the clover or the snow!
　　　What cares he? he cannot know:
　　　　Lay him low!

Fold him in his country's stars,
　　Roll the drum and fire the volley!
What to him are all our wars,
　　What but death-bemocking folly?
　　　Lay him low, lay him low,
　　　In the clover or the snow!
　　　What cares he? he cannot know:
　　　　Lay him low!

Leave him to God's watching eye;
　　Trust him to the hand that made him.
Mortal love weeps idly by:
　　God alone has power to aid him.
　　　Lay him low, lay him low,
　　　In the clover or the snow!
　　　What cares he? he cannot know:
　　　　Lay him low!

—George Henry Boker.

BARBARA FRIETCHIE

U P from the meadows rich with corn,
　Clear in the cool September morn,

The clustered spires of Frederick stand
Green-walled by the hills of Maryland.

138

Round about them orchards sweep,
Apple and peach tree fruited deep,

Fair as the garden of the Lord
To the eyes of the famished rebel horde,

On that pleasant morn of the early fall,
When Lee marched over the mountain wall,—

Over the mountains winding down,
Horse and foot, into Frederick town.

Forty flags with their silver stars,
Forty flags with their crimson bars,

Flapped in the morning wind: the sun
Of noon looked down, and saw not one.

Up rose old Barbara Frietchie then,
Bowed with her fourscore years and ten;

Bravest of all in Frederick town,
She took up the flag the men hauled down;

In her attic window the staff she set,
To show that one heart was loyal yet.

Up the street came the rebel tread,
Stonewall Jackson riding ahead.

Under his slouched hat left and right
He glanced; the old flag met his sight.

"Halt!"—the dust-brown ranks stood fast.
"Fire!"—out blazed the rifle-blast.

It shivered the window, pane and sash;
It rent the banner with seam and gash.

Quick, as it fell, from the broken staff
Dame Barbara snatched the silken scarf;

She leaned far out on the window-sill,
And shook it forth with a royal will.

" Shoot, if you must, this old gray head,
But spare your country's flag," she said.

A shade of sadness, a blush of shame,
Over the face of the leader came;

The nobler nature within him stirred
To life at that woman's deed and word:

" Who touches a hair of yon gray head
Dies like a dog! March on!" he said.

All day long through Frederick street
Sounded the tread of marching feet:

All day long that free flag tossed
Over the heads of the rebel host;

Ever its torn folds rose and fell
On the loyal winds that loved it well;

And through the hill-gaps sunset light
Shone over it with a warm good-night.

Barbara Frietchie's work is o'er,
And the Rebel rides on his raids no more.

Honour to her! and let a tear
Fall for her sake on Stonewall's bier.

Over Barbara Frietchie's grave,
Flag of Freedom and Union, wave!

Peace and order and beauty draw
Round thy symbol of light and law;

And ever the stars above look down
On thy stars below in Frederick town!
                    —*John Greenleaf Whittier.*

THE VICTOR OF ANTIETAM

WHEN tempest winnowed grain from bran,
        And men were looking for a man,
Authority called you to the van,
                McClellan!
Along the line the plaudits ran,
As later when Antietam's cheers began.

Through storm-cloud and eclipse must move
Each cause and man, dear to the stars and Jove;
Nor always can the wisest tell
Deferred fulfilment from the hopeless knell—
The struggler from the floundering ne'er-do-well.
A pall-cloth on the Seven Days fell,
                McClellan—
Unprosperously heroical!
Who could Antietam's wreath foretell?

Authority called you; then, in mist
And loom of jeopardy—dismissed.
But staring peril soon appalled;
You, the Discarded, she recalled—

Recalled you, nor endured delay;
And forth you rode upon a blasted way,
Arrayed Pope's rout, and routed Lee's array,
      McClellan!
Your tent was choked with captured flags that day,
      McClellan.
Antietam was a telling fray.

Recalled you; and she heard your drum
Advancing through the ghastly gloom.
You manned the wall, you propped the Dome,
You stormed the powerful stormer home,
      McClellan!
Antietam's cannon long shall boom.

At Alexandria, left alone,
      McClellan!
Your veterans sent from you, and thrown
To fields and fortunes all unknown—
What thoughts were yours, revealed to none,
While faithful still you laboured on—
Hearing the far Manassas gun!
      McClellan,
Only Antietam could atone.

You fought in the front (an evil day,
      McClellan)—
The forefront of the first assay;
The Cause went sounding, groped its way;
The leadsmen quarrelled in the bay;
Quills thwarted swords; divided sway;
The rebel flushed in his lusty May:
You did your best, as in you lay,
      McClellan.
Antietam's sun-burst sheds a ray.

Your medalled soldiers love you well,
> McClellan!

Name your name, their true hearts swell;
With you they shook dread Stonewall's spell,
With you they braved the blended yell
Of rebel and maligner fell;
With you in shame or fame they dwell,
> McClellan!

Antietam-braves a brave can tell.

And when your comrades (now so few,
> McClellan—

Such ravage in deep files they rue)
Meet round the board, and sadly view
The empty places; tribute due
They render to the dead—and you!
Absent and silent o'er the blue;
The one-armed lift the wine to you,
> McClellan,

And great Antietam's cheers renew.

—*Herman Melville.*

THE EAGLE OF CORINTH

DID you hear of the fight at Corinth,
How we whipped out Price and Van Dorn?
Ah! that day we earned our rations
(Our cause was God's and the Nation's,
Or we 'd have come out forlorn!)
A long and terrible day!
And, at last, when night grew gray,
By the hundreds, there they lay,
(Heavy sleepers, you 'd say)—
That would n't wake on the morn.

143

Our staff was bare of a flag,
We did n't carry a rag
　In those brave marching days—
Ah, no, but a finer thing!
With never a cord or string,
An eagle, of ruffled wing,
　And an eye of awful gaze.
The grape it rattled like hail,
The minies were dropping like rain,
　The first of a thunder-shower—
　　The wads were blowing like chaff,
(There was pounding, like floor and flail,
　All the front of our line!)
So we stood it, hour after hour—
　But our eagle, he felt fine!
　　'T would have made you cheer and laugh,
To see, through that iron gale,
How the old fellow 'd swoop and sail
Above the racket and roar—
To right and to left he 'd soar,
　But ever came back, without fail,
　　And perched on his standard-staff.

All that day, I tell you true,
　They had pressed us, steady and fair,
　Till we fought in street and square—
(The affair, you might think, looked blue),
　But we knew we had them there!
Our works and batteries were few,
Every gun, they 'd have sworn, they knew—
But, you see, there was one or two
　We had fixed for them, unaware.

　They reckon they 've got us now!
　　For the next half hour 't will be warm—
　Aye, aye, look yonder!—I vow,
If they were n't Secesh, how I 'd love them!

Only see how grandly they form,
(Our eagle whirling above them,)
To take Robinett by storm!
They 're timing!—it can't be long—
Now for the nub of the fight!
(You may guess that we held our breath,
By the Lord, 't is a splendid sight!
A column two thousand strong
Marching square to the death!

On they came, in solid column,
For once, no whooping nor yell—
(Ah, I dare say they felt solemn!)
Front and flank—grape and shell—
Our batteries pounded away!
And the minies hummed to remind 'em
They had started on no child's play!
Steady they kept a-going,
But a grim wake settled behind 'em—
From the edge of the *abattis,*
(Where our dead and dying lay
Under fence and fallen tree),
Up to Robinett, all the way
The dreadful swath kept growing!
'T was butternut, flecked with gray.

Now for it, at Robinett!
Muzzle to muzzle we met—
(Not a breath of bluster or brag,
Not a lisp for quarter or favour)—
Three times, there, by Robinett,
With a rush, their feet they set
On the logs of our parapet,
And waved their bit of a flag—
What could be finer or braver!
But our cross-fire stunned them in flank,

They melted, rank after rank—
(O'er them, with terrible poise,
    Our Bird did circle and wheel!)
        Their whole line began to waver—
Now for the bayonet, boys!
    On them with the cold steel!

Ah, well—you know how it ended—
    We did for them, there and then,
    But their pluck, throughout, was splendid.
(As I said before, I could love them!)
        They stood, to the last, like men—
Only a handful of them
        Found the way back again.

Red as blood, o'er the town,
    The angry sun went down,
        Firing flag-staff and vane—
And our eagle—as for him,
There, all ruffled and grim,
        He sat, o'erlooking the slain!

Next morning, you 'd have wondered
    How we had to drive the spade!
    There, in great trenches and holes,
    (Ah, God rest their poor souls!)
We piled some fifteen hundred,
        Where that last charge was made!

Sad enough, I must say.
    No mother to mourn and search,
No priest to bless or to pray—
We buried them where they lay,
    Without a rite of the church—
But our eagle, all that day,
    Stood solemn and still on his perch.

'T is many a stormy day
  Since, out of the cold, bleak North,
  Our great War Eagle sailed forth
To swoop o'er battle and fray.
Many and many a day
  O'er charge and storm hath he wheeled,
  Foray and foughten field,
    Tramp, and volley, and rattle!—
Over crimson trench and turf,
Over climbing clouds of surf,
Through tempest and cannon-rack,
  Have his terrible pinions whirled—
    (A thousand fields of battle!
    A million leagues of foam!)

But our Bird shall yet come back,
  He shall soar to his eyrie-home—
And his thunderous wings be furled,
In the gaze of a gladdened world,
  On the Nation's loftiest Dome.

—Henry Howard Brownell.

AT FREDERICKSBURG

G OD send us peace, and keep red strife away;
    But should it come, God send us men and steel!
The land is dead that dare not face the day
  When foreign danger threats the common weal.

Defenders strong are they that homes defend;
  From ready arms the spoiler keeps afar,
Well blest the country that has sons to lend
  From trades of peace to learn the trade of war.

Thrice blest the nation that has every son
    A soldier, ready for the warning sound;
Who marches homeward when the fight is done,
    To swing the hammer and to till the ground.

Call back that morning, with its lurid light,
    When through our land the awful war-bell tolled;
When lips were mute, and women's faces white
    As the pale cloud that out from Sumter rolled.

Call back that morn: an instant all were dumb,
    As if the shot had struck the Nation's life;
Then cleared the smoke, and rolled the calling drum,
    And men streamed in to meet the coming strife.

They closed the ledger and they stilled the loom,
    The plough left resting in the prairie farm;
They saw but " Union " in the gathering gloom;
    The tearless women helped the men to arm;

Brigades from towns,—each village sent its band:
    German and Irish, every race and faith;
There was no question then of native land,
    But—love the Flag and follow it to death.

No need to tell their tale: through every age
    The splendid story shall be sung and said;
But let me draw one picture from the page,
    For words of song embalm the hero dead.

.   .   .   .   .

The smooth hill is bare, and the cannons are planted,
    Like Gorgon fates shading its terrible brow;
The word has been passed that the stormers are wanted,
    And Burnside's battalions are mustering now.

The armies stand by to behold the dread meeting;
　The work must be done by a desperate few;
The black-mouthed guns on the height give them greet-
　　ing,
　From gun-mouth to plain every grass blade in view.

Strong earthworks are there, and the rifles behind them
　Are Georgia militia,—an Irish brigade—
Their caps have green badges, as if to remind them
　Of all the brave record their country has made.

The stormers go forward,—the Federals cheer them;
　They breast the smooth hillside,—the black mouths are
　　dumb;
The riflemen lie in the works till they near them,
　And cover the stormers as upward they come.

Was ever a death-march so grand and so solemn?
　At last, the dark summit with flame is enlined;
The great guns belch doom on the sacrificed column
　That reels from the height, leaving hundreds behind.

The armies are hushed,—there is no cause for cheering:
　The fall of brave men to brave men is a pain.
Again come the stormers! and as they are nearing,
　The flame-sheeted rifle-lines reel back again.

And so till full noon come the Federal masses—
　Flung back from the height, as the cliff flings a wave;
Brigade on brigade to the death-struggle passes,
　No wavering rank till it steps on the grave.

Then comes a brief lull, and the smoke-pall is lifted,
　The green of the hillside no longer is seen;
The dead soldiers lie as the sea-weed is drifted,
　The earthworks still held by the badges of green.

Have they quailed? is the word. No: again they are
    forming—
    Again comes a column to death and defeat!
What is it in these who shall now do the storming
    That makes every Georgian spring to his feet?

"O God! what a pity!" they cry in their cover,
    As rifles are readied and bayonets made tight;
"'T is Meagher and his fellows! their caps have green
    clover;
    'T is Greek to Greek now for the rest of the fight!"

Twelve hundred the column, their rent flag before them,
    With Meagher at their head, they have dashed at the
    hill!
Their foemen are proud of the country that bore them;
    But, Irish in love, they are enemies still.

Out rings the fierce word, "Let them have it!" The
    rifles
    Are emptied point-blank in the hearts of the foe:
It is green against green, but a principle stifles
    The Irishman's love in the Georgian's blow.

The column has reeled, but it is not defeated;
    In front of the guns they re-form and attack;
Six times they have done it, and six times retreated,
    Twelve hundred they came, and two hundred go back.

Two hundred go back with the chivalrous story;
    The wild day is closed in the night's solemn shroud
A thousand lie dead, but their death was a glory
    That calls not for tears, the Green Badges are proud!

Bright honour be theirs who for honour were fearless,
　Who charged for their flag to the grim cannon's
　　mouth;
And honour to them who were true but not tearless—
　Who bravely that day kept the cause of the South!

The quarrel is done,—God avert such another!
　The lesson it brought us we should evermore heed.
Who loveth the flag is a man and a brother,
　No matter what birth or what race or what creed.
　　　　　　　　　—John Boyle O'Reilly.

LITTLE GIFFEN

O UT of the focal and foremost fire—
　　Out of the hospital walls as dire;
Smitten of grape-shot and gangrene,
(Eighteenth battle, and *he* sixteen;)
Spectre, such as you seldom see,
Little Giffen of Tennessee!

" Take him?—and welcome!" the surgeon said,
" Much your doctor can help the dead!"
And so we took him, and brought him where
The balm was sweet on the summer air;
　And we laid him down on a wholesome bed,
Utter Lazarus, heel to head!

Weary war with the bated breath,
Skeleton boy against skeleton Death.
Months of torture, how many such!
Weary weeks of the stick and crutch!
Still a glint in the steel-blue eye
Spoke of a spirit that would not die!

And did n't! nay, more! in death's despite
The crippled skeleton learned to write!
" Dear mother," at first, of course; and then,
" Dear captain "—enquiring about " the men."
Captain's answer—" Of eighty and five,
Giffen and I are left alive! "

" Johnston 's pressed at the front, they say! "
Little Giffen was up and away.
A tear, his first, as he bade good bye,
Dimmed the glint of his steel-blue eye:
" I 'll write, if spared." There was news of fight,
But none of Giffen! he did not write!

I sometimes fancy that, were I king
Of the princely Knights of the Golden Ring,
With the song of the minstrel in mine ear,
And the tender legend that trembles here,
I 'd give the best on his bended knee,
The whitest soul of my chivalry,
For little Giffen of Tennessee!

—*Francis Orrery Ticknor.*

BOSTON HYMN

THE word of the Lord by night
To the watching Pilgrims came,
As they sat by the seaside,
And filled their hearts with flame.

God said, I am tired of kings,
I suffer them no more;
Up to my ear the morning brings
The outrage of the poor.

Think ye I made this ball
  A field of havoc and war,
Where tyrants great and tyrants small
  Might harry the weak and poor?

My angel—his name is Freedom—
  Choose him to be your king;
He shall cut pathways east and west,
  And fend you with his wing.

Lo! I uncover the land,
  Which I hid of old time in the west,
As the sculptor uncovers the statue
  When he has wrought his best;

I show Columbia, of the rocks
  Which dip their foot in the seas,
And soar to the air-borne flocks
  Of clouds and the boreal fleece.

I will divide my goods;
  Call in the wretch and slave;
None shall rule but the humble,
  And none but Toil shall have.

I will have never a noble,
  No lineage counted great;
Fishers and choppers and ploughmen
  Shall constitute a state.

Go, cut down trees in the forest
  And trim the straightest boughs;
Cut down trees in the forest
  And build me a wooden house.

Call the people together,
    The young men and the sires,
The digger in the harvest-field,
    Hireling and him that hires;

And here in a pine state-house
    They shall choose men to rule
In every needful faculty,
    In church and state and school.

Lo, now! if these poor men
    Can govern the land and sea,
And make just laws below the sun,
    As planets faithful be.

And ye shall succour men;
    'T is nobleness to serve;
Help them who cannot help again:
    Beware from right to swerve.

I break your bonds and masterships,
    And I unchain the slave:
Free be his heart and hand henceforth
    As wind and wandering wave.

I cause from every creature
    His proper good to flow;
As much as he is and doeth,
    So much he shall bestow.

But, laying hands on another,
    To coin his labour and sweat,
He goes in pawn to his victim
    For eternal years in debt.

To-day unbind the captive,
  So only are ye unbound;
Lift up a people from the dust,
  Trump of their rescue, sound!

Pay ransom to the owner
  And fill the bag to the brim.
Who is the owner? The slave is owner,
  And ever was. Pay him.

O North! give him beauty for rags,
  And honour, O South! for his shame;
Nevada! coin thy golden crags
  With Freedom's image and name.

Up! and the dusky race
  That sat in darkness long,—
Be swift their feet as antelopes,
  And as behemoth strong.

Come, East and West and North,
  By races, as snow-flakes,
And carry my purpose forth,
  Which neither halts nor shakes.

My will fulfiled shall be,
  For, in daylight or in dark,
My thunderbolt has eyes to see
  His way home to the mark.
                    —*Ralph Waldo Emerson.*

THE DEATH OF SLAVERY

O THOU great Wrong, that, through the slow-paced
    years,
Didst hold thy millions fettered, and didst wield

The scourge that drove the labourer to the field,
And turn a stony gaze on human tears,
    Thy cruel reign is o'er;
    Thy bondmen crouch no more
In terror at the menace of thine eye;
    For He who marks the bounds of guilty power,
Long-suffering, hath heard the captive's cry,
    And touched his shackles at the appointed hour,
And lo! they fall, and he whose limbs they galled
Stands in his native manhood, disenthralled.

A shout of joy from the redeemed is sent;
    Ten thousand hamlets swell the hymn of thanks;
    Our rivers roll exulting, and their banks
Send up hosannas to the firmament!
        Fields where the bondman's toil
        No more shall trench the soil.
Seem now to bask in a serener day;
    The meadow-birds sing sweeter, and the airs
Of heaven with more caressing softness play,
    Welcoming man to liberty like theirs.
A glory clothes the land from sea to sea,
For the great land and all its coasts are free.

Within that land wert thou enthroned of late,
    And they by whom the nation's laws were made,
    And they who filled its judgment-seats obeyed
Thy mandate, rigid as the will of Fate.
        Fierce men at thy right hand,
        With gesture of command,
Gave forth the word that none might dare gainsay;
    And grave and reverend ones, who loved thee not,
Shrank from thy presence, and in blank dismay
    Choked down, unuttered, the rebellious thought;
While meaner cowards, mingling with thy train,
Proved, from the book of God, thy right to reign.

Great as thou wert, and feared from shore to shore,
  The wrath of Heaven o'ertook thee in thy pride;
  Thou sitt'st a ghastly shadow; by thy side
Thy once strong arms hang nerveless evermore.
    And they who quailed but now
    Before thy lowering brow,
Devote thy memory to scorn and shame,
  And scoff at the pale, powerless thing thou art.
And they who ruled in thine imperial name,
  Subdued, and standing sullenly apart,
Scowl at the hands that overthrew thy reign,
And shattered at a blow the prisoner's chain.

Well was thy doom deserved; thou didst not spare
  Life's tenderest ties, but cruelly didst part
  Husband and wife, and from the mother's heart
Didst wrest her children, deaf to shriek and prayer;
    Thy inner lair became
    The haunt of guilty shame;
Thy lash dropped blood; the murderer, at thy side,
  Showed his red hands, nor feared the vengeance due.
Thou didst sow earth with crimes, and, far and wide,
  A harvest of uncounted miseries grew,
Until the measure of thy sins at last
Was full, and then the avenging bolt was cast!

Go now, accursed of God, and take thy place
  With hateful memories of the elder time,
  With many a wasting plague, and nameless crime,
And bloody war that thinned the human race;
    With the Black Death, whose way
    Through wailing cities lay,
Worship of Moloch, tyrannies that built
  The Pyramids, and cruel creeds that taught
To avenge a fancied guilt by deeper guilt—

Death at the stake to those that held them not.
Lo! the foul phantoms, silent in the gloom
Of the flown ages, part to yield thee room.

I see the better years that hasten by
  Carry thee back into that shadowy past,
  Where, in the dusty spaces, void and vast,
The graves of those whom thou hast murdered lie.
    The slave-pen, through whose door
    Thy victims pass no more,
Is there, and there shall the grim block remain
  At which the slave was sold; while at thy feet
Scourges and engines of restraint and pain
  Moulder and rust by thine eternal seat.
There, mid the symbols that proclaim thy crimes,
Dwell thou, a warning to the coming times.

—William Cullen Bryant.

MOSBY AT HAMILTON

DOWN Loudon Lanes, with swinging reins
    And clash of spur and sabre,
And bugling of the battle horn
  Sixscore and eight we rode at morn,
  Sixscore and eight of Southern born,
    All tried in love and labour.

Full in the sun at Hamilton,
  We met the South's invaders;
Who, over fifteen hundred strong,
  'Mid blazing homes had marched along
All night, with Northern shout and song
    To crush the rebel raiders.

Down Loudon Lanes, with streaming manes,
  We spurred in wild March weather;

And all along our war-scarred way
The graves of Southern heroes lay,
Our guide-posts to revenge that day,
   As we rode grim together.

Old tales still tell some miracle
   Of saints in holy writing—
But who shall say while hundreds fled
Before the few that Mosby led,
 Unless the noblest of our dead
   Charged with us then when fighting?

While Yankee cheers still stunned our ears,
   Of troops at Harper's Ferry,
While Sheridan led on his Huns,
And Richmond rocked to roaring guns,
We felt the South still had some sons
   She would not scorn to bury.
                        —*Madison Cawein.*

JOHN PELHAM

JUST as the spring came laughing through the strife,
   With all its gorgeous cheer,
In the bright April of historic life,
   Fell the great cannoneer.

The wondrous lulling of a hero's breath
   His bleeding country weeps;
Hushed in the alabaster arms of Death,
   Our young Marcellus sleeps.

Nobler and grander than the Child of Rome
   Curbing his chariot steeds,

The knightly scion of a Southern home
    Dazzled the land with deeds.

Gentlest and bravest in the battle-brunt,
    The champion of the truth,
He bore his banner to the very front
    Of our immortal youth.

A clang of sabres 'mid Virginian snow,
    The fiery pang of shells,—
And there's a wail of immemorial woe
    In Alabama dells.

The pennon drops that led the sacred band
    Along the crimson field;
The meteor blade sinks from the nerveless hand
    Over the spotless shield.

We gazed and gazed upon that beauteous face;
    While round the lips and eyes,
Couched in their marble slumber, flashed the grace
    Of a divine surprise.

O mother of a blessed soul on high!
    Thy tears may soon be shed;
Think of thy boy with princes of the sky,
    Among the Southern dead!

How must he smile on this dull world beneath,
    Fevered with swift renown,—
He, with the martyr's amaranthine wreath
    Twining the victor's crown!

               —*James Ryder Randall.*

THE BATTLE OF CHARLESTON HARBOUR

TWO hours, or more, beyond the prime of the blithe April
    day
The Northmen's mailed "Invincibles" steamed up fair
    Charleston Bay;
They came in sullen file, and slow, low-breasted wave,
Black as a midnight on the front of storm, and silent as the
    grave.

A thousand warrior-hearts beat high as those dread monsters
    drew
More closely to the game of death across the breezeless blue;
And twice ten thousand hearts of those who watch the scene
    afar
Thrill in the awful hush that bides the battle's broadening
    star.

Each gunner, moveless by his gun, with rigid aspect stands,
The ready flintlocks firmly grasped in bold, untrembling
    hands;
So moveless in their marble calm, their stern, heroic guise,
They look like forms of statued stone with burning human
    eyes!

Our banners on the outmost walls, with stately rustling fold,
Flash back from arch and parapet the sunlight's ruddy
    gold;—
They mount to the deep roll of drums, and widely echoing
    cheers,
And then, once more, dark, breathless, hushed, wait the grim
    cannoneers.

Onward, in sullen file, and slow, low-glooming on the wave,
Near, nearer still, the haughty fleet glides silent as the grave,

When, shivering the portentous calm o'er startled flood and
    shore,
Broke from the sacred Island Fort the thunder-wrath of
    yore!

Ha! brutal Corsairs! though ye come thrice-cased in iron
    mail,
Beware the storm that 's opening now, God's vengeance
    guides the hail!
Ye strive, the ruffian types of Might, 'gainst law and truth
    and Right;
Now quail beneath a sturdier Power, and own a mightier
    Might!

The storm has burst! and while we speak, more furious,
    wilder, higher,
Dart from the circling batteries a hundred tongues of fire;
The waves gleam red, the lurid vault of heaven seems rent
    above—
Fight on, O knightly gentlemen, for faith, and home, and
    love!

There 's not, in all that line of flame, one soul that would not
    rise,
To seize the victor's wreath of blood, though Death must give
    the prize;
There 's not, in all this anxious crowd that throngs the
    ancient town,
A maid who does not yearn for power to strike one foeman
    down!

The conflict deepens! Ship by ship the proud Armada
    sweeps,
Where fierce from Sumter's raging breast the volleyed light-
    ning leaps;

And ship by ship, raked, overborne, ere burned the sunset
    light,
Crawls in the gloom of baffled hate beyond the field of fight!

O glorious Empress of the Main! from out thy storied spires
Thou well mayst peal thy bells of joy, and light thy festal
    fires,—
Since Heaven this day hath striven for thee, hath nerved thy
    dauntless sons,
And thou in clear-eyed faith hast seen God's angels near the
    guns!

                                            —*Paul Hamilton Hayne.*

RUNNING THE BATTERIES

A MOONLESS night—a friendly one;
    A haze dimmed the shadowy shore
As the first lampless boat slid silent on;
    Hist! and we spake no more;
We but pointed, and, stilly to what we saw.

We felt the dew, and seemed to feel
    The secret like a burden laid.
The first boat melts; and a second keel
    Is blent in the foliage shade—
Their midnight rounds have the rebel officers made?

Unspied as yet.   A third—a fourth—
    Gunboat and transport in Indian file
Upon the war-path, smooth from the North;
    But the watch may they hope to beguile?
The manned river-batteries stretch far mile on mile.

A flame leaps out; they are seen;
　　Another and another gun roars;
We tell the course of the boats through the screen
　　By each further fort that pours,
And we guess how they jump from their beds on those
　　shrouded shores.

Converging fires.　We speak, though low:
　　" That blastful furnace can they thread? "
" Why, Shadrach, Meshach, and Abednego
　　Came out all right, we read;
The Lord, be sure, he helps his people, Ned."

How we strain our gaze.　On bluffs they shun
　　A golden growing flame appears—
Confirms to a silvery steadfast one:
　　" The town is afire! " crows Hugh: "three cheers! "
Lot stops his mouth: " Nay, lad, better three tears."

A purposed light; it shows our fleet;
　　Yet a little late in its searching ray,
So far and strong, that in phantom cheat
　　Lank on the deck our shadows lay;
The shining flag-ship stings their guns to furious play.

How dread to mark her near the glare
　　And glade of death the beacon throws
Athwart the racing waters there;
　　One by one each plainer grows,
Then speeds a blazoned target to our gladdened foes.

The impartial cresset lights as well
　　The fixed forts to the boats that run;
And, plunged from the ports, their answers swell
　　Back to each fortress dun:
Ponderous words speaks every monster guns.

Fearless they flash through gates of flame,
  The salamanders hard to hit,
Though vivid shows each bulky frame;
  And never the batteries intermit,
Nor the boat's huge guns; they fire and flit.

Anon a lull. The beacon dies:
  "Are they out of that strait accurst?"
But other flames now dawning rise,
  Not mellowly brilliant like the first,
But rolled in smoke, whose whitish volumes burst.

A baleful brand, a hurrying torch
  Whereby anew the boats are seen—
A burning transport all alurch!
  Breathless we gaze; yet still we glean
Glimpses of beauty as we eager lean.

The effulgence takes an amber glow
  Which bathes the hillside villas far;
Affrighted ladies mark the show
  Painting the pale magnolia—
The fair, false, Circe light of Civil War.

The barge drifts doomed, a plague-strick one.
  Shoreward in yawls the sailors fly.
But the gauntlet now is nearly run,
  The spleenful forts by fits reply,
And the burning boat dies down in morning sky.

All out of range. Adieu, Messieurs!
  Jeers, as it speeds, our parting gun.
So burst we through our barriers
  And menaces every one.
So Porter proved himself a brave man's son.
                              —*Herman Melville.*

HOOKER'S ACROSS

HOOKER 's across! Hooker 's across!
Standards and guidons and lance-pennons toss
Over the land where he points with his blade,
Bristle the hill-top, and fill up the glade.
Who would not follow a leader whose blood
Has swelled, like our own, the battle's red flood?
Who bore what we suffered, our wound and our pain,—
Bore them with patience, and dares them again?
                    Hooker 's across!

Hooker 's across! Hooker 's across!
River of death, you shall make up our loss!
Out of your channel we summon each soul,
Over whose body your dark billows roll;
Up from your borders we summon the dead,
From valleys and hills where they struggled and bled,
To joy in the vengeance the traitors shall feel
At the roar of our guns and the rush of our steel!
                    Hooker 's across!

Hooker 's across! Hooker 's across!
Fears to the wind, with our standards, we toss,
Moving together, straight on, with one breath,
Down to the outburst of passion and death.
Oh, in the depths of our spirits we know
If we fail now in the face of the foe,
Flee from the field with our flag soiled and dim,
We may return, but 't will not be with him!
                    Hooker 's across!
                    —*George Henry Boker.*

KEENAN'S CHARGE

THE sun had set;
   The leaves with dew were wet—
Down fell a bloody dusk
 On the woods, that second of May,
Where Stonewall's corps, like a beast of prey,
Tore through, with angry tusk.

"They 've trapped us, boys!"—
Rose from our flank a voice.
With a rush of steel and smoke
On came the Rebels straight,
Eager as love and wild as hate:
And our line reeled and broke;

Broke and fled.
No one stayed—but the dead!
With curses, shrieks, and cries,
Horses and wagons and men
Tumbled back through the shuddering glen,
And above us the fading skies.

There 's one hope, still—
Those batteries parked on the hill!
"Battery, wheel!" ('mid the roar),
"Pass pieces; fix prolonge to fire
Retiring. Trot!" In the panic dire
A bugle rings "Trot"—and no more.

The horses plunged,
The cannon lurched and lunged,
To join the hopeless rout.
But suddenly rode a form
Calmly in front of the human storm,
With a stern, commanding shout:

"Align those guns!"
(We knew it was Pleasanton's.)
The cannoneers bent to obey,
And worked with a will, at his word,
And the black guns moved as if *they* had heard,
But ah, the dread delay!

"To wait is crime;
O God, for ten minutes' time!"
The general looked around.
There Keenan sat, like a stone,
With his three hundred horse alone—
Less shaken than the ground.

"Major, your men?"—
"Are soldiers, General."—"Then,
Charge, Major! Do your best:
Hold the enemy back, at all cost,
Till my guns are placed;—else the army is lost.
You die to save the rest!"

By the shrouded gleam of the western skies,
Brave Keenan looked in Pleasanton's eyes
For an instant—clear, and cool, and still;
Then, with a smile, he said: "I will."
"Cavalry, charge!" Not a man of them shrank.
Their sharp, full cheer, from rank on rank,
Rose joyously, with a willing breath,
Rose like a greeting hail to death.

Then forward they sprang, and spurred, and clashed;
Shouted the officers, crimson-sashed;
Rode well the men, each brave as his fellow,
In their faded coats of the blue and yellow;
And above in the air, with an instinct true,
Like a bird of war their pennon flew.

With clank of scabbards and thunder of steeds,
And blades that shine like sunlit reeds,
And strong brown faces bravely pale
For fear their proud attempt shall fail,
Three hundred Pennsylvanians close
On twice ten thousand gallant foes.

Line after line the troopers came
To the edge of the wood that was ringed with flame;
Rode in, and sabred, and shot—and fell:
Nor came one back his wounds to tell.
And full in the midst rose Keenan, tall
In the gloom, like a martyr awaiting his fall,
While the circle-stroke of his sabre, swung
Round his head, like a halo there, luminous hung.
Line after line; aye, whole platoons,
Struck dead in their saddles, of brave dragoons,
By the maddened horses were onward borne
And into the vortex flung, trampled and torn;
As Keenan fought with his men, side by side.
So they rode, till there were no more to ride.
But over them, lying there, shattered and mute,
What deep echo rolls?—'T is a death salute
From the cannon in place; for, heroes, you braved
Your fate not in vain: the army was saved!

Over them now—year following year—
Over their graves, the pine-cones fall,
And the whippoorwill chants his spectre-call;
But they stir not again; they raise no cheer:
They have ceased. But their glory shall never cease,
Nor their light be quenched in the light of peace.
The rush of their charge is resounding still,
That saved the army at Chancellorsville.

—George Parsons Lathrop.

STONEWALL JACKSON'S WAY

COME, stack arms, men! Pile on the rails,
  Stir up the camp-fire bright;
No matter if the canteen fails,
  We 'll make a roaring night.
Here Shenandoah brawls along,
There burly Blue Ridge echoes strong,
To swell the brigade's rousing song
  Of " Stonewall Jackson's way."

We see him now,—the queer slouched hat
  Cocked o'er his eye askew;
The shrewd, dry smile, the speech so pat,
  So calm, so blunt, so true.
The " Blue-Light Elder " knows 'em well;
Says he, " That 's Banks,—he 's fond of shell;
Lord save his soul! we 'll give him ——; " well,
  That 's " Stonewall Jackson's way."

Silence! ground arms! kneel all! caps off!
  Old Massa's going to pray.
Strangle the fool that dares to scoff!
  Attention! it 's his way.
Appealing from his native sod,
In forma pauperis to God,
" Lay bare Thine arm; stretch forth Thy rod!
  Amen! " That's " Stonewall's way."

He 's in the saddle now. Fall in!
  Steady! the whole brigade!
Hill 's at the ford cut off; we 'll win
  His way out, ball and blade!
What matter if our shoes are worn?
What matter if our feet are torn?
" Quick-step! we 're with him before morn! "
  That 's " Stonewall Jackson's way."

The sun's bright lances rout the mists
  Of morning, and, by George!
Here 's Longstreet struggling in the lists,
  Hemmed in an ugly gorge.
Pope and his Yankees, whipped before,
" Bay'nets and grape! " hear Stonewall roar;
" Charge, Stuart! Pay off Ashby's score! "
  In " Stonewall Jackson's way."

Ah! Maiden, wait and watch and yearn
  For news of Stonewall's band!
Ah! Widow, read, with eyes that burn,
  That ring upon thy hand.
Ah! Wife, sew on, pray on, hope on;
Thy life shall not be all forlorn;
The foe had better ne'er been born
  That gets in " Stonewall's way."

                    —*John Williamson Palmer.*

DEATH OF STONEWALL JACKSON

NOT midst the lightning of the stormy fight,
  Not in the rush upon the vandal foe,
Did kingly Death, with his resistless might,
  Lay the great leader low.

His warrior soul its earthly shackles broke
  In the full sunhine of a peaceful town;
When all the storm was hushed, the trusty oak
  That propped our cause went down.

Though his alone the blood that flecks the ground,
  Recording all his grand, heroic deeds,
Freedom herself is writhing with the wound,
  And all the country bleeds.

He entered not the Nation's Promised Land
  At the red belching of the cannon's mouth;
But broke the House of Bondage with his hand—
  The Moses of the South!

O gracious God! not gainless is the loss:
  A glorious sunbeam gilds thy sternest frown;
And while his country staggers 'neath the Cross,
  He rises with the Crown.

                  —Henry Lynden Flash.

THE BLACK REGIMENT

DARK as the clouds of even,
  Ranked in the western heaven,
Waiting the breath that lifts
All the dread mass, and drifts
Tempest and falling brand
Over a ruined land,—
So still and orderly,
Arm to arm, knee to knee,
Waiting the great event,
Stands the black regiment.

Down the long dusky line
Teeth gleam and eyeballs shine;
And the bright bayonet,
Bristling and firmly set,
Flashed with a purpose grand,
Long ere the sharp command
Of the fierce rolling drum
Told them their time had come,
Told them what work was sent
For the black regiment.

"Now," the flag-sergeant cried,
"Though death and hell betide,
Let the whole nation see
If we are fit to be
Free in this land; or bound
Down, like the whining hound,—
Bound with red stripes of pain
In our old chains again!"
Oh, what a shout there went
From the black regiment!

"Charge!" trump and drum awoke;
Onward the bondmen broke;
Bayonet and sabre-stroke
Vainly opposed their rush.
Through the wild battle's crush,
With but one thought aflush,
Driving their lords like chaff,
In the guns' mouths they laugh,
Or at the slippery brands,
Leaping with open hands,
Down they tear man and horse,
Down in their awful course;
Trampling with bloody heel
Over the crashing steel,
All their eyes forward bent,
Rushed the black regiment.

"Freedom!" their battle-cry,—
"Freedom! or leave to die!"
Ah! and they meant the word,
Not as with us 't is heard,
Not a mere party-shout:
They gave their spirits out;
Trusted the end to God,
And on the gory sod

Rolled in triumphant blood.
Glad to strike one free blow,
Whether for weal or woe;
Glad to breathe one free breath,
Though on the lips of death;
Praying—alas! in vain!—
That they might fall again,
So they could once more see
That burst to liberty!
This was what "freedom" lent
To the black regiment.

Hundreds on hundreds fell;
But they are resting well;
Scourges and shackles strong
Never shall do them wrong.
Oh, to the living few,
Soldiers, be just and true!
Hail them as comrades tried;
Fight with them side by side;
Never, in field or tent,
Scorn the black regiment!

—*George Henry Boker.*

RIDING WITH KILPATRICK

DAWN peered through the pines as we dashed at the ford;
   Afar the grim guns of the infantry roared;
There were miles yet of dangerous pathway to pass,
And Mosby might menace, and Stuart might mass;
But we mocked every doubt, laughing danger to scorn,
As we quaffed with a shout from the wine of the morn;
Those who rode with Kilpatrick to valour were born.

How we chafed at delay! How we itched to be on!
How we yearned for the fray where the battle-reek shone!
It was *forward,* not *halt,* stirred the fire in our veins,
When our horses' feet beat to the click of the reins;
It was *charge,* not *retreat,* we were wonted to hear;
It was *charge,* not *retreat,* that was sweet to the ear;
Those who rode with Kilpatrick had never felt fear!

At last the word came, and troop tossed it to troop,
Two squadrons deployed with a falcon-like swoop;
While swiftly the others in echelons formed,
For there, just ahead, was the line to be stormed.
The trumpets rang out; there were guidons ablow;
The white summer sun set out sabres aglow;
Those who rode with Kilpatrick charged straight at the foe!

We swept like the whirlwind; we closed; at the shock
The sky seemed to reel and the earth seemed to rock;
Steel clashed upon steel with a deafening sound,
While a redder than rose-stain encrimsoned the ground;
If we gave back a space from the fierce pit of hell,
We were rallied again by a voice like a bell.
Those who rode with Kilpatrick rode valiantly well.

Rang sternly his orders from out of the wrack:
Reform there, New Yorkers! You, " Harris Light," back!
Come on, men of Maine! We will conquer or fall!
Now, forward, boys, forward! and follow me all!
A Bayard in boldness, a Sidney in grace,
A lion to lead and a stag-hound to chase—
Those who rode with Kilpatrick looked Death in the face!

Though brave were our foemen, they faltered and fled;
Yet that was no marvel when such as he led!
Long ago, long ago, was that desperate day!
Long ago, long ago, strove the Blue and the Gray!

Praise God that the red sun of battle is set!
That our hand-clasp is loyal and loving—and yet
Those who rode with Kilpatrick can never forget!

—Clinton Scollard.

GREENCASTLE JENNY

OH, Greencastle streets were a stream of steel
    With the slanted muskets the soldiers bore,
And the scared earth muttered and shook to feel
    The tramp and the rumble of Longstreet's Corps;
The bands were blaring *The Bonny Blue Flag,*
    And the banners borne were a motley many;
And watching the gray column wind and drag
    Was a slip of a girl—we 'll call her Jenny.

A slip of a girl—what needs her name?—
    With her cheeks aflame and her lips aquiver,
As she leaned and looked with a loyal shame
    On the steady flow of the steely river:
Till a storm grew black in her hazel eyes
    Time had not tamed, nor a lover sighed for;
And she ran and she girded her, apron-wise,
    With the flag she loved and her brothers died for.

Out of the doorway they saw her start
    (Pickett's Virginians were marching through),
The hot little foolish hero-heart
    Armoured with stars and the sacred blue.
Clutching the folds of red and white
    Stood she and bearded those ranks of theirs,
Shouting shrilly with all her might,
    "Come and take it, the man that dares!"

Pickett's Virginians were passing through;
    Supple as steel and brown as leather,
Rusty and dusty of hat and shoe,

Wonted to hunger and war and weather;
Peerless, fearless, an army's flower!
  Sterner soldiers the world saw never,
Marching lightly, that summer hour,
  To death and failure and fame for ever.

Rose from the rippling ranks a cheer;
  Pickett saluted, with bold eyes beaming,
Sweeping his hat like a cavalier,
  With his tawny locks in the warm wind streaming.
Fierce little Jenny! her courage fell,
  As the firm lines flickered with friendly laughter,
And Greencastle streets gave back the yell
  That Gettysburg slopes gave back soon after.

So they cheered for the flag they fought
  With the generous glow of the stubborn fighter,
Loving the brave as the brave men ought,
  And never a finger was raised to fright her:
So they marched, though they knew it not,
  Through the fresh green June to the shock infernal,
To the hell of the shell and the plunging shot,
  And the charge that has won them a name eternal.

And she felt at last, as she hid her face
  There had lain at the root of her childish daring
A trust in the men of her own brave race,
  And a secret faith in the foe's forbearing.
And she sobbed, till the roll of the rumbling gun
  And the swinging tramp of the marching men
Where a memory only, and day was done,
  And the stars in the fold of the blue again.

Thank God that the day of the sword is done,
  And the stars in the fold of the blue again!
                                    —*Helen Gray Cone.*

GETTYSBURG

THERE was no union in the land,
  Though wise men laboured long
With links of clay and ropes of sand
  To bind the right and wrong.

There was no temper in the blade
  That once could cleave a chain;
Its edge was dull with touch of trade
  And clogged with rust of gain.

The sand and clay must shrink away
  Before the lava tide;
By blows and blood and fire assay
  The metal must be tried.

Here sledge and anvil met, and when
  The furnace fiercest roared,
God's undiscerning workingmen
  Reforged His people's sword.

Enough for them to ask and know
  The moment's duty clear—
The bayonets flashed it there below,
  The guns proclaimed it here:

To do and dare, and die at need,
  But while life lasts, to fight—
For right or wrong a simple creed,
  But simplest for the right.

They faltered not who stood that day
  And held this post of dread;
Nor cowards they who wore the gray
  Until the gray was red.

For every wreath the victor wears
　　The vanquished half may claim;
And every monument declares
　　A common pride and fame.

We raise no altar stones to Hate,
　　Who never bowed to Fear:
No province crouches at our gate,
　　To shame our triumph here.

Here standing by a dead wrong's grave
　　The blindest now may see,
The blow that liberates the slave
　　But sets the master free!

When ills beset the nation's life
　　Too dangerous to bear,
The sword must be the surgeon's knife,
　　Too merciful to spare.

O Soldier of our common land,
　　'T is thine to bear that blade
Loose in the sheath, or firm in hand,
　　But ever unafraid.

When foreign foes assail our right,
　　One nation trusts to thee—
To wield it well in worthy fight—
　　The sword of Meade and Lee!
　　　　　　　　—*James Jeffrey Roche.*

HIGH TIDE AT GETTYSBURG

A CLOUD possessed the hollow field,
　　The gathering battle's smoky shield:
Athwart the gloom the lightning flashed,

And through the cloud some horsemen dashed,
And from the heights the thunder pealed.

Then, at the brief command of Lee
Moved out that matchless infantry,
    With Pickett leading grandly down,
    To rush against the roaring crown
Of those dread heights of destiny.

Far heard above the angry guns,
A cry across the tumult runs;
    The voice that rang through Shiloh's woods
    And Chickamauga's solitudes,
The fierce South cheering on her sons!

Ah, how the withering tempest blew
Against the front of Pettigrew!
    A Khamsin wind that scorched and singed
    Like that infernal flame that fringed
The British squares at Waterloo!

A thousand fell where Kemper led;
A thousand died where Garnett bled:
    In blinding flame and strangling smoke
    The remnant through the batteries broke
And crossed the works with Armistead.

"Once more in Glory's van with me!"
Virginia cried to Tennessee:
    "We two together, come what may,
    Shall stand upon these works to-day!"
The reddest day in history.

Brave Tennessee! In reckless way
Virginia heard her comrades say:
    "Close round this rent and riddled rag!"

What time she set her battle-flag
Amid the guns of Doubleday.

But who shall break the guards that wait
Before the awful face of Fate?
   The tattered standards of the South
   Were shrivelled at the cannon's mouth,
And all her hopes were desolate.

In vain the Tennesseean set
His breast against the bayonet;
   In vain Virginia charged and raged,
   A tigress in her wrath uncaged,
Till all the hill was red and wet!

Above the bayonets, mixed and crossed,
Men saw a gray, gigantic ghost
   Receding through the battle-cloud,
   And heard across the tempest loud
The death-cry of a nation lost!

The brave went down! Without disgrace
They leaped to Ruin's red embrace;
   They only heard Fame's thunders wake,
   And saw the dazzling sunburst break
In smiles on Glory's bloody face!

They fell, who lifted up a hand
And bade the sun in heaven to stand;
   They smote and fell, who set the bars
   Against the progress of the stars,
And stayed the march of Motherland.

They stood, who saw the future come
On through the fight's delirium;
   They smote and stood, who held the hope

Of nations on that slippery slope,
Amid the cheers of Christendom!

God lives! He forged the iron will,
That clutched and held that trembling hill!
   God lives and reigns! He built and lent
   The heights for Freedom's battlement,
Where floats her flag in triumph still!

Fold up the banner! Smelt the guns!
Love rules. Her gentler purpose runs.
   A mighty mother turns in tears,
   The pages of her battle years,
Lamenting all her fallen sons!

                 —*Will Henry Thompson.*

A TENT SCENE

OUR generals sat in their tent one night,
   On the Mississippi's banks,
Where Vicksburg sullenly still held out
   Against the assaulting ranks.

They could hear the firing as they talked,
   Long after set of sun;
And the blended noise of a thousand guns
   In the distance seemed as one.

All at once Sherman started to his feet,
   And listened to the roar,
His practiced ear had caught a sound,
   That he had not heard before.

" They have mounted another gun on the walls;
   'T is new," he said, " I know;

I can tell the voice of a gun, as a man
    Can tell the voice of his foe!

"What! not a soul of you hears but me?
    No matter, I am right;
Bring me my horse! I must silence this
    Before I sleep to-night!"

He was gone; and they listened to the ring
    Of hoofs on the distant track;
Then talked and wondered for a while,—
    In an hour he was back.

"Well, General! what is the news?" they cried,
    As he entered flushed and worn;
"We have picked their gunners off, and the gun
    Will be dislodged at morn!"

—Phœbe Cary.

VICKSBURG

FOR sixty days and upwards
    A storm of shell and shot
Rained round as in a flaming shower,
    But still we faltered not!
"If the noble city perish,"
    Our grand young leader said,
"Let the only walls the foe shall scale
    Be ramparts of the dead!"

For sixty days and upwards
    The eye of heaven waxed dim,
And e'en throughout God's holy morn,
    O'er Christian prayer and hymn,
Arose a hissing tumult,
    As if the fiends of air

Strove to engulf the voice of faith
  In the shrieks of their despair.

There was wailing in the houses,
  There was trembling on the marts,
While the tempest raged and thundered,
  'Mid the silent thrill of hearts;
But the Lord, our shield, was with us,
  And ere a month had sped,
Our very women walked the streets,
  With scarce one throb of dread.

And the little children gambolled—
  Their faces purely raised,
Just for a wondering moment,
  As the huge bombs whirled and blazed!
Then turned with silvery laughter
  To the sports which children love,
Thrice-mailed in the sweet, instinctive thought
  That the good God watched above.

Yet the hailing bolts fell faster
  From scores of flame-clad ships,
And, above us, denser, darker,
  Grew the conflict's wild eclipse;
Till a solid cloud closed o'er us,
  Like a type of doom and ire,
Whence shot a thousand, quivering tongues
  Of forked and vengeful fire.

But the unseen hands of angels
  Those death-shafts warned aside,
And the dove of heavenly mercy
  Ruled o'er the battle-tide;
In the houses ceased the wailing,
  And through the war-scarred marts

The people strode with step of hope
    To the music in their hearts.
                    —*Paul Hamilton Hayne.*

THE DRAFT RIOT

IS it the wind, the many-tongued, the weird,
    That cries in sharp distress about the eaves?
Is it the wind whose gathering shout is heard
    With voice of peoples myriad like the leaves?
Is it the wind? Fly to the casement, quick,
And when the roar comes thick,
            Fling wide the sash,
            Await the crash!

Nothing. Some various solitary cries,—
    Some sauntering woman's short hard laugh,
Or honester, a dog's bark,—these arise
    From lamplit street up to this free flag-staff:
Nothing remains of that low threatening sound;
The wind raves not the eaves around.
            Clasp casement to,—
            You heard not true.

Hark there again! a roar that holds a shriek!
    But not without—no, from below it comes:
What pulses up from solid earth to wreak
    A vengeful word on towers and lofty domes?
What angry booming doth the trembling ear,
Glued to the stone wall, hear—
            So deep, no air
            Its weight can bear?

Grieve! 't is the voice of ignorance and vice,—
    The rage of slaves who fancy they are free:

Men who would keep men slaves at any price,
  Too blind their own black manacles to see.
Grieve! 't is that grisly spectre with a torch,
Riot—that bloodies every porch,
        Hurls justice down
        And burns the town.
                    —*Charles De Kay.*

THE HERO OF FORT WAGNER

FORT WAGNER! that is a place for us
    To remember well, my lad!
For us, who were under the guns, and know
  The bloody work we had.

I should not speak to one so young,
  Perhaps, as I do to you;
But you are a soldier's son, my boy,
  And you know what soldiers do.

And when peace comes to our land again,
  And your father sits in his home,
You will hear such tales of war as this,
  For many a year to come.

We were repulsed from the Fort, you know,
  And saw our heroes fall,
Till the dead were piled in bloody heaps
  Under the frowning wall.

Yet crushed as we were and beaten back,
  Our spirits never bowed;
And gallant deeds that day were done
  To make a soldier proud.

Brave men were there, for their country's sake
  To spend their latest breath;
But the bravest was one who gave his life
  And his body after death.

No greater words than his dying ones
  Have been spoken under the sun;
Not even his, who brought the news
  On the field at Ratisbon.

I was pressing up, to try if yet
  Our men might take the place,
And my feet had slipped in his oozing blood
  Before I saw his face.

His face! it was black as the skies o'erhead
  With the smoke of the angry guns;
And a gash in his bosom showed the work
  Of our country's traitor sons.

Your pardon, my poor boy! I said,
  I did not see you here;
But I will not hurt you as I pass;
  I 'll have a care; no fear!

He smiled; he had only strength to say
  These words, and that was all:
"I 'm done gone, Massa; step on me;
  And you can scale the wall!"

—Phœbe Cary.

MEMORIÆ POSITUM

BENEATH the trees,
  My lifelong friends in this dear spot,
Sad now for eyes that see them not,

I hear the autumnal breeze
Wake the dry leaves to sigh for gladness gone,
Whispering vague omens of oblivion,
    Hear, restless as the seas,
Time's grim feet rustling through the withered grace
Of many a spreading realm and strong-stemmed race,
    Even as my own through these.

    Why make we moan
  For loss that doth enrich us yet
  With upward yearnings of regret?
    Bleaker than unmossed stone
Our lives were but for this immortal gain
Of unstilled longing and inspiring pain!
    As thrills of long-hushed tone
Live in the viol, so our souls grow fine
With keen vibrations from the touch divine
    Of noble natures gone.

    'T were indiscreet
  To vex the shy and sacred grief
  With harsh obtrusions of relief;
    Yet, Verse, with noiseless feet,
Go whisper: "*This* death hath far choicer ends
Than slowly to impearl in hearts of friends;
    Thus obsequies 't is meet
Not to seclude in closets of the heart,
But, church-like, with wide doorways to impart
    Even to the heedless street."

    Brave, good, and true,
I see him stand before me now,
And read again on that young brow,
    Where every hope was new,
How sweet were life! Yet, by the mouth firm-set,
And look made up for Duty's utmost debt,

I could divine he knew
That death within the sulphurous hostile lines,
In the mere wreck of nobly-pitched designs,
Plucks heart's-ease, and not rue.

Happy their end
Who vanish down life's evening stream
Placid as swans that drift in dream
Round the next river-bend!
Happy long life, with honour at the close,
Friends' painless tears, the softened thought of foes!
And yet, like him, to spend
All at a gush, keeping our first faith sure
From mid-life's doubt and eld's contentment poor,
What more could Fortune send?

Right in the van,
On the red rampart's slippery swell,
With heart that beat a charge, he fell,
Foeward, as fits a man;
But the high soul burns on to light men's feet
Where death for noble ends makes dying sweet;
His life her crescent's span
Orbs full with share in their undarkening days
Who ever climbed the battailous steeps of praise
Since valour's praise began.

His life's expense
Hath won him coëternal youth
With the immaculate prime of Truth;
While we, who make pretence
At living on, and wake and eat and sleep,
And life's stale trick by repetition keep,
Our fickle permanence
(A poor leaf-shadow on a brook, whose play

Of busy idlesse ceases with our day)
    Is the mere cheat of sense.

     We bide our chance,
    Unhappy, and make terms with Fate
    A little more to let us wait;
     He leads for ay the advance,
Hope's forlorn-hopes that plant the desperate good
For nobler Earths and days of manlier mood;
     Our wall of circumstance
Cleared at a bound, he flashes o'er the fight
A saintly shape of flame, to cheer the right
     And steel each wavering glance.

     I write of one,
    While with dim eyes I think of three;
    Who weeps not others fair and brave as he?
     Ah, when the fight is won,
Dear Land, whom triflers now make bold to scorn
(Thee! from whose forehead Earth awaits her morn)
     How nobler shall the sun
Flame in thy sky, how braver breathe thy air,
That thou bred'st children who for thee could dare
     And die as thine have done.
                 —*James Russell Lowell.*

LINCOLN AT GETTYSBURG

AFTER the eyes that looked, the lips that spake
    Here, from the shadows of impending death,
    Those words of solemn breath,
    What voice may fitly break
The silence, doubly hallowed, left by him?
We can but bow the head, with eyes grown dim,
And, as a Nation's litany, repeat
The phrase his martyrdom hath made complete,

Noble as then, but now more sadly sweet;
"Let us, the Living, rather dedicate
Ourselves to the unfinished work, which they
Thus far advanced so nobly on its way,
   And save the perilled State!
Let us, upon this field where they, the brave,
Their last full measure of devotion gave,
Highly resolve they have not died in vain!—
That, under God, the Nation's later birth
   Of Freedom, and the people's gain
Of their own Sovereignty, shall never wane
And perish from the circle of the earth!"
From such a perfect text, shall Song aspire
   To light her faded fire,
   And into wandering music turn
Its virtue, simple, sorrowful, and stern?
His voice all elegies anticipated;
   For, whatsoe'er the strain,
   We hear that one refrain:
"We consecrate ourselves to them, the Consecrated!"
              —*Bayard Taylor.*

THE BATTLE ABOVE THE CLOUDS

BY the banks of Chattanooga watching with a soldier's
   heed,
In the chilly autumn morning, gallant Grant was on his
   steed:
For the foe had climbed above him with the banners of their
   band,
And the cannon swept the river from the hills of Cumber-
   land.

Like a trumpet rang his orders: "Howard, Thomas, to the
   bridge!

One brigade aboard the Dunbar, storm the heights of Mis-
 sion Ridge!
On the left, the ledges, Sherman, charge and hurl the rebels
 down!
Hooker, take the steeps of Lookout and the slope before the
 town!"

Fearless, from the northern summit, looked the traitors,
 where they lay,
On the gleaming Union army, marshalled as for muster-day,
Till the sudden shout of battle thundered upward from the
 farms
And they dropped their idle glasses in a sudden rush to
 arms.

Then together up the highlands, surely, swiftly, swept the
 lines,
And the clang of war above them swelled with loud and
 louder signs,
Till the loyal peaks of Lookout in the tempest seemed to
 throb,
And the star-flag of our country soared in smoke o'er Or-
 chard Knob.

Day and night and day returning, ceaseless shock and
 ceaseless change,
Still the furious mountain conflict burst and burned along
 the range,
While with battle's cloud of sulphur mingled heaven's mist
 of rain,
Till the ascending squadrons vanished from the gazers on
 the plain.

From the boats upon the river, from the tents upon the
 shore,
From the roofs of yonder city anxious eyes the clouds
 explore:

But no rift amid the darkness shows them fathers, brothers,
    sons,
While they trace the viewless struggle by the echo of the
    guns.

Upward! charge for God and country! up! Ah! they
    rush, they rise,
Till the faithful meet the faithless in the never-clouded
    skies,
And the battle-field is bloody where a dew-drop never falls,
For a voice of tearless justice to a tearless vengeance calls.

And the heaven is wild with shouting; fiery shot and bayonet
    keen
Gleam and glance where freedom's angels battle in the blue
    serene.
Charge and volley fiercely follow, and the tumult in the air
Tells of right in mortal grapple with rebellion's strong de-
    spair.

They have conquered! God's own legions! Well their foes
    might be dismayed,
Standing in the mountain temple 'gainst the terrors of His
    aid;
And the clouds might fitly echo pæan loud and parting gun,
When, from upper light and glory, sank the traitor host,
    undone.

They have conquered! Through the region where our
    brothers plucked the palm,
Rings the noise with which they won it with the sweetness
    of a psalm;
And our wounded, sick, and dying hear it in their crowded
    wards,
And they whisper, "Heaven is with us! lo, our battle is the
    Lord's!"

And our famished captive heroes locked in Richmond's
    prison-hells
List those guns of cloudland booming glad as freedom's
    morning bells,
Lift their haggard eyes, and panting, with their cheeks
    against the bars,
Feel God's breath of hope, and see it playing with the
    Stripes and Stars.

Tories, safe in serpent-treason, startle as those airy cheers,
And that wild, ethereal war-drum fall like doom upon their
    ears;
And that rush of cloud-borne armies, rolling back the na-
    tion's shame,
Frights them with its sound of judgment and the flash of
    angry flame.

Widows weeping by their firesides, loyal sires despondent
    grown,
Smile to hear their country's triumph from the gate of
    Heaven blown,
And the patriot's poor children wonder, in their simple hearts
    to know
In the land above the thunder our embattled champions go.
                   —*Theron Brown.*

CHATTANOOGA

A KINDLING impulse seized the host
    Inspired by heaven's elastic air;
Their hearts outran their General's plan,
    Though Grant commanded there—
    Grant, who without reserve can dare;
And, "Well, go on and do your will,"
    He said, and measured the mountain then:
So master-riders fling the rein—
    But you must know your men.

On yester-morn in grayish mist,
  Armies like ghosts on hills had fought,
And rolled from the cloud their thunders loud
  The Cumberlands far had caught:
  To-day the sunlit steeps are sought.
Grant stood on cliffs whence all was plain,
  And smoked as one who feels no cares;
But mastered nervousness intense
  Alone such calmness wears.

The summit-cannon plunge their flame
  Sheer down the primal wall,
But up and up each linking troop
  In stretching festoons crawl—
  Nor fire a shot. Such men appall
The foe, though brave. He, from the brink,
  Looks far along the breadth of slope,
And sees two miles of dark dots creep,
  And knows they mean the cope.

He sees them creep. Yet here and there
  Half hid 'mid leafless groves they go;
As men who ply through traceries high
  Of turreted marbles show—
  So dwindle these to eyes below.
But fronting shot and flanking shell
  Sliver and rive the inwoven ways;
High tops of oaks and high hearts fall,
  But never the climbing stays.

From right to left, from left to right
  They roll the rallying cheer—
Vie with each other, brother with brother,
  Who shall the first appear—
  What colour-bearer with colours clear
In sharp relief, like sky-drawn Grant,

Whose cigar must now be near the stump—
While in solitude, his back
　　Heaps slowly to a hump.

Near and more near; till now the flags
　　Run like a catching flame;
And one flares highest, to peril nighest—
　　He means to make a name;
　　Salvos! they give him his fame.
The staff is caught, and next the rush,
　　And then the leap where death has led;
Flag answering flag along the crest,
　　And swarms of Rebels fled.

But some who gained the envied Alp,
　　And—eager, ardent, earnest there—
Dropped into Death's wide-open arms,
　　Quelled on the wing like eagles struck in air—
　　For ever they slumber, young and fair,
The smile upon them as they died;
　　Their end attained—that end, a height;
Life was to them a dream fulfilled,
　　And death a starry night.
　　　　　　　　　　　　—*Herman Melville.*

ULRIC DAHLGREN

A FLASH of light across the night,
　　An eager face, an eye afire:
O lad so true, you yet may rue
　　The courage of your deep desire!

" Nay, tempt me not; the way is plain—
'T is but the coward checks his rein;
　　For there they lie,
196

And there they cry
For whose dear sake 't were joy to die!"

He bends unto his saddle-bow,
   The steeds they follow two and two;
Their flanks are wet with foam and sweat,
   Their riders' locks are damp with dew.

"O comrades, haste! the way is long,
The dirge it drowns the battle song;
   The hunger preys,
   The famine slays,
An awful horror veils our ways!"

Beneath the pall of prison wall
   The rush of hoofs they seem to hear;
From loathsome guise they lift their eyes,
   And beat their bars and bend their ear.

"Ah, God be thanked! our friends are nigh;
He wills it not that thus we die;
   O fiends accurst
   Of Want and Thirst,
Our comrades gather—do your worst!"

A sharp affright runs through the night,
   An ambush stirred, a column reined;
The hurrying steed has checked his speed,
   His smoking flanks are crimson stained.

O noble son of noble sire,
Thine ears are deaf to our desire!
   O knightly grace
   Of valiant race,
The grave is honour's trysting-place!

O life so pure! O faith so sure!
  O heart so brave, and true, and strong!
With tips of flame is writ your name,
  In annalled deed and storied song!

It flares across the solemn night,
It glitters in the radiant light;
  A jewel set,
  Unnumbered yet,
In our Republic's coronet!
          —*Kate Brownlee Sherwood.*

THE BATTLE OF THE WILDERNESS

THERE he stood, the grand old hero, great Virginia's
    godlike son—
Second unto none in glory, equal of her Washington!—
Gazing on his line of battle as it wavered to and fro,
'Neath the front and flank advances of the almost conquer-
    ing foe:
Calm as was that clear May morning ere the furious death
    roar broke
From the iron-throated war-lions crouching 'neath their
    clouds of smoke;
Cool as though the battle raging was but mimicry of fight,
Each brigade an ivory castle and each regiment a knight.
Chafing in reserve beside him two brigades of Texans lay,
All impatient for their portion in the fortune of the day.
Shot and shell are 'mong them falling, yet unmoved they
    silent stand,
Longing—eager for the battle, but awaiting his command.
Suddenly he rode before them as the forward line gave way,
Raised his hat with courtly gesture—"Follow me and save
    the day."
But as though by terror stricken, still and silent stood that
    troop
Who were wont to rush to battle with a fierce avenging
    whoop;

It was but a single moment, then a murmur through them
    ran,
Heard above the cannon's roaring, as it passed from man
    to man,
Heard above the cannon's roaring, as it passed from man
       to man,
"You go back and we'll go forward," now the waiting
    leader hears,
Mixed with deep impatient sobbing as of strong men moved
    to tears.
Once again he gave the order "I will lead you on the foe";
Then through all their line of battle rang a loud determined
    "No!"
Quick as thought a gallant Major, with a firm and vise-like
    grasp,
Seized the General's bridle, shouting, "Forward, boys, I'll
    hold him fast."
Then again the hat was lifted, "Sir, I am the older man,
Loose my bridle, I will lead them," in a measured tone and
    calm.
Trembling with suppressed emotion, with intense excitement
    hot,
In a quivering voice the Texan, "You shall not, sir, *you
    shall not!*"
By them swept the charging squadron with a loud exultant
    cheer,
"We'll retake the salient, General, if you'll watch us from
    the rear."
And they kept their word right nobly sweeping every foe
    away,
With that grand grey head uncovered watching how they
    saved the day.
But the godlike calm was shaken, which the battle could
    not move,
By this true spontaneous token of his soldiers' childlike
    love.   —*Mary Tenella.*

ZEST FOR INVASION

BOOM! and a crash! as our cannon flash—
  Our columns are under way,
Tramp, tramp, tramp, out of the camp
  On this sunny seventh of May;
Victory behind, blown on the wind,
  And our banners gayly float,
With a hip, hurray! as we march away
  With a blade at Georgia's throat.

Into the Gap without a mishap,
  Where the buzzards roost and fly,
Down in the Run, bayonet and gun,
  Up again to the sky,
With a steady tread, Atlanta ahead,
  We enter the plain below,
Where Wheeler's horse deploy in force—
  Hurrah! for the fleeing foe.

Fort and redoubt have fallen in the rout,
  Ours every mountain crag;
The creeks have run red, Johnston has fled,
  Dalton is under the flag;
Naught but defeat, dismay, and retreat
  Shall fall to Johnston's part,
With a hip, hurray! now Sherman 's away
  With his sword at Georgia's heart.
                    —*Clement V. Zane.*

OBSEQUIES OF STUART

WE could not pause, while yet the noontide air
  Shook with the cannonade's incessant pealing,
The funeral pageant fitly to prepare—
  A nation's grief revealing.

200

The smoke, above the glimmering woodland wide
  That skirts our southward border in its beauty,
Marked where our heroes stood and fought and died
    For love and faith and duty.

And still, what time the doubtful strife went on,
  We might not find expression for our sorrow;
We could but lay our dear dumb warrior down,
    And gird us for the morrow.

One weary year agone, when came a lull
  With victory in the conflict's stormy closes,
When the glad spring, all flushed and beautiful,
    First mocked us with her roses,

With dirge and bell and minute-gun, we paid
  Some few poor rites—an inexpressive token
Of a great people's pain—to Jackson's shade,
    In agony unspoken.

No wailing trumpet and no tolling bell,
  No cannon, save the battle's boom receding,
When Stuart to the grave we bore, might tell,
    With hearts all crushed and bleeding.

The crisis suited not with pomp, and she
  Whose anguish bears the seal of consecration
Had wished his Christian obsequies should be
    Thus void of ostentation.

Only the maidens came, sweet flowers to twine
  Above his form so still and cold and painless,
Whose deeds upon our brightest record shine,
    Whose life and sword were stainless.

They well remembered how he loved to dash
  Into the fight, festooned from summer bowers;
How like a fountain's spray his sabre's flash
    Leaped from a mass of flowers.

And so we carried to his place of rest
  All that of our great Paladin was mortal:
The cross, and not the sabre, on his breast,
    That opes the Heavenly portal.

No more of tribute might to us remain;
  But there will come a time when Freedom's martyrs
A richer guerdon of renown shall gain
    Than gleams in stars and garters.

I hear from out that sunlit land which lies
  Beyond these clouds that gather darkly o'er us,
The happy sounds of industry arise
    In swelling peaceful chorus.

And mingling with these sounds, the glad acclaim
  Of millions undisturbed by war's afflictions,
Crowning each martyr's never-dying name
    With grateful benedictions.

In some fair future garden of delights,
  Where flowers shall bloom and song-birds sweetly warble,
Art shall erect the statues of our knights
    In living bronze and marble.

And none of all that bright heroic throng
  Shall wear to far-off time a semblance grander,
Shall still be decked with fresher wreaths of song,
    Than this beloved commander.

The Spanish legend tells us of the Cid,
    That after death he rode erect, sedately,
Along his lines, even as in life he did,
        In presence yet more stately:

And thus our Stuart, at this moment, seems
    To ride out of our dark and troubled story
Into the region of romance and dreams,
        A realm of light and glory;

And sometimes, when the silver bugles blow,
    That ghostly form, in battle reappearing,
Shall lead his horsemen headlong on the foe,
        In victory careering!
                        —*John Randolph Thompson.*

DEATH OF GENERAL LEONIDAS POLK

A FLASH from the edge of the hostile trench,
    A puff of smoke, a roar,
Whose echo shall roll from the Kennesaw hills
    To the farthermost Christian shore,
Proclaims to the world that the warrior-priest
    Will battle for right no more.

And that for a cause which is sanctified
    By the blood of martyrs unknown—
A cause for which they gave their lives,
    And for which he gave his own—
He kneels, a meek ambassador,
    At the foot of the Father's throne.

And up to the courts of another world,
    Which angels alone have trod,
He lives, away from the din and strife

Of this blood-besprinkled sod—
Crowned with the amaranthine wreath
That is worn by the blessed of God.

—*Harry Lynden Flash.*

THE "KEARSARGE"

SUNDAY in Old England:
  In gray churches everywhere
The calm of low responses,
  The sacred hush of prayer.

Sunday in Old England;
  And summer winds that went
O'er the pleasant fields of Sussex,
  The garden lands of Kent,

Stole into dim church windows
  And passed the oaken door,
And fluttered open prayer-books
  With cannon's awful roar.

Sunday in New England:
  Upon a mountain gray
The wind-bent pines are swaying
  Like giants at their play;

Across the barren lowlands,
  Where men find scanty food,
The north wind brings its vigour
  To homesteads plain and rude.

Ho, land of pine and granite!
  Ho, hardy northland breeze!
Well have you trained the manhood
  That shook the Channel seas,

When o'er those storied waters
  The iron war-bolts flew,
And through Old England's churches
  The summer breezes blew;

While in our other England
  Stirred one gaunt rocky steep,
When rode her sons as victors,
  Lords of the lonely deep.
                    —*Silas Weir Mitchell.*

LOGAN AT PEACH TREE CREEK

YOU know that day at Peach Tree Creek,
  When the Rebs with their circling, scorching wall
Of smoke-hid cannon and sweep of flame
Drove in our flanks, back! back! and all
Our toil seemed lost in the storm of shell—
That desperate day McPherson fell!

Our regiment stood in a little glade
Set round with half-grown red oak trees—
An awful place to stand, in full fair sight,
While the minie bullets hummed like bees,
And comrades dropped on either side—
That fearful day McPherson died!

The roar of the battle, steady, stern,
Rung in our ears. Upon our eyes
The belching cannon smoke, the half-hid swing
Of deploying troops, the groans, the cries,
The hoarse commands, the sickening smell—
That blood-red day McPherson fell!

But we stood there!—when out from the trees,
Out of the smoke and dismay to the right
Burst a rider—His head was bare, his eye
Had a blaze like a lion fain for fight;
His long hair, black as the deepest night
Streamed out on the wind. And the might
Of his plunging horse was a tale to tell,
And his voice rang high like a bugle's swell;

"Men, the enemy hem us on every side;
We 'll whip 'em yet! Close up that breach—
Remember your flag—don't give an inch!
The right flank 's gaining and soon will reach—
Forward boys, and give 'em hell!"—
Said Logan after McPherson fell.

We laughed and cheered and the red ground shook,
As the general plunged along the line
Through the deadliest rain of screaming shells;
For the sound of his voice refreshed us all,
And we filled the gap like a roaring tide,
And saved the day McPherson died!

But that was twenty years ago,
And part of a horrible dream now past.
For Logan, the lion, the drums throb low
And the flag swings low on the mast;
He has followed his mighty chieftain through
The mist-hung stream, where gray and blue
One colours stand,
And North to South extends the hand.
It 's right that deeds of war and blood
Should be forgot, but, spite of all,
I think of Logan, now, as he rode
That day across the field; I hear the call
Of his trumpet voice—see the battle shine

In his stern, black eyes, and down the line
Of cheering men, I see him ride,
As on the day McPherson died.
                    —*Hamlin Garland.*

A DIRGE FOR McPHERSON

A RMS reversed and banners craped—
        Muffled drums;
Snowy horses sable-draped—
    McPherson comes.
        But tell us, shall we know him more,
        Lost-Mountain and lone Kenesaw?

Brave the sword upon the pall—
    A gleam in gloom;
So a bright name lighteth all
    McPherson's doom.

Bear him through the chapel-door—
    Let priest in stole
Pace before the warrior
    Who led.   Bell—toll!

Lay him down, within the nave,
    The Lesson read—
Man is noble, man is brave,
    But man 's—a weed.

Take him up again and wend
    Graveward, nor weep:
There 's a trumpet that shall rend
    This Soldier's sleep.

Pass the ropes the coffin round,
    And let descend;

Prayer and volley—let it sound
  McPherson's end.
    True fame is his, for life is o'er—
    Sarpedon of the mighty war.
                 —Herman Melville.

THE BAY-FIGHT

THREE days through sapphire seas we sailed—
  The steady Trade blew strong and free,
The Northern Light his banners paled,
The Ocean Stream our channels wet,
  We rounded low Canaveral's lee,
And passed the isles of emerald set
  In blue Bahama's turquoise sea.

By reef and shoal obscurely mapped,
  And hauntings of the gray sea-wolf,
The palmy Western Key lay lapped
  In the warm washing of the Gulf.

But weary to the hearts of all
  The burning glare, the barren reach,
Of Santa Rosa's withered beach,
  And Pensacola's ruined wall.

And weary was the long patrol,
  And thousand miles of shapeless strand,
From Brazos to San Blas that roll
  Their driftless dunes of desert sand.

Yet, coastwise, as we cruised or lay,
  The land-breeze still, at nightfall bore
By beach and fortress-guarded bay
  Sweet odours from the enemy's shore.

Fresh from the forest solitudes,
  Unchallenged of his sentry lines,
The bursting of his cypress buds,
  And the warm fragrance of his pines.

Ah, never braver bark and crew,
  Nor bolder Flag a foe to dare,
Had left a wake on ocean blue
  Since Lion-Heart sailed Trence-le-mer!

But little gain by that dark ground
  Was ours, save, sometime, freer breath
For friend or brother strangely found,
  'Scaped from the drear domain of death.

And little venture for the bold,
  Or laurel for our valiant Chief,
  Save some blockaded British thief,
Full fraught with murder in his hold.

Caught unawares at ebb or flood,
  Or dull bombardment, day by day,
  With fort and earthwork, far away,
Low couched in sullen leagues of mud.

A weary time, but to the strong,
  The day at last, as ever, came;
And the volcano, laid so long,
  Leaped forth in thunder and in flame.

"Man your starboard battery!"
  Kimberly shouted.
The ship, with her hearts of oak,
Was going, mid roar and smoke,
      On to victory!
  None of us doubted—
  No, not our dying—
  Farragut's flag was flying!

Gaines growled low on our left,
  Morgan roared on our right—
Before us, gloomy and fell,
With breath like the fume of hell,
Lay the Dragon of iron shell,
  Driven at last to the fight!

Ha, old ship! do they thrill,
  The brave two hundred scars
  You got in the River-Wars?
That were leeched with clamorous skill,
  (Surgery savage and hard),
Splinted with bolt and beam,
Probed in scarfing and seam,
  Rudely linted and tarred
With oakum and boiling pitch,
And sutured with splice and hitch,
  At the Brooklyn Navy-Yard!

Our lofty spars were down,
To bide the battle's frown
(Wont of old renown)—
But every ship was drest
In her bravest and her best,
As if for a July day;
Sixty flags and three,
As we floated up the bay—
At every peak and mast-head flew
The brave Red, White, and Blue,—
We were eighteen ships that day.

With hawsers strong and taut,
The weaker lashed to port,
  On we sailed, two by two—
That if either a bolt should feel
Crash through caldron or wheel,

Fin of bronze or sinew of steel,
  Her mate might bear her through.

Forging boldly ahead,
The great Flag-ship led,
  Grandest of sights!
On her lofty mizzen flew
Our Leader's dauntless blue,
  That had waved o'er twenty fights—
So we went, with the first of the tide,
  Slowly, 'mid the roar
  Of the rebel guns ashore
And thunder of each full broadside.

Ah, how poor the prate
Of statute and state,
  We once held with these fellows—
Here on the flood's pale green,
  Hark, how he bellows,
  Each bluff old Sea-lawyer!
Talk to them, Dahlgren,
  Parrott, and Sawyer!

On, in the whirling shade
  Of the cannon's sulphury breath
  We drew to the line of Death
That our devilish foe had laid—
Meshed in a horrible net,
  And baited villanous well,
Right in our path were set
  Three hundred traps of hell!

And there, O sight forlorn—
  There, while the cannon
  Hurtled and thundered—
  (Ah, what ill raven
Flapped o'er the ship that morn?)

Caught by the under-death
In the drawing of a breath,
    Down went dauntless Craven,
    He and his hundred!
A moment we saw her turret,
    A little heel she gave,
And a thin white spray went o'er her
    Like the crest of a breaking wave—
In that great iron coffin,
    The channel for their grave,
    The fort their monument,
(Seen afar in the offing,)
Ten fathom deep lie Craven,
    And the bravest of our brave.

Then in that deadly track
A little the ships held back,
Closing up in their stations;—
There are minutes that fix the fate
Of battles and of nations
(Christening the generations),
When valour were all too late,
If a moment's doubt be harboured;—
From the main-top, bold and brief,
Came the word of our grand old Chief—
    "Go on!"—'t was all he said—
Our helm was put to starboard,
    And the *Hartford* passed ahead.

Ahead lay the *Tennessee,*
    On our starboard bow he lay,
With his mail-clad consorts three,
    (The rest had run up the Bay)—
There he was, belching flame from his bow,
And the steam from his throat's abyss
Was a Dragon's maddened hiss—

In sooth a most cursèd craft!—
In a sullen ring at bay
By the Middle Ground they lay,
  Raking us fore and aft.

Trust me, our berth was hot,
Ah, wickedly well they shot;
How their death-bolts howled and stung!
  And the water batteries played
  With their deadly cannonade
Till the air around us rung;
So the battle raged and roared—
Ah, had you been aboard
  To have seen the fight we made!
How they leaped, the tongues of flame
  From the cannon's fiery lip!
How the broadsides, deck and frame
  Shook the great ship!

And how the enemy's shell
  Came crashing, heavy and oft,
  Clouds of splinters flying aloft
And falling in oaken showers.
But ah, the pluck of the crew!
Had you stood on that deck of ours
You had seen what men can do.

Still, as the fray grew louder,
  Boldly we worked and well,
Steadily came the powder,
  Steadily came the shell,
And if tackle or truck found hurt,
  Quickly they cleared the wreck,
And the dead were laid to port,
  All a-row, on our deck.

Never a nerve that failed,
Never a cheek that paled,
Not a tinge of gloom or pallor—
There was bold Kentucky grit,
And the Old Virginia valour
And the daring Yankee wit.

There were blue eyes from turfy Shannon,
There were black orbs from palmy Niger—
But there, alongside of the cannon,
Each man fought like a tiger!

A little, once, it looked ill,
Our consort began to burn—
They quenched the flames with a will
But our men were falling still,
And still the fleet was astern.

Right abreast of the Fort
In an awful shroud they lay,
Broadsides thundering away,
And lightning from every port;
Scene of glory and dread!
A storm-cloud all aglow
With flashes of fiery red,
The thunder raging below,
And the forest of flags o'erhead!

So grand the hurly and roar,
So fiercely their broadsides blazed,
The regiments fighting ashore
Forgot to fire as they gazed.
There, to silence the foe,
Moving grimly and slow,
They loomed in that deadly wreath,
Where the darkest batteries frowned,—

Death in the air all around,
And the black torpedoes beneath!

And now, as we looked ahead,
  All for'ard, the long white deck
Was growing a strange dull red;
  But soon, as once and agen
Fore and aft we sped,
  (The firing to guide or check,)
You could hardly choose but tread
  On the ghastly human wreck,
(Dreadful gobbet and shred
  That a minute ago were men!)

Red, from mainmast to bitts!
  Red, on bulwark and wale—
Red, by combing and hatch—
  Red, o'er netting and rail!

And ever, with steady con,
  The ship forged slowly by,—
And ever the crew fought on,
  And their cheers rang loud and high.

Grand was the sight to see
  How by their guns they stood,
Right in front of our dead
  Fighting square abreast—
  Each brawny arm and chest
All spotted with black and red,
  Chrism of fire and blood!

Worth our watch, dull and sterile,
  Worth all the weary time—
Worth the woe and the peril,
  To stand in that strait sublime!

Fear? A forgotten form!
 Death? A dream of the eyes!
We were atoms in God's great storm
 That roared through the angry skies.

One only doubt was ours,
One only dread we knew,—
Could the day that dawned so well
Go down for the Darker Powers?
Would the fleet get through?
And ever the shot and shell
Came with the howl of hell,
The splinter-clouds rose and fell,
And the long line of corpses grew,—
Would the fleet win through?

They are men that never will fail
 (How aforetime they 've fought!)
But Murder may yet prevail—
 They may sink as Craven sank.
 Therewith, one hard, fierce thought
Burning on heart and lip,
Ran, like fire through the ship—
 Fight her, to the last plank!

A dimmer renown might strike
 If Death lay square alongside,—
But the old Flag has no like,
 She must fight, whatever betide;—
When the War is a tale of old,
 And this day's story is told,
They shall hear how the *Hartford* died!

But, as we ranged ahead,
 And the leading ships worked in,
 Losing their hope to win

The enemy turned and fled—
And one seeks a shallow reach,
   And another, winged in her flight,
      Our mate, brave Jouett, brings in—
   And one, all torn in the fight,
Runs for a wreck on the beach,
   Where her flames soon fire the night.

And the *Ram,* when well up the Bay,
   And we looked that our stems should meet,
(He had us fair for a prey,)
Shifting his helm midway,
   Sheered off and ran for the fleet;
There, without skulking or sham,
   He fought them, gun for gun,
And ever he sought to ram,
   But could finish never a one.

From the first of the iron shower
   Till we sent our parting shell,
'T was just one savage hour
   Of the roar and the rage of hell.

With the lessening smoke and thunder,
   Our glasses around we aim—
What is that burning yonder?
   Our *Philippi,*—aground and in flame!

Below, 't was still all a-roar,
As the ships went by the shore,
   But the fire of the fort had slacked,
(So fierce their volleys had been)—
And now, with a mighty din,
The whole fleet came grandly in,
   Though sorely battered and wracked.

So, up the Bay we ran,
   The Flag to port and ahead,

And a pitying rain began
  To wash the lips of our dead.

A league from the Fort we lay,
  And deemed that the end must lag;
When lo! looking down the Bay,
  There flaunted the Rebel Rag—
The *Ram* is again under way,
  And heading dead for the Flag!

Steering up with the stream,
  Boldly his course he lay,
Though the fleet all answered his fire,
And, as he still drew nigher,
Ever on bow and beam
  Our Monitors pounded away—
  How the *Chickasaw* hammered away!

Quickly breasting the wave,
  Eager the prize to win,
First of us all the brave
  Monongahela went in
Under full head of steam,
Twice she struck him abeam,
Till her stem was a sorry work,
  (She might have run on a crag!)
The *Lackawanna* hit fair,
He flung her aside like a cork,
  And still he held for the Flag.

High in the mizzen shroud
  (Lest the smoke his sight o'erwhelm),
Our Admiral's voice rang loud,
  " Hard-a-starboard your helm!
Starboard! and run him down!"
  Starboard it was—and so,
Like a black squall's lifting frown,

One mighty bow bore down
  On the iron beak of the Foe.

We stood on the deck together,
  Men that had looked on death
In battle and stormy weather—
  Yet a little we held our breath,
  When, with the hush of death,
The great ships drew together.

Our Captain strode to the bow,
  Drayton, courtly and wise,
  Kindly cynic, and wise,
(You hardly had known him now,—
  The flame of fight in his eyes!)
His brave heart eager to feel
How the oak would tell on the steel!

But, as the space grew short,
  A little he seemed to shun us,
Out peered a form grim and lanky,
  And a voice yelled: "Hard-a-port!
Hard-a-port!—here 's the damned Yankee
  Coming right down on us!"

He sheered, but the ships ran foul
With a gnarring shudder and growl—
  He gave us a deadly gun;
But as he passed in his pride,
(Rasping right alongside!)
  The Old Flag, in thunder tones,
Poured in her port broadside,
Rattling his iron hide,
  And cracking his timber bones!

Just then, at speed on the *Foe,*
　With her bow all weathered and brown,
　The great *Lackawanna* came down,
Full tilt, for another blow;
We were forging ahead,
　She reversed—but, for all our pains,
Rammed the old *Hartford* instead,
　Just for'ard the mizzen-chains!

Ah! how the masts did buckle and bend,
　And the stout hull ring and reel,
As she took us right on end!
　(Vain were engine and wheel,
　She was under full steam)—
With the roar of a thunder-stroke
Her two thousand tons of oak
　Brought up on us, right abeam!

A wreck, as it looked, we lay—
(Rib and plankshear gave way
　To the stroke of that giant wedge!)
Here, after all, we go—
The old ship is gone!—ah, no,
　But cut to the water's edge.

Never mind, then—at him again!
　His flurry now can't last long;
He 'll never again see land,
Try *that* on him, Marchand!
　On him again, brave Strong!

Heading square at the hulk,
　Full on his beam we bore;
But the spine of the huge Sea-hog
Lay on the tide, like a log,
　He vomited flame no more.

By this he had found it hot—
    Half the fleet, in an angry ring,
    Closed round the hideous thing,
Hammering with solid shot,
And bearing down, bow on bow—
    He had but a minute to choose;
Life or renown? which now
    Will the Rebel Admiral lose?

Cruel, haughty and cold,
He ever was strong and bold,
    Shall he shrink from a wooden stem?
He will think of that brave band
He sank in the *Cumberland*—
    Aye, he will sink like them.

Nothing left but to fight
Boldly his last sea-fight!
Can he strike? By Heaven, 't is true!
Down comes the traitor Blue,
And up goes the captive White!

Up went the White! Ah, then
The hurrahs that once and again
Rang from three thousand men
All flushed and savage with fight!
Our dead lay cold and stark;
But our dying, down in the dark,
Answered as best they might,
Lifting their poor lost arms,
And cheering for God and Right!

Ended the mighty noise,
Thunder of forts and ships.
Down we went to the hold,
Oh, our dear dying boys!
How we pressed their poor brave lips

(Ah, so pallid and cold!)
And held their hands to the last
(Those who had hands to hold).

Still thee, O woman heart!
(So strong an hour ago);
If the idle tears must start,
'T is not in vain they flow.

They died, our children dear,
On the drear berth-deck they died,—
Do not think of them here—
Even now their footsteps near
The immortal, tender sphere
(Land of love and cheer!
Home of the Crucified).

And the glorious deed survives;
Our threescore, quiet and cold,
Lie thus, for a myriad lives
And treasure-millions untold
(Labour of poor men's lives,
Hunger of weans and wives,
Such is the war-wasted gold).

Our ship and her fame to-day
Shall float on the storied Stream
When mast and shroud have crumbled away,
And her long white deck is a dream.

One daring leap in the dark,
Three mortal hours at the most,—
And hell lies stiff and stark
On a hundred leagues of coast.

For the mighty Gulf is ours,—
The bay is lost and won,
An Empire is lost and won!

Land, if thou yet hast flowers,
Twine them in one more wreath
Of tenderest red and white
(Twine buds of glory and death!),
For the brows of our brave dead,
For thy Navy's noblest son.

Joy, O Land, for thy sons,
Victors by flood and field!
The traitor walls and guns
Have nothing left but to yield
(Even now they surrender!).

And the ships shall sail once more,
And the clouds of war sweep on
To break on the cruel shore;—
But Craven is gone,
He and his hundred are gone.

The flags flutter up and down
At sunrise and twilight dim,
The cannons menace and frown,—
But never again for him,
Him and the hundred.

The Dahlgrens are dumb,
Dumb are the mortars;
Never more shall the drum
Beat to colours and quarters,—
The great guns are silent.

O brave heart and loyal!
Let all your colours dip;—

Mourn him proud ship!
From main deck to royal.
God rest our Captain,
Rest our lost hundred!

Droop flag and pennant!
What is your pride for?
Heaven, that he died for,
Rest our Lieutenant,
Rest our brave threescore!

.   .   .   .   .

O Mother Land! this weary life
    We led, we lead, is 'long of thee;
Thine the strong agony of strife,
    And thine the lonely sea.

Thine the long decks all slaughter-sprent,
    The weary rows of cots that lie
With wrecks of strong men, marred and rent,
    'Neath Pensacola's sky.

And thine the iron caves and dens
    Wherein the flame our war-fleet drives;
The fiery vault, whose breath is man's
    Most dear and precious lives!

Ah, ever when the storm sublime
    Dread Nature clears our murky air,
Thus in the crash of falling crime
    Some lesser guilt must share.

Full red the furnace fires must glow
    That melt the ore of mortal kind;

The mills of God are grinding slow,
　　But ah, how close they grind!

To-day the Dahlgren and the drum
　　Are dread Apostles of His Name;
His kingdom here can only come
　　By chrism of blood and flame.

Be strong: already slants the gold
　　Athwart these wild and stormy skies:
From out this blackened waste, behold
　　What happy homes shall rise!

But see thou we no traitor gloze,
　　No striking hands with Death and Shame,
Betray the sacred blood that flows
　　So freely for thy name.

And never fear a victor foe—
　　Thy children's hearts are strong and high;
Nor mourn too fondly; well they know
　　On deck or field to die.

Nor shalt thou want one willing breath,
　　Though, ever smiling round the brave,
The blue sea bear us on to death,
　　The green were one wide grave.
　　　　　　　　—Henry Howard Brownell.

FARRAGUT

FARRAGUT, Farragut,
　　Old Heart of Oak,
Daring Dave Farragut,
　　Thunderbolt stroke,
Watches the hoary mist
　　Lift from the bay,

Till his flag, glory-kissed,
  Greets the young day.

Far, by gray Morgan's walls,
  Looms the black fleet.
Hark, deck to rampart calls
  With the drums' beat!
Buoy your chains overboard,
  While the steam hums;
Men! to the battlement,
  Farragut comes.

See, as the hurricane
  Hurtles in wrath
Squadrons of clouds amain
  Back from its path!
Back to the parapet,
  To the guns' lips,
Thunderbolt Farragut
  Hurls the black ships.

Now through the battle's roar
  Clear the boy sings,
"By the mark fathoms four,"
  While his lead swings.
Steady the wheelmen five
  "Nor' by east keep her,"
"Steady," but two alive:
  How the shells sweep her!

Lashed to the mast that sways
  Over red decks,
Over the flame that plays
  Round the torn wrecks,
Over the dying lips
  Framed for a cheer,

Farragut leads his ships,
  Guides the line clear.

On by heights cannon-browed,
  While the spars quiver;
Onward still flames the cloud
  Where the hulks shiver.
See, yon fort's star is set,
  Storm and fire past.
Cheer him, lads—Farragut,
  Lashed to the mast!

Oh! while the Atlantic's breast
  Bears a white sail,
While the Gulf's towering crest
  Tops a green vale;
Men thy bold deeds shall tell,
  Old Heart of Oak,
Daring Dave Farragut,
  Thunderbolt stroke!
          —William Tucker Meredith.

SHERIDAN'S RIDE

UP from the south at break of day,
  Bringing to Winchester fresh dismay,
The affrighted air with a shudder bore,
Like a herald in haste, to the chieftain's door,
The terrible grumble, and rumble, and roar,
Telling the battle was on once more,
And Sheridan twenty miles away.

And wider still those billows of war
Thundered along the horizon's bar;
And louder yet into Winchester rolled
The roar of that red sea uncontrolled,

Making the blood of the listener cold,
As he thought of the stake in that fiery fray,
And Sheridan twenty miles away.

But there is a road from Winchester town,
A good, broad highway leading down;
And there, through the flush of the morning light,
A steed as black as the steeds of night,
Was seen to pass, as with eagle flight.
As if he knew the terrible need,
He stretched away with his utmost speed;
Hills rose and fell; but his heart was gay,
With Sheridan fifteen miles away.

Still sprung from those swift hoofs, thundering south,
The dust, like smoke from the cannon's mouth;
Or the trail of a comet, sweeping faster and faster,
Foreboding to traitors the doom of disaster.
The heart of the steed, and the heart of the master
Were beating like prisoners assaulting their walls,
Impatient to be where the battle-field calls;
Every nerve of the charger was strained to full play,
With Sheridan only ten miles away.

Under his spurning feet, the road
Like an arrowy Alpine river flowed,
And the landscape sped away behind
Like an ocean flying before the wind,
And the steed, like a bark fed with furnace ire,
Swept on, with his wild eye full of fire.
But, lo! he is nearing his heart's desire;
He is snuffing the smoke of the roaring fray,
With Sheridan only five miles away.

The first that the general saw were the groups
Of stragglers, and then the retreating troops;
What was done? what to do? a glance told him both,
Then striking his spurs with a terrible oath,
He dashed down the line, 'mid a storm of huzzas,
And the wave of retreat checked its course there, because
The sight of the master compelled it to pause.
With foam and with dust the black charger was gray;
By the flash of his eye, and his red nostril's play,
He seemed to the whole great army to say,
"I have brought you Sheridan all the way,
From Winchester down, to save the day."

Hurrah, hurrah for Sheridan!
Hurrah, hurrah for horse and man!
And when their statues are placed on high,
Under the dome of the Union sky,—
The American soldiers' Temple of Fame,
There, with the glorious general's name,
Be it said, in letters both bold and bright:
"Here is the steed that saved the day
By carrying Sheridan into the fight,
From Winchester,—twenty miles away!"
                              —*Thomas Buchanan Read.*

"ALBEMARLE" CUSHING

JOY in rebel Plymouth town, in the spring of 'sixty-four,
    When the *Albemarle* down on the Yankee frigates bore,
With the saucy Stars and Bars at her main;
    When she smote the *Southfield* dead, and the stout *Miami*
        quailed,
And the fleet in terror fled when their mighty cannon hailed
    Shot and shell on her iron back in vain,
Till she slowly steamed away to her berth at Plymouth pier,

And their quick eyes saw her sway with her great beak
    out of gear,
And the colour of their courage rose again.

All the summer lay the ram,
    Like a wounded beast at bay,
While the watchful squadron swam
    In the harbour night and day,
Till the broken beak was mended, and the weary vigil ended,
    And her time was come again to smite and slay.

Must they die, and die in vain,
    Like a flock of shambled sheep?
Then the Yankee grit and brain
    Must be dead or gone to sleep,
And our sailors' gallant story of a hundred years of glory
    Let us sell for a song, selling cheap!

Cushing, scarce a man in years,
    But a sailor thoroughbred,
"With a dozen volunteers
    I will sink the ram," he said.
"At the worst 't is only dying." And the old commander,
    sighing,
    "'T is to save the fleet and flag—go ahead!"

    .   .   .   .

Bright the rebel beacons blazed
    On the river left and right;
Wide awake their sentries gazed
    Through the watches of the night;
Sharp their challenge rang, and fiery came the rifle's quick
    inquiry,
    As the little launch swung into the light.

Listening ears afar had heard;
    Ready hands to quarters sprung,

The *Albemarle* awoke and stirred,
    And her howitzers gave tongue;
Till the river and the shore echoed back the mighty roar,
When the portals of her hundred-pounders swung.

    Will the swordfish brave the whale,
        Doubly girt with boom and chain?
    Face the shrapnel's iron hail?
        Dare the livid leaden rain?
Ah! that shell has done its duty; it has spoiled the Yankee's
        beauty;
    See her turn and fly with half her madmen slain.

    High the victor's taunting yell
        Rings above the battle roar,
    And they bid her mock farewell
        As she seeks the farther shore,
Till they see her sudden swinging, crouching for the leap
        and springing
    Back to boom and chain and bloody fray once more.

    Now the Southern captain, stirred
        By the spirit of his race,
    Stops the firing with a word,
        Bids them yield, and offers grace.
Cushing, laughing, answers, "No! we are here to fight!"
        and so
    Swings the dread torpedo spar to its place.

    Then the great ship shook and reeled,
        With a wounded, gaping side,
    But her steady cannon pealed
        Ere she settled in the tide,
And the Roanoke's dull flood ran full red with Yankee blood,
    When the fighting *Albemarle* sunk and died.

Woe in rebel Plymouth town when the *Albemarle* fell,
   And the saucy flag went down that had floated long and
      well,
Nevermore from her stricken deck to wave.
   For the fallen flag a sigh, for the fallen foe a tear!
Never shall their glory die while we hold our glory dear,
   And the hero's laurels live on his grave.
Link their Cooke's with Cushing's name; proudly call them
      both our own;
Claim their valour and their fame for America alone—
   Joyful mother of the bravest of the brave!

                              —*James Jeffrey Roche.*

SHERMAN'S MARCH TO THE SEA

OUR camp fires shone bright on the mountain
      That frowned on the river below,
As we stood by our guns in the morning,
   And eagerly watched for the foe;
When a rider came out of the darkness
   That hung over mountain and tree,
And shouted, "Boys, up and be ready!
   For Sherman will march to the Sea!"

Then cheer upon cheer for bold Sherman
   Went up from each valley and glen,
And the bugles re-echoed the music
   That came from the lips of the men;
For we knew that the stars in our banner
   More bright in their splendour would be,
And that blessings from Northland would greet us,
   When Sherman marched down to the sea.

Then forward, boys! forward to battle!
   We marched on our wearisome way,
We stormed the wild hills of Resaca—

God bless those who fell on that day!
Then Kenesaw, dark in its glory,
  Frowned down on the flag of the free;
But the East and the West bore our standard
  And Sherman marched down to the sea.

Still onward we pressed, till our banners
  Swept out from Atlanta's grim walls,
And the blood of the patriot dampened
  The soil where the traitor flag falls;
We paused not to weep for the fallen,
  Who slept by each river and tree,
Yet we twined them a wreath of the laurel,
  As Sherman marched down to the sea.

Oh, proud was our army that morning,
  That stood where the pine darkly towers,
When Sherman said, " Boys, you are weary,
  But to-day fair Savannah is ours!"
Then sang we the song of our chieftain,
  That echoed o'er river and lea,
And the stars in our banner shone brighter
  When Sherman marched down to the sea.

            —*Samuel H. M. Byers.*

MARCHING THROUGH GEORGIA

BRING the good old bugle, boys, we 'll sing another song—
  Sing it with a spirit that will start the world along—
Sing it as we used to sing it fifty thousand strong,
    While we were marching through Georgia.

Chorus

  "Hurrah! Hurrah! we bring the jubilee!
    Hurrah! Hurrah! the flag that makes you free!"
  So we sang the chorus from Atlanta to the sea,
    While we were marching through Georgia.

How the darkeys shouted when they heard the joyful sound!
How the turkeys gobbled which our commissary found!
How the sweet potatoes even started from the ground,
　　　While we were marching through Georgia.

Yes, and there were Union men who wept with joyful tears,
When they saw the honoured flag they had not seen for years;
Hardly could they be restrained from breaking forth in cheers
　　　While we were marching through Georgia.

"Sherman's dashing Yankee boys will never reach the
　　　coast!"
So the saucy rebels said—and 't was a handsome boast,
Had they not forgot, alas! to reckon on a host,
　　　While we were marching through Georgia.

So we made a thoroughfare for Freedom and her train,
Sixty miles in latitude—three hundred to the main;
Treason fled before us, for resistance was in vain,
　　　While we were marching through Georgia.
　　　　　　　　　　—*Henry Clay Work.*

THE SONG OF SHERMAN'S ARMY

A PILLAR of fire by night,
　　A pillar of smoke by day,
Some hours of march—then a halt to fight,
　　And so we hold our way;
Some hours of march—then a halt to fight,
　　As on we hold our way.

Over mountain and plain and stream,
 To some bright Atlantic bay,
With our arms aflash in the morning beam,
 We hold our festal way;
 With our arms aflash in the morning beam,
 We hold our checkless way!

There is terror wherever we come,
 There is terror and wild dismay
When they see the Old Flag and hear the drum
 Announce us on the way;
 When they see the Old Flag and hear the drum
 Beating time to our onward way;

Never unlimber a gun
 For those villainous lines in gray,
Draw sabres! and at 'em upon the run!
 'T is thus we clear our way,
 Draw sabres, and soon you will see them run,
 As we hold our conquering way.

The loyal, who long have been dumb,
 Are loud in their cheers to-day;
And the old men out on their crutches come,
 To see us hold our way;
 And the old men out on their crutches come,
 To bless us on our way.

Around us in rear and flanks,
 Their futile squadrons play,
With a sixty-mile front of steady ranks,
 We hold our checkless way;
 With a sixty-mile front of serried ranks,
 Our banner clears the way.

Hear the spattering fire that starts
From the woods and copses gray,
There is just enough fighting to quicken our hearts
As we frolic along the way!
There is just enough fighting to warm our hearts
As we rattle along the way.

Upon different roads abreast
The heads of our columns gay,
With fluttering flags, all forward pressed,
Hold on their conquering way.
With fluttering flags to victory pressed,
We hold our glorious way.

Ah, traitors! who bragged so bold
In the sad war's early day,
Did nothing predict you should ever behold
The Old Flag come this way?
Did nothing predict you should yet behold
Our banner come back this way?

By heaven! 't is a gala march,
'T is a picnic or a play;
Of all our long war 't is the crowning arch,
Hip, hip! for Sherman's way!
Of all our long war this crowns the arch—
For Sherman and Grant, hurrah!

—*Charles Graham Halpine.*

SAVANNAH

THOU hast not drooped thy stately head,
Thy woes a wondrous beauty shed!

Not like a lamb to slaughter led,
But with the lion's monarch tread,
Thou comest to thy battle bed.
　　Savannah! O Savannah!

Thine arm of flesh is girded strong;
The blue veins swell beneath thy wrong;
To thee the triple cords belong
Of woe and death and shameless wrong,
And spirit vaunted long, too long!
　　Savannah! O Savannah!

No blood-stains spot thy forehead fair;
Only the martyr's blood is there;
It gleams upon thy bosom bare,
It moves thy deep, deep soul to prayer,
And tunes a dirge for thy sad ear,
　　Savannah! O Savannah!

Thy clean white hand is opened wide
For weal or woe, thou Freedom Bride;
The sword-sheath sparkles at thy side,
Thy plighted troth, whate'er betide,
Thou hast but Freedom for thy guide,
　　Savannah! O Savannah!

What though the heavy storm-cloud lowers
Still at thy feet the old oak towers;
Still fragrant are thy jessamine bowers,
And things of beauty, love, and flowers
Are smiling o'er this land of ours,
　　My sunny home, Savannah!

There is no film before thy sight,—
Thou seest woe and death and night,
And blood upon thy banner bright;

But in thy full wrath's kindled might
What carest thou for woe or night?
  My rebel home, Savannah!

Come—for the crown is on thy head!
Thy woes a wondrous beauty shed;
Not like a lamb to slaughter led,
But with the lion's monarch tread,
Oh! come unto thy battle bed,
  Savannah! O Savannah!
                    —*Alethea S. Burroughs.*

LAUS DEO!

IT is done!
  Clang of bell and roar of gun
Send the tidings up and down.
  How the belfries rock and reel!
  How the great guns, peal on peal,
Fling the joy from town to town!

  Ring, O bells!
  Every stroke exulting tells
Of the burial hour of crime.
  Loud and long, that all may hear,
  Ring for every listening ear
Of Eternity and Time!

  Let us kneel:
  God's own voice is in that peal,
And this spot is holy ground.
  Lord, forgive us! What are we,
  That our eyes this glory see,
  That our ears have heard the sound!

For the Lord
On the whirlwind is abroad;
In the earthquake He has spoken;
He has smitten with His thunder
The iron walls asunder,
And the gates of brass are broken!

Loud and long
Lift the old exulting song;
Sing with Miriam by the sea,
He has cast the mighty down;
Horse and rider sink and drown;
"He hath triumphed gloriously!"

Did we dare,
In our agony of prayer,
Ask for more than He has done?
When was ever His right hand
Over any time or land
Stretched as now beneath the sun?

How they pale,
Ancient myth and song and tale,
In this wonder of our days,
When the cruel rod of war
Blossoms white with righteous law,
And the wrath of man is praise!

Blotted out!
All within and all about
Shall a fresher life begin;
Freer breathe the universe
As it rolls its heavy curse
On the dead and buried sin!

It is done!
  In the circuit of the sun
Shall the sound thereof go forth.
  It shall bid the sad rejoice,
  It shall give the dumb a voice,
It shall belt with joy the earth!

  Ring and swing,
  Bells of joy! On morning's wing
Send the song of praise abroad!
  With a sound of broken chains
  Tell the nations that He reigns,
Who alone is Lord and God!
                    —*John Greenleaf Whittier.*

CHARLESTON

CALMLY beside her tropic strand,
  An empress, brave and loyal,
I see the watchful city stand,
  With aspect sternly royal;
She knows her mortal foe draws near,
  Armoured by subtlest science,
Yet deep, majestical, and clear,
  Rings out her grand defiance.
Oh, glorious is thy noble face,
  Lit up by proud emotion,
And unsurpassed thy stately grace,
  Our warrior Queen of Ocean!

First from thy lips the summons came,
  Which roused our South to action,
And, with the quenchless force of flame,
  Consumed the demon, Faction;

First, like a rush of sovereign wind,
    That rends dull waves asunder,
Thy prescient warning struck the blind,
    And woke the deaf with thunder;
They saw, with swiftly kindling eyes,
    The shameful doom before them,
And heard, borne wild from northern skies,
    The death-gale hurtling o'er them:

Wilt thou, whose virgin banner rose,
    A morning star of splendour,
Quail when the war-tornado blows,
    And crouch in base surrender?
Wilt thou, upon whose loving breast
    Our noblest chiefs are sleeping,
Yield thy dead patriots' place of rest
    To scornful alien keeping?
No! while a life-pulse throbs for fame,
    Thy sons will gather round thee,
Welcome the shot, the steel, the flame,
    If honour's hand hath crowned thee.

Then fold about thy beauteous form
    The imperial robe thou wearest,
And front with regal port the storm
    Thy foe would dream thou fearest;
If strength, and will, and courage fail
    To cope with ruthless numbers,
And thou must bend, despairing, pale,
    Where thy last hero slumbers,
Lift the red torch, and light the fire
    Amid those corpses gory,
And on thy self-made funeral pyre,
    Pass from the world to glory.
                    —*Paul Hamilton Hayne.*

THE SURRENDER OF THE ARMY OF NORTHERN VIRGINIA

HAVE we wept till our eyes were dim with tears,
　Have we borne the sorrows of four long years
　　Only to meet this sight?
O merciful God! can it really be
This downfall awaits our gallant Lee
　　And the cause we counted right?

Have we known this bitter, bitter pain,
Have all our dear ones died in vain?
　　Has God forsaken quite?
Is this the answer to every prayer,
This anguish of untold despair,
　　This spirit-scathing blight?

Heart-broken we kneel on the bloody sod,
We hide from the wrath of our angry God,
　　Who bows us in the dust.
We heed not the sneer of the insolent foe,
But that Thou, O God! should forsake us so,
　　In whom was our only trust!

Even strong men weep! the men who stand
Fast in defence of our native land,
　　These gallant hearts and brave;
They wept not the souls who fighting fell,
For the hero's death became them well,
　　And they feared not the hero's grave.

They have marched through long and stormy nights,
They have borne the brunt of a hundred fights,
　　And their courage never failed;
Hunger and cold, and the summer heat;

They have felt on the march and the long retreat,
  Yet their brave hearts never quailed.

Now all these hardships seem real bliss,
Compared with a grief of a scene like this,
  This speechless, this wordless woe;
That Lee, at the head of his faithful band,
The flower and pride of our Southern land,
  Must yield to the hated foe.

The conquered foe of a hundred fields,
The foe that, conquering, the laurel yields
  Lee's sad, stern brow to grace;
For he, with the pain of defeat in his heart,
Will bear in history the nobler part,
  And fill the loftier place.

Scatter the dust on each bowed head,
Happy, thrice happy, the honoured dead
    Who sleep their last long sleep!
For we who live in the coming years,
Beholding days ghastly with phantom fears,
    What can we do but weep?
                              —*Florence Anderson.*

THE SWORD OF ROBERT LEE

FORTH from its scabbard, pure and bright,
    Flashed the sword of Lee!
Far in the front of the deadly fight,
High o'er the brave in the cause of right,
Its stainless sheen, like a beacon light,
    Led us to victory!

Out of its scabbard, where full long,
  It slumbered peacefully,
Roused from its rest by the battle's song,
Shielding the feeble, smiting the strong,
Guarding the right, avenging the wrong,
  Gleamed the sword of Lee.

Forth from its scabbard, high in air
  Beneath Virginia's sky;
And they who saw it gleaming there,
And knew who bore it, knelt to swear
That where that sword led they would dare
  To follow—and to die.

Out of its scabbard! Never hand
  Waved sword from stain as free,
No purer sword led braver band,
Nor braver bled for a brighter land,
Nor brighter land had a cause so grand,
  Nor cause a chief like Lee!

Forth from its scabbard! How we prayed
  That sword might victor be!
And when our triumph was delayed,
And many a heart grew sore afraid,
We still hoped on while gleamed the blade
  Of noble Robert Lee.

Forth from its scabbard all in vain
  Bright flashed the sword of Lee;
'T is shrouded now in its sheath again,
It sleeps the sleep of our noble slain,
Defeated, yet without a stain,
  Proudly and peacefully.

                              —*Abram Joseph Ryan.*

WHEN LILACS LAST IN THE DOORYARD
BLOOMED

WHEN lilacs last in the dooryard bloomed,
    And the great star early drooped in the western sky
        in the night,
I mourned, and yet shall mourn with ever-returning spring.

Ever-returning spring, trinity sure to me you bring,
Lilacs blooming perennial and drooping star in the west,
And thought of him I love.

O powerful western fallen star!
O shades of night—O moody, tearful night!
O great star disappeared—O the black murk that hides the
        star!
O cruel hand that holds me powerless—O helpless soul of me!
O harsh surrounding cloud that will not free my soul.

In the dooryard fronting an old farm-house near the white-
        washed palings,
Stands the lilac-bush tall-growing with heart-shaped leaves
        of rich green,
With many a pointed blossom rising delicate, with the per-
        fume strong I love,
With every leaf a miracle—and from this bush in the door-
        yard,
With delicate-coloured blossoms and heart-shaped leaves of
        rich green,
A sprig with its flower I break.
In the swamp in secluded recesses,
A shy and hidden bird is warbling a song.

Solitary the thrush,
The hermit withdrawn to himself, avoiding the settlements,
Sings by himself a song.
Song of the bleeding throat,
Death's outlet song of life, (for well, dear brother, I know,
If thou wast not granted to sing thou would'st surely die).

Over the breast of the spring, the land, amid cities,
Amid lanes and through old woods, where lately the violets
     peeped from the ground, spotting the gray debris,
Amid the grass in the fields each side of the lanes, passing
     the endless grass,
Passing the yellow-speared wheat, every grain from its
     shroud in the dark-brown fields uprisen,
Passing the apple-tree blows of white and pink in the
     orchards,
Carrying a corpse to where it shall rest in the grave,
Night and day journeys a coffin.

Coffin that passes through lanes and streets,
Through day and night with the great cloud darkening the
     land,
With the pomp of the inlooped flags with the cities draped
     in black,
With the show of the States themselves as of crape-veiled
     women standing,
With processions long and winding and the flambeaus of the
     night,
With the countless torches lit, with the silent sea of faces
     and the unbared heads,
With the waiting depot, the arriving coffin, and the sombre
     faces,

With dirges through the night, and the thousand voices rising
    strong and solemn,
With all the mournful voices of the dirges poured around the
    coffin,
The dim-lit churches and the shuddering organs—where amid
    these you journey,
With the tolling, tolling bells' perpetual clang,
Here, coffin that slowly passes,
I give you my sprig of lilac.

(Nor for you, for one alone,
Blossoms and branches green to coffins all I bring,
For fresh as the morning, thus would I chant a song for you,
    O sane and sacred death.

All over bouquets of roses,
O death, I cover you over with roses and early lilies,
But mostly and now the lilac that blooms the first,
Copious I break, I break the sprigs from the bushes
With loaded arms I come, pouring for you,
For you and the coffins all of you, O death.)

O western orb sailing the heaven,
Now I know what you must have meant as a month since I
    walked,
As I walked in silence the transparent shadowy night,
As I saw you had something to tell as you bent to me night
    after night,
As you drooped from the sky low down as if to my side,
    (while the other stars all looked on,)
As we wandered together the solemn night, (for something,
    I know not what, kept me from sleep),

As the night advanced, and I saw on the rim of the west how
     full you were of woe,
As I stood on the rising ground in the breeze in cool trans-
     parent night,
As I watched where you passed and was lost in the nether-
     ward black of the night,
As my soul in its trouble dissatisfied sank, as where you, sad
     orb,
Concluded, dropt in the night, and was gone.

Sing on there in the swamp,
O singer bashful and tender! I hear your notes, I hear your
     call,
I hear, I come presently, I understand you,
But a moment I linger, for the lustrous star has detained me,
The star my departing comrade holds and detains me.

O how shall I warble myself for the dead one there I loved?
And how shall I deck my song for the large sweet soul that
     has gone?
And what shall my perfume be for the grave of him I love?

Sea-winds blow, from east and west,
Blown from the Eastern sea and blown from the Western sea,
     till there on the prairies meeting,
These and with these and the breath of my chant,
I 'll perfume the grave of him I love.

O what shall I hang on the chamber walls?
And what shall the pictures be that I hang on the walls,
To adorn the burial-house of him I love?
Pictures of growing spring and farms and homes,

With Fourth-month eve at sundown, and the gray smoke
lucid and bright,
With floods of the yellow gold of the gorgeous, indolent,
sinking sun, burning, expanding the air,
With fresh sweet herbage under foot, and the pale green
leaves of the trees prolific,
In the distance the flowing glaze, the breast of the river, with
a wind-dapple here and there,
With ranging hills on the banks, and many a line against the
sky, and shadows,
And the city at hand with dwellings so dense, and stacks of
chimneys,
And all the scenes of life and the workshops, and the work-
men homeward returning.

Lo, body and soul—this land,
My own Manhattan with spires, and the sparkling and hurry-
ing tides, and the ships,
The varied and ample land, the South and the North in the
light, Ohio's shores and flashing Missouri,
And ever the far-spreading prairies covered with grass and
corn.

Lo, the most excellent sun so calm and haughty,
The violet and purple morn with just-felt breezes,
The gentle soft-born measureless light,
The miracle spreading, bathing all, fulfilled the noon,
The coming eve delicious, the welcome night and the stars,
Over my cities shining all, enveloping man and land.

Sing on, sing on, you gray-brown bird!
Sing from the swamps, the recesses; pour your chant from
the bushes,
Limitless out of the dusk, out of the cedars and pines.

Sing on, dearest brother, warble your reedy song,
Loud human song, with voice of uttermost woe.

O liquid and free and tender!
O wild and loose to my soul—O wondrous singer!
You only I hear—yet the star holds me, (but will soon
    depart),
Yet the lilac with mastering odour holds me.

Now while I sat in the day and looked forth,
In the close of the day with its light and the fields of spring,
    and the farmers preparing their crops,
In the large unconscious scenery of my land with its lakes
    and forests,
In the heavenly aerial beauty, (after the perturbed winds and
    the storms),
Under the arching heavens of the afternoon swift passing,
    and the voices of children and women,
The many-moving sea-tides, and I saw the ships how they
    sailed,
And the summer approaching with richness, and the fields
    all busy with labour,
And the infinite separate houses, how they all went on, each
    with its meals and the minutiæ of daily usages,
And the streets how their throbbings throbbed, and the cities
    pent—lo, then and there,
Falling upon them all and among them all, enveloping me
    with the rest,
Appeared the cloud, appeared the long black trail,
And I knew death, its thought, and the sacred knowledge of
    death.

Then with the knowledge of death as walking one side of me,
And the thought of death close-walking the other side of me,

And I in the middle as with companions, and as holding the
        hands of companions,
I fled forth to the hiding receiving night that talks not,
Down to the shores of the water, the path by the swamp in
        the dimness,
To the solemn shadowy cedars and ghostly pines so still.

And the singer so shy to the rest received me,
The gray-brown bird I know received us comrades three,
And he sang the carol of death, and a verse for him I love.

From deep secluded recesses,
From the fragrant cedars and the ghostly pines so still,
Came the carol of the bird.

And the charm of the carol rapt me,
As I held as if by their hands my comrades in the night,
And the voice of my spirit tallied the song of the bird.

Come, lovely and soothing death,
Undulate round the world, serenely arriving, arriving
In the day, in the night, to all, to each,
Sooner or later, delicate death.

Praised be the fathomless universe,
For life and joy, and for objects and knowledge curious,
And for love, sweet love—but praise! praise! praise!
For the sure-enwinding arms of cool-enfolding death.

Dark mother, always gliding near with soft feet,
Have none chanted for thee a chant of fullest welcome?

Then I chant it for thee, I glorify thee above all,
I bring thee a song that when thou must indeed come, come
      unfalteringly.

Approach, strong deliveress!
When it is so, when thou hast taken them, I joyously sing the
      dead,
Lost in the loving floating ocean of thee,
Laved in the flood of thy bliss, O death.

From me to thee glad serenades,
Dances for thee I propose, saluting thee, adornments and
      feasting for thee,
And the sights of the open landscape and the highspread sky
      are fitting,
And life and the fields, and the huge and thoughtful night.

The night in silence under many a star,
The ocean shore and the husky whispering wave whose voice
      I know,
And the soul turning to thee, O vast and well-veiled death,
And the body gratefully nestling close to thee.

Over the tree-tops I float thee a song,
Over the rising and sinking waves, over the myriad fields and
      the prairies wide,
Over the dense-packed cities all and the teeming wharves and
      ways,
I float this carol with joy, with joy to thee, O death.

To the tally of my soul,
Loud and strong kept up the gray-brown bird,
With pure deliberate notes spreading, filling the night.

Loud in the pines and cedars dim,
Clear in the freshness moist and the swamp-perfume,
And I with my comrades there in the night.

While my sight that was bound in my eyes unclosed,
As to long panoramas of visions.
And I saw askant the armies,
I saw as in noiseless dreams hundreds of battle-flags,
Borne through the smoke of battles and pierced with missiles
        I saw them,
And carried hither and yon through smoke, and torn and
        bloody,
And at last but a few shreds left on the staffs, (and all in
        silence),
And the staffs all splintered and broken.

I saw battle corpses, myriads of them,
And white skeletons of young men, I saw them;
I saw the débris and débris of all the slain soldiers of the
        war,
But I saw they were not as was thought,
They themselves were fully at rest, they suffered not,
The living remained and suffered, the mother suffered,
And the wife and the child and the musing comrade suffered,
And the armies that remained suffered.

Passing the vision, passing the night,
Passing, unloosing the hold of my comrades' hands,
Passing the song of the hermit bird and the tallying song of
        my soul,
Victorious song, death's outlet song, yet varying ever-altering
        song,
As low and wailing, yet clear, the notes rising and falling,
        flooding the night,

Sadly sinking and fainting, as warning and warning, and yet
again bursting with joy,
Covering the earth and filling the spread of heaven,
As that powerful psalm in the night I heard from recesses,
Passing, I leave thee, lilac with heart-shaped leaves,
O leave thee there in the door-yard, blooming, returning with
spring.

I cease from my song for thee,
From my gaze on thee in the west, fronting the west, com-
muning with thee,
O comrades lustrous, with silver face in the night.

Yet each to keep and all, retrievements out of the night,
The song the wondrous chant of the gray-brown bird,
And the tallying chant, the echo aroused in my soul,
With the lustrous and drooping star with the countenance
full of woe,
With the holders holding my hand nearing the call of the
bird,
Comrades mine and I in the midst, and their memory ever to
keep, for the dead I loved so well,
For the sweetest, wisest soul of all my days and lands—and
this for his dear sake,
Lilac and star and bird twined with the chant of my soul,
There in the fragrant pines and the cedars dusk and dim.
—Walt Whitman.

ABRAHAM LINCOLN

OH, slow to smite and swift to spare,
Gentle and merciful and just!
Who, in the fear of God, didst bear
The sword of power, a nation's trust!

In sorrow by thy bier we stand,
　　Amid the awe that hushes all,
And speak the anguish of a land
　　That shook with horror at thy fall.

Thy task is done; the bond are free:
　　We bear thee to an honoured grave,
Whose proudest monument shall be
　　The broken fetters of the slave.

Pure was thy life; its bloody close
　　Hath placed thee with the sons of light,
Among the noble host of those
　　Who perished in the cause of Right.

　　　　　　　　　—*William Cullen Bryant.*

O CAPTAIN! MY CAPTAIN!

O CAPTAIN! my Captain! our fearful trip is done;
　　The ship has weathered every rack, the prize we sought
　　　is won;
The port is near, the bells I hear, the people all exulting,
While follow eyes the steady keel, the vessel grim and daring:
　　But O heart! heart! heart!
　　　O the bleeding drops of red,
　　　　Where on the deck my Captain lies,
　　　　　Fallen cold and dead!

O Captain! my Captain! rise up and hear the bells;
Rise up—for you the flag is flung—for you the bugle trills;
For you bouquets and ribboned wreaths—for you the shores
　　a-crowding;
For you they call, the swaying mass, their eager faces
　　turning;
　　　Here Captain! dear father!
　　　　This arm beneath your head;

It is some dream that on the deck
    You 've fallen cold and dead.

My Captain does not answer, his lips are pale and still;
My father does not feel my arm, he has no pulse nor will:
The ship is anchored safe and sound, its voyage closed and
    done;
From fearful trip the victor ship comes in with object won:
    Exult, O shores, and ring, O bells!
      But I, with mournful tread,
        Walk the deck my Captain lies,
          Fallen cold and dead.

                —*Walt Whitman.*

PEACE

O LAND, of every land the best—
    O Land whose glory shall increase;
Now in your whitest raiment drest
    For the great festival of peace:

Take from your flag its fold of gloom,
    And let it float undimmed above,
Till over all our vales shall bloom,
    The sacred colours that we love.

On mountain high, in valley low,
    Set Freedom's living fires to burn;
Until the midnight sky shall show
    A redder pathway than the morn.

Welcome, with shouts of joy and pride,
    Your veterans from the war-path's track;
You gave your boys, untrained, untried;
    You bring them men and heroes back!

And shed no tear, though think you must
    With sorrow of the martyred band;
Not even of him whose hallowed dust
    Has made our prairies holy land.

Though by the places where they fell,
    The places that are sacred ground,
Death, like a sullen sentinel,
    Paces his everlasting round.

Yet when they set their country free
    And gave her traitors fitting doom,
They left their last great enemy,
    Baffled, beside an empty tomb.

Not there, but risen, redeemed, they go
    Where all the paths are sweet with flowers;
They fought to give us peace, and lo!
    They gained a better peace than ours.
                                —*Phœbe Cary.*

THE CONQUERED BANNER

FURL that banner! for 't is weary,
        Round its staff 't is drooping dreary,
    Furl it, fold it,—it is best;
    For there 's not a man to wave it,
    And there 's not a sword to save it,
    And there 's not a hand to lave it
    In the blood that heroes gave it,
    And its foes now scorn and brave it.
        Furl it, hide it—let it rest!

Take that banner down! 't is tattered;
Broken is its staff and shattered,
And the valiant hosts are scattered

257

Over whom it fluttered high.
Oh, 't is hard for us to fold it!
Hard to think there 's none to hold it;
Hard that those who once unrolled it
     Now must furl it with a sigh.

Furl that banner—furl it sadly;
Once ten thousand hailed it gladly,
And ten thousand wildly, madly
     Swore it should for ever wave.
Swore that foemen's swords should never
Hearts like theirs entwined dissever,
And that flag should float for ever
     O'er their freedom, or their grave.

Furl it, for the hands that grasped it
And the hearts that fondly clasped it
     Cold and dead are lying low;
And that banner—it is trailing,
While around it sounds the wailing
     Of its people in their woe.
For, though conquered, they adore it,
Love the cold, dead hands that bore it,
Weep for those who fell before it,
Pardon those who trailed and tore it;
And oh, wildly they deplore it
     Now to furl and fold it so.

Furl that banner! True, 't is gory,
Yet 't is wreathed around with glory,
And 't will live in song and story
     Though its folds are in the dust;
For its fame, on brightest pages,
Penned by poets and by sages,
Shall go sounding down the ages.
     Furl its folds, though now we must.

Furl that banner, softly, slowly;
Treat it gently—it is holy,
  For it droops above the dead;
Touch it not—unfurl it never,
Let it droop there, furled for ever,
  For its people's hopes are fled.

                              —*Abram Joseph Ryan.*

A SECOND REVIEW OF THE GRAND ARMY

I READ last night of the Grand Review
  In Washington's chiefest avenue—
Two hundred thousand men in blue,
  I think they said was the number,—
Till I seemed to hear their trampling feet,
The bugle blast and the drum's quick beat,
The clatter of hoofs in the stony street,
The cheers of people who came to greet,
And the thousand details that to repeat
  Would only my verse encumber,—
Till I fell in a revery, sad and sweet,
  And then to a fitful slumber.

When, lo! in a vision I seemed to stand
In the lonely Capitol. On each hand
Far stretched the portico; dim and grand
Its columns ranged, like a martial band
Of sheeted spectres whom some command
  Had called to a last reviewing.
And the streets of the city were white and bare,
No footfall echoed across the square;
But out of the misty midnight air
I heard in the distance a trumpet blare,
And the wandering night-winds seemed to bear
  The sound of a far tattooing.

Then I held my breath with fear and dread;
For into the square, with a brazen tread,
There rode a figure whose stately head
  O'erlooked the review that morning,
That never bowed from its firm-set seat
When the living column passed its feet,
Yet now rode steadily up the street
  To the phantom bugle's warning:

Till it reached the Capitol square, and wheeled,
And there in the moonlight stood revealed
A well-known form that in State and field
  Had led our patriot sires;
Whose face was turned to the sleeping camp,
Afar through the river's fog and damp,
That showed no flicker, nor waning lamp,
  Nor wasted bivouac fires.

And I saw a phantom army come,
With never a sound of fife or drum,
But keeping time to a throbbing hum
  Of wailing and lamentation:
The martyred heroes of Malvern Hill,
Of Gettysburg and Chancellorsville,
The men whose wasted figures fill
  The patriot graves of the nation.

And there came the nameless dead,—the men
Who perished in fever-swamp and fen,
The slowly-starved of the prison-pen;
  And, marching beside the others,
Came the dusky martyrs of Pillow's fight,
With limbs enfranchised and bearing bright:
I thought—perhaps 't was the pale moonlight—
  They looked as white as their brothers!

And so all night marched the Nation's dead,
With never a banner above them spread,
Nor a badge, nor a motto brandishèd;
No mark—save the bare uncovered head
    Of the silent bronze Reviewer;
With never an arch save the vaulted sky;
With never a flower save those that lie
On the distant graves—for love could buy
    No gift that was pure or truer.

So all night long swept the strange array;
So all night long, till the morning gray,
I watched for one who had passed away,
    With a reverent awe and wonder,—
Till a blue cap waved in the lengthening line,
And I knew that one who was kin of mine
Had come; and I spake—and lo! that sign
    Awakened me from my slumber.

                  —Francis Bret Harte.

ODE RECITED AT THE HARVARD COMMEMORATION

WEAK-WINGED is song,
    Nor aims at that clear-ethered height
Whither the brave deed climbs for light:
    We seem to do them wrong,
Bringing our robin's-leaf to deck their hearse
Who in warm life-blood wrote their nobler verse,
Our trivial song to honour those who come
With ear attuned to strenuous trump and drum,
And shaped in squadron-strophes their desire,
Lives battle-odes whose lines were steel and fire:
    Yet sometimes feathered words are strong,
A gracious memory to buoy up and save
From Lethe's dreamless ooze, the common grave
    Of the unventurous throng.

To-day our Reverend Mother welcomes back
 Her wisest Scholars, those who understood
The deeper teaching of her mystic tome,
  And offered their fresh lives to make it good:
    No lore of Greece or Rome,
No science peddling with the names of things,
Or reading stars to find inglorious fates,
    Can lift our life with wings
Far from Death's idle gulf that for the many waits,
    And lengthen out our dates
With that clear fame whose memory sings
In manly hearts to come, and nerves them and dilates:
Nor such thy teaching, Mother of us all!
    Not such the trumpet-call
    Of thy diviner mood,
    That could thy sons entice
From happy homes and toils, the fruitful nest
Of those half-virtues which the world calls best,
    Into War's tumult rude;
    But rather far that stern device
The sponsors chose that round thy cradle stood
   In the dim, unventured wood,
   The VERITAS that lurks beneath
   The letter's unprolific sheath,
  Life of whate'er makes life worth living,
Seed-grain of high emprise, immortal food,
  One heavenly thing whereof earth hath the giving.

Many loved Truth, and lavished life's best oil
  Amid the dust of books to find her,
Content at last, for guerdon of their toil,
  With the cast mantle she hath left behind her;
   Many in sad faith sought for her,
   Many with crossed hands sighed for her;
   But these, our brothers, fought for her,

At life's dear peril wrought for her,
So loved her that they died for her,
Tasting the raptured fleetness
Of her divine completeness:
Their higher instinct knew
Those love her best who to themselves are true,
And what they dare to dream of, dare to do;
They followed her and found her
Where all may hope to find,
Not in the ashes of the burnt-out mind,
But beautiful, with danger's sweetness round her.
Where faith made whole with deed
Breathes its awakening breath
Into the lifeless creed,
They saw her plumed and mailed
With sweet, stern face unveiled,
And all-repaying eyes, look proud on them in death.

Our slender life runs rippling by, and glides
Into the silent hollow of the past;
What is there that abides
To make the next age better for the last?
Is earth too poor to give us
Something to live for here that shall outlive us?
Some more substantial boon
Than such as flows and ebbs with Fortune's fickle moon?
The little that we see
From doubt is never free;
The little that we do
Is but half-nobly true;
With our laborious hiving
What men call treasure, and the gods call dross,
Life seems a jest of Fate's contriving,
Only secure in every one's conniving,
A long account of nothings paid with loss,

Where we poor puppets, jerked by unseen wires,
  After our little hour of strut and rave,
With all our pasteboard passions and desires,
Loves, hates, ambitions, and immortal fires,
  Are tossed pell-mell together in the grave.
  But stay! no age was e'er degenerate,
  Unless men held it at too cheap a rate,
  For in our likeness still we shape our fate.
    Ah, there is something here
  Unfathomed by the cynic's sneer,
  Something that gives our feeble light
  A high immunity from Night,
  Something that leaps life's narrow bars
To claim its birthright with the hosts of Heaven;
  A seed of sunshine that can leaven
  Our earthly dullness with the beams of stars,
      And glorify our clay
  With light from fountains elder than the Day;
    A conscience more divine than we,
    A gladness fed with secret tears,
    A vexing, forward-reaching sense
    Of some more noble permanence;
      A light across the sea,
Which haunts the soul and will not let it be,
Still beaconing from the heights of unregenerate years.

      Whither leads the path
      To ampler fates that leads?
      Not down through flowery meads,
      To reap an aftermath
    Of youth's vainglorious weeds,
    But up the steep, amid the wrath
  And shock of deadly-hostile creeds,
  Where the world's best hope and stay
By battle's flashes gropes a desperate way,

And every turf the fierce foot clings to bleeds.
   Peace hath her not ignoble wreath,
    Ere yet the sharp, decisive word
Light the black lips of cannon, and the sword
      Dreams in its easeful sheath;
But some day the live coal behind the thought,
     Whether from Baäl's stone obscene,
     Or from the shrine serene
     Of God's pure altar brought,
Bursts up in flame; the war of tongue and pen
Learns with what deadly purpose it was fraught,
And, helpless in the fiery passion caught,
Shakes all the pillared state with shock of men:
Some day the soft Ideal that we wooed
Confronts us fiercely, foe-beset, pursued,
And cries reproachful: "Was it then my praise,
And not myself was loved? Prove now thy truth;
I claim of thee the promise of thy youth;
Give me thy life, or cower in empty phrase,
The victim of thy genius, not its mate!"
   Life may be given in many ways,
   And loyalty to Truth be sealed
As bravely in the closet as the field,
    So bountiful is Fate;
    But then to stand beside her,
    When craven churls deride her,
To front a lie in arms and not to yield,
    This shows, methinks, God's plan
    And measure of a stalwart man,
    Limbed like the old heroic breeds,
    Who stands self-poised on manhood's solid earth,
   Not forced to frame excuses for his birth,
Fed from within with all the strength he needs.

Such was he, our Martyr-Chief,
   Whom late the Nation he had led,

With ashes on her head,
Wept with the passion of an angry grief:
Forgive me, if from present things I turn
To speak what in my heart will beat and burn,
And hang my wreath on his world-honoured urn.
　　Nature, they say, doth dote,
　　And cannot make a man
　　Save on some worn-out plan,
　　Repeating us by rote:
For him her Old-World moulds aside she threw,
　　And choosing sweet clay from the breast
　　Of the unexhausted West,
With stuff untainted shaped a hero new,
Wise, steadfast in the strength of God, and true.
　　How beautiful to see
Once more a shepherd of mankind indeed,
Who loved his charge, but never loved to lead;
One whose meek flock the people joyed to be,
　　Not lured by any cheat of birth,
　　But by his clear-grained human worth,
And brave old wisdom of sincerity!
　　They knew that outward grace is dust;
　　They could not choose but trust
In the sure-footed mind's unfaltering skill,
　　And supple-tempered will
That bent like perfect steel to spring again and thrust.
　　His was no lonely mountain-peak of mind,
　　Thrusting to thin air o'er our cloudy bars,
　　A sea-mark now, now lost in vapours blind;
　　Broad prairie rather, genial level-lined,
　　Fruitful and friendly for all human kind,
Yet also nigh to heaven and loved of loftiest stars.
　　Nothing of Europe here,
Or, then, of Europe fronting mornward still,
　　Ere any names of Serf and Peer

Could Nature's equal scheme deface
And thwart her genial will;
Here was a type of the true elder race,
And one of Plutarch's men talked with us face to face.
   I praise him not; it were too late;
And some innative weakness there must be
In him who condescends to victory
Such as the Present gives, and cannot wait,
   Safe in himself as in a fate.
      So always firmly he:
      He knew to bide his time,
      And can his fame abide,
Still patient in his simple faith sublime,
      Till the wise years decide.
   Great captains, with their guns and drums,
      Disturb our judgment for the hour,
      But at last silence comes;
   These all are gone, and, standing like a tower,
   Our children shall behold his fame.
      The kindly-earnest, brave, foreseeing man,
Sagacious, patient, dreading praise, not blame,
New birth of our new soil the first American.

   Long as man's hope insatiate can discern
      Or only guess some more inspiring goal
      Outside of Self, enduring as the pole,
   Along whose course the flying axles burn
   Of spirits bravely-pitched, earth's manlier brood;
      Long as below we cannot find
   The meed that stills the inexorable mind;
   So long this faith to some ideal Good,
   Under whatever mortal names it masks,
   Freedom, Law, Country, this ethereal mood

That thanks the Fates for their severer tasks,
  Feeling its challenged pulses leap,
  While others skulk in subterfuge cheap,
And, set in Danger's van, has all the boon it asks,
  Shall win man's praise and woman's love,
  Shall be a wisdom that we set above
All other skills and gifts to culture dear,
  A virtue round whose forehead we inwreathe
  Laurels that with a living passion breathe
When other crowns grow, while we twine them, sear.
  What brings us thronging these high rites to pay,
And seal these hours the noblest of our year,
  Save that our brothers found this better way?

  We sit here in the Promised Land
That flows with Freedom's honey and milk;
  But 't was they won it, sword in hand,
Making the nettle danger soft for us as silk.
  We welcome back our bravest and our best;
  Ah me! not all! some come not with the rest,
Who went forth brave and bright as any here!
I strive to mix some gladness with my strain,
      But the sad strings complain,
      And will not please the ear:
I sweep them for a pæan, but they wane
      Again and yet again
Into a dirge, and die away, in pain.
In these brave ranks I only see the gaps,
Thinking of dear ones whom the dumb turf wraps,
Dark to the triumph which they died to gain:
    Fitlier may others greet the living,
    For me the past is unforgiving;
                    268

I with uncovered head
Salute the sacred dead,
Who went, and who return not.—Say not so!
'T is not the grapes of Canaan that repay,
But the high faith that failed not by the way;
Virtue treads paths that end not in the grave;
No ban of endless night exiles the brave;
And to the saner mind
We rather seem the dead that stayed behind.
Blow, trumpets, all your exultations blow!
For never shall their aureoled presence lack:
I see them muster in a gleaming row,
With ever-youthful brows that nobler show;
We find in our dull road their shining track;
In every nobler mood
We feel the orient of their spirit glow,
Part of our life's unalterable good,
Of all our saintlier aspiration;
They come transfigured back,
Secure from change in their high-hearted ways,
Beautiful evermore, and with the rays
Of morn on their white Shields of Expectation!

But is there hope to save
Even this ethereal essence from the grave?
What ever 'scaped Oblivion's subtle wrong
Save a few clarion names, or golden threads of song?
Before my musing eye
The mighty ones of old sweep by,
Disvoiced now and insubstantial things,
As noisy once as we; poor ghosts of kings,
Shadows of empire wholly gone to dust,

And many races, nameless long ago,
To darkness driven by that imperious gust
Of ever-rushing Time that here doth blow:
O visionary world, condition strange,
Where naught abiding is but only Change,
Where the deep-bolted stars themselves still shift and range!
Shall we to more continuance make pretence?
Renown builds tombs; a life-estate is Wit;
And, bit by bit,
The cunning years steal all from us but woe;
Leaves are we, whose decays no harvest sow.
But, when we vanish hence,
Shall they lie forceless in the dark below,
Save to make green their little length of sods,
Or deepen pansies for a year or two,
Who now to us are shining-sweet as gods?
Was dying all they had the skill to do?
That were not fruitless: but the Soul resents
Such short-lived service, as if blind events
Ruled without her, or earth could so endure;
She claims a more divine investiture
Of longer tenure than Fame's airy rents;
Whate'er she touches doth her nature share;
Her inspiration haunts the ennobled air,
Gives eyes to mountains blind,
Ears to the deaf earth, voices to the wind,
And her clear trump sings succour everywhere
By lonely bivouacs to the wakeful mind;
For soul inherits all that soul could dare:
Yea, Manhood hath a wider span
And larger privilege of life than man.
The single deed, the private sacrifice,
So radiant now through proudly-hidden tears,
Is covered up erelong from mortal eyes
With thoughtless drift of the deciduous years;

But that high privilege that makes all men peers,
　　That leap of heart whereby a people rise
　　　　Up to a noble anger's height,
And, flamed on by the Fates, not shrink, but grow more
　　　bright,
　　　That swift validity in noble veins,
　　　　Of choosing danger and disdaining shame,
　　　　　Of being set on flame
　　　By the pure fire that flies all contact base
But wraps its chosen with angelic might,
　　　These are imperishable gains,
　　Sure as the sun, medicinal as light,
　　These hold great futures in their lusty reins
And certify to earth a new imperial race.

　　　Who now shall sneer!
　　　Who dare again to say we trace
　　　Our lines to a plebeian race?
　　　　Roundhead and Cavalier!
Dumb are those names erewhile in battle loud;
Dream-footed as the shadow of a cloud,
　　　They flit across the ear:
That is best blood that hath most iron in 't.
To edge resolve with, puring without stint
　　　For what makes manhood dear.
　　　Tell us not of Plantagenets,
Hapsburgs, and Guelfs, whose thin bloods crawl
Down from some victor in a border-brawl!
　　　How poor their outworn coronets,
Matched with one leaf of that plain civic wreath
Our brave for honour's blazon shall bequeath
　　Through whose desert a rescued Nation sets
Her heel on treason, and the trumpet hears
Shout victory, tingling Europe's sullen ears
　　With vain resentments and more vain regrets!

Not in anger, not in pride,
Pure from passion's mixture rude
Ever to base earth allied,
But with far heard gratitude,
Still with heart and voice renewed,
To heroes living and dear martyrs dead,
The strain should close that consecrates our brave.
Lift the heart and lift the head!
Lofty be its moods and grave,
Not without a martial ring,
Not without a prouder tread
And a peal of exultation:
Little right has he to sing
Through whose heart in such an hour
Beats no march of conscious power,
Sweeps no tumult of elation!
'T is no Man we celebrate,
By his country's victories great,
A hero half, and half the whim of Fate,
But the pith and marrow of a Nation
Drawing force from all her men,
Highest, humblest, weakest, all,
For her time of need, and then
Pulsing it again through them,
Till the basest can no longer cower,
Feeling his soul spring up divinely tall,
Touched but in passing by her mantle-hem.
Come back, then, noble pride, for 't is her dower
How could poet ever tower,
If his passions, hopes, and fears,
If his triumphs and his tears,
Kept not measure with his people?
Boom, cannon, boom to all the winds and waves!
Clash out, glad bells, from every rocking steeple!
Banners, adance with triumph, bend your staves!

And from every mountain-peak
Let beacon-fire to answering beacon speak,
Katahdin tell Monadnock, Whiteface he,
And so leap on in light from sea to sea,
Till the glad news be sent
Across a kindling continent,
Making earth feel more firm and air breathe braver:
" Be proud! for she is saved, and all have helped to
save her!
She that lifts up the manhood of the poor,
She of the open soul and open door,
With room about her heart for all mankind!
The fire is dreadful in her eyes no more;
From her bold front the helm she doth unbind,
Sends all her handmaid armies back to spin,
And bids her navies, that so lately hurled
Their crashing battle, hold their thunders in,
Swimming like birds of calm along the unharmful shore.
No challenge sends she to the elder world,
That looked askance and hated; a light scorn
Plays o'er her mouth, as round her mighty knees
She calls her children back, and waits the morn
Of noble day, enthroned between her subject seas."

Bow down, dear Land, for thou hast found release!
Thy God, in those distempered days,
Hath taught thee the sure wisdom of His ways,
And through thine enemies hath wrought thy peace!
Bow down in prayer and praise!
No poorest in thy borders but may now
Lift to the juster skies a man's enfranchised brow.
O Beautiful! my Country! ours once more!
Smoothing thy gold of war-dishevelled hair
O'er such sweet brows as never other wore,
And letting thy set lips,

Freed from wrath's pale eclipse,
The rosy edges of their smile lay bare,
What words divine of lover or of poet
Could tell our love and make thee know it,
Among the Nations bright beyond compare?
    What were our lives without thee?
    What all our lives to save thee?
    We reck not what we gave thee;
    We will dare to doubt thee,
But ask whatever else, and we will dare.
                —*James Russell Lowell.*

THE CABLE HYMN

O LONELY bay of Trinity,
  O dreary shores, give ear!
Lean down unto the white-lipped sea
  The voice of God to hear!

From world to world His couriers fly,
  Thought-winged and shod with fire;
The angel of His stormy sky
  Rides down the sunken wire.

What saith the herald of the Lord?
  "The world's long strife is done;
Close wedded by that mystic cord,
  Its continents are one.

"And one in heart, as one in blood,
  Shall all her peoples be;
The hands of human brotherhood
  Are clasped beneath the sea.

"Through Orient seas, o'er Afric's plain
    And Asian mountains borne,
The vigour of the Northern brain
    Shall nerve the world outworn.

"From clime to clime, from shore to shore,
    Shall thrill the magic thread;
The new Prometheus steals once more
    The fire that wakes the dead."

Throb on, strong pulse of thunder! beat
    From answering beach to beach;
Fuse nations in thy kindly heat,
    And melt the chains of each!

Wild terror of the sky above,
    Glide tamed and dumb below!
Bear gently, Ocean's carrier-dove,
    Thy errands to and fro.

Weave on, swift shuttle of the Lord,
    Beneath the deep so far,
The bridal robe of earth's accord,
    The funeral shroud of war!

For lo! the fall of Ocean's wall
    Space mocked and time outrun;
And round the world the thought of all
    Is as the thought of one!

The poles unite, the zones agree,
    The tongues of striving cease;
As on the Sea of Galilee
    The Christ is whispering, Peace!

                    —*John Greenleaf Whittier.*

KU-KLUX

WE have sent him seeds of the melon's core,
And nailed a warning upon his door;
By the Ku-Klux laws we can do no more.

Down in the hollow, 'mid crib and stack,
The roof of his low-porched house looms black,
Not a line of light at the doorsill's crack.

Yet arm and mount! and mask and ride!
The hounds can sense though the fox may hide!
And for a word too much men oft have died.

The clouds blow heavy towards the moon.
The edge of the storm will reach it soon.
The killdee cries and the lonesome loon.

The clouds shall flush with a wilder glare
Than the lightning makes with his angled flare,
When the Ku-Klux verdict is given there.

In the pause of the thunder rolling low,
A rifle's answer—who shall know
From the wind's fierce hurl and the rain's black blow?

Only the signature written grim
At the end of the message brought to him,—
A hempen rope and a twisted limb.

So arm and mount! and mask and ride!
The hounds can sense though the fox may hide!
And for a word too much men oft have died.

—Madison Cawein.

MEMORIAL DAY

UNTO this hallowed spot, where sleep
   The brave, the fair, the honoured dead,
Let youthful hands sweet garlands bear
   And strow them o'er each silent head.

O tender hearts, too young to reap
   The care which bore a soldier's sigh,
Gather the roses and strow them o'er
   These graves where truth and honour lie.
                  —Gordon Coogler.

THE BLUE AND THE GRAY

BY the flow of the inland river,
   Whence the fleets of iron had fled,
Where the blades of the grave-grass quiver,
   Asleep are the ranks of the dead:
      Under the sod and the dew;
        Waiting the judgement day;
      Under the one, the Blue,
        Under the other, the Gray.

These in the robings of glory,
   Those in the gloom of defeat,
All with the battle-blood gory,
   In the dusk of eternity meet:
      Under the sod and the dew;
        Waiting the judgement day;
      Under the laurel, the Blue,
        Under the willow, the Gray.

From the silence of sorrowful hours
   The desolate mourners go,
Lovingly laden with flowers,

Alike for the friend and foe:
   Under the sod and the dew;
      Waiting the judgement day;
   Under the roses, the Blue,
      Under the lilies, the Gray.

So with an equal splendour,
   The morning sun-rays fall,
With a touch impartially tender,
   On the blossoms blooming for all:
      Under the sod and the dew,
         Waiting the judgement day;
      Broidered with gold, the Blue,
         Mellowed with gold, the Gray.

So, when the summer calleth
   On forest and field of grain,
With an equal murmur falleth
   The cooling drip of the rain:
      Under the sod and the dew,
         Waiting the judgement day;
      Wet with the rain, the Blue,
         Wet with the rain, the Gray.

Sadly, but not with upbraiding,
   The generous deed was done;
In the storm of the years now fading
   No braver battle was won:
      Under the sod and the dew,
         Waiting the judgement day;
      Under the blossoms, the Blue,
         Under the garlands, the Gray.

No more shall the war-cry sever,
   Or winding rivers be red;
They banish our anger for ever

When they laurel the graves of our dead!
Under the sod and the dew,
Waiting the judgement day;
Love and tears for the Blue,
Tears and love for the Gray.
—*Francis Miles Finch.*

REUNITED

SURER than thy own white snow,
Nobler than thy mountain's height,
Deeper than the ocean's flow,
Stronger than thy own proud might;
O Northland, to thy sister land
Was late thy mercy's generous deed and grand.

Nigh twice ten years the sword was sheathed;
Its mist of green o'er the battle-plain
For nigh two decades spring had breathed;
And yet the crimson lifeblood stain
From passive swards had never paled,
Nor fields, where all were brave and some had failed.

Between the Northland, bride of snow,
And Southland, brightest sun's fair bride,
Swept, deepening ever in its flow,
The stormy wake, in war's dark tide:
No hand might clasp across the tears,
And blood, and anguish of four deathless years.

When summer, like a rose in bloom,
Had blossomed from the bud of spring,
Oh! who could deem the dews of doom
Upon the blushing lips could cling?
And who believe in fragrant light
Would e'er be freighted with the breath of blight?

Yet o'er the Southland crept the spell,
  That e'en from out its brightness spread;
And prostrate, powerless, she fell,
  Rachel-like, amid her dead.
Her bravest, fairest, purest, best,
The waiting grave would welcome as its guest.

The Northland, strong in love, and great,
  Forgot the stormy days of strife;
Forgot that souls with dreams of hate,
  Or unforgiveness, e'er were rife.
Forgotten was each thought and hushed,
Save—she was generous and her foe was crushed.

No hand might clasp, from land to land;
  Yea! there was one to bridge the tide;
For at the touch of Mercy's hand
  The North and South stood side by side:
The Bride of Snow, the Bride of Sun,
In Charity's espousals are made one.

"Thou givest back my sons again,"
  The Southland to the Northland cries;
"For all my dead, on battle plain,
  Thou bidst my dying now uprise:
I still my sobs, I cease my tears,
And thou hast recompensed my anguished years.

"Blessings on thine every wave,
  Blessings on thine every shore,
Blessings that from sorrows save,
  Blessings giving more and more,
For all thou gav'st thy sister land,
O Northland, in thy generous deed and grand."
                              —*Abram Joseph Ryan.*

ALASKA

ICE built, ice bound, and ice bounded,
　Such cold seas of silence! such room!
Such snow-light, such sea-light confounded
　With thunder that smites like doom!
Such grandeur! such glory! such gloom!
Hear that boom! Hear that deep distant boom
　Of an avalanche hurled
　Down this unfinished world!

Ice seas! and ice summits! ice spaces
　In splendour of white, as God's throne!
Ice worlds to the poles! and ice places
　Untracked, and unnamed, and unknown!
Hear that boom! Hear the grinding, the groan
Of the ice-gods in pain! Hear the moan
　Of yon ice-mountain hurled
　Down this unfinished world.

—Joaquin Miller.

THE PACIFIC RAILWAY

'TIS done—the wondrous thoroughfare,
　Type of that Highway all divine!
No ancient wonder can compare
　With this, in grandeur of design.
For, 't was no visionary scheme
　To immortalize the builder's name;
No impulse rash, no transient dream
　Of some mere worshipper of Fame.

Rare common sense conceived the plan,
　For working out a lasting good—
The full development of Man;
　The growth of human brotherhood!

281

And lo! by patient toil and care,
   The work with rare success is crowned;
And nations, yet to be, will share
   In blessings that shall e'er abound.

Across a continent's expanse,
   The lengthening track now runs secure,
O'er which the Iron Horse shall prance,
   So long as earth and time endure!
His course extends from East to West—
   From where Atlantic billows roar,
To where the quiet waters rest,
   Beside the far Pacific shore.

Proud Commerce, by Atlantic gales
   Tossed to and fro,—her canvas rent—
Will gladly furl her wearied sails,
   And glide across a continent.
Through smiling valleys, broad and free,
   O'er rivers wide, or mountain-crest,
Her course shall swift and peaceful be,
   Till she has reached the farthest West.

And e'en the treasures of the East,
   Diverted from their wonted track,—
With safety gained, with speed increased,—
   Will follow in her footsteps back.
And thus the Nations, greatly blest,
   Will share another triumph, won,
That links yet closer East and West—
   The rising and the setting sun!

This glorious day with joy we greet!
   May Faith abound, may Love increase,
And may this highway, now complete,
   Be the glad harbinger of Peace!

God bless the Work, that it may prove
  The source of greater good in store,
When Man shall heed the law of Love,
  And Nations shall learn war no more.
                              —*C. R. Ballard.*

ISRAEL FREYER'S BID FOR GOLD

ZOUNDS! How the price went flashing through
  Wall Street, William, Broad Street, New!
All the specie in all the land
Held in one Ring, by a giant hand—
For millions more, it was ready to pay,
And throttle the street on hangman's day.
Up from the gold-pit's nether hell,
While the innocent fountain rose and fell,
Loud and higher the bidding rose,
And the bulls, triumphant, faced their foes.
It seemed as if Satan himself were in it;
Lifting it—one per cent. a minute—
Through the bellowing broker, there amid,
Who made the terrible, final bid!

    Higher over all, and ever higher,
      Was the voice of Israel Freyer,—
A doleful knell in the storm-swept mart,—
" Five millions more! and for any part
      I 'll give One Hundred and Sixty! "

Israel Freyer—the Government Jew—
Good as the best—soaked through and through
With credit gained in the year he sold
Our Treasury's precious hoard of gold;
Now through his thankless mouth rings out
The leaguers' last and cruellest shout!
Pity the shorts? Not they, indeed,
While a single rival's left to bleed!

283

Down come dealers in silks and hides,
Crowding the Gold Room's rounded sides,
Jostling, trampling each other's feet,
Uttering groans in the outer street;
Watching, with upturned faces pale,
The scurrying index mark its tale;
 Hearing the bid of Israel Freyer,—
 That ominous voice, would it never tire?
" Five millions more!—for any part
(If it breaks your firm, if it cracks your heart),
 " I 'll give One Hundred and Sixty! "

One Hundred and Sixty! Can't be true!
What will the bears-at-forty do?
How will the merchants pay their dues?
How will the country stand the news?
What 'll the banks—but listen! hold!
In screwing upward the price of gold
To that dangerous, last, particular peg,
They have killed their Goose with the Golden Egg!
Just there the metal came pouring out,
All ways at once, like a water-spout,
Or a rushing, gushing, yellow flood,
That drenched the bulls wherever they stood!
Small need to open the Washington main,
Their coffer-dams were burst with the strain!
 It came by runners, it came by wire,
 To answer the bid of Israel Freyer,
It poured in millions from every side,
And almost strangled him as he cried,—
 " I 'll give One Hundred and Sixty! "

Like Vulcan after Jupiter's kick,
Or the aphoristical Rocket's stick,
Down, down, down, the premium fell,
Faster than this rude rhyme can tell!

Thirty per cent. the index slid,
Yet Freyer still kept making his bid,—
" One Hundred and Sixty for any part ! "
—The sudden ruin had crazed *his* heart,
Shattered his senses, cracked his brain,
And left him crying again and again,—
Still making his bid at the market's top
(Like the Dutchman's leg that never could stop),
" One Hundred and Sixty—Five Millions more ! "
Till they dragged him, howling, off the floor.

    The very last words that seller and buyer
    Heard from the mouth of Israel Freyer—
A cry to remember long as they live—
Were, " I 'll take Five Millions more ! I 'll give—
    I 'll give One Hundred and Sixty ! "

Suppose (to avoid the appearance of evil)
There 's such a thing as a Personal Devil,
It would seem that his Highness here got hold,
For once, of a bellowing Bull in Gold !
Whether bull or bear, it would n't much matter
Should Israel Freyer keep up his clatter
On earth or under it (as, they say
He is doomed) till the general Judgement Day,
When the Clerk, as he cites him to answer for 't,
Shall bid him keep silence in that Court !
But it matters most, as it seems to me,
That my countrymen, great and strong and free,
So marvel at fellows who seem to win,
That if even a Clown can only begin
By stealing a railroad, and use its purse
For cornering stocks and gold, or—worse—
For buying a Judge and Legislature,
And sinking still lower poor human nature,

285

The gaping public, whatever befall,
Will swallow him, tandem, harlots, and all!
While our rich men drivel and stand amazed
At the dust and pother his gang have raised,
And make us remember a nursery tale
Of the four-and-twenty who feared one snail.

What 's bred in the bone will breed, you know;
Clowns and their trainers, high and low,
Will cut such capers, long as they dare,
While honest Poverty says its prayer.
But tell me what prayer or fast can save
Some hoary candidate for the grave,
The market's wrinkled Giant Despair,
Muttering, brooding, scheming there,—
Founding a college or building a church
Lest Heaven should leave him in the lurch!
Better come out in the rival way,
Issue your scrip in open day,
And pour your wealth in the grimy fist
Of some gross-mouthed, gambling pugilist;
Leave toil and poverty where they lie,
Pass thinkers, workers, artists, by.
Your pot-house fag from his counters bring
And make him into a Railway King!
Between such Gentiles and such Jews
Little enough one finds to choose;
Either the other will buy and use,
Eat the meat and throw him the bone,
And leave him to stand the brunt alone.

—Let the tempest come, that 's gathering near,
And give us a better atmosphere!
—Edmund Clarence Stedman.

CALIFORNIA'S GREETING TO SEWARD

WE know him well: no need of praise,
    Or bonfire from the windy hill
To light to softer paths and ways
    The world-worn man we honour still;

No need to quote those truths he spoke
    That burned through years of war and shame,
While History carves with surer stroke
    Across our map his noonday fame;

No need to bid him show the scars
    Of blows dealt by the Scæan gate,
Who lived to pass its shattered bars,
    And see the foe capitulate;

Who lived to turn his slower feet,
    Toward the western setting sun,
To see his harvest all complete,
    His dream fulfilled, his duty done,—

The one flag streaming from the pole,
    The one faith borne from sea to sea,—
For such a triumph, and such goal,
    Poor must our human greeting be.

Ah! rather that the conscious land
    In simpler ways salute the Man,—
The tall pines bowing where they stand,
    The bared head of El Capitan,

The tumult of the waterfalls,
    Pohono's kerchief in the breeze,
The waving from the rocky walls,
    The stir and rustle of the trees;

Till, lapped in sunset skies of hope,
   In sunset lands by sunset seas,
The Young World's Premier treads the slope
   Of sunset years in calm and peace.

—*Francis Bret Harte.*

THE OLD ADMIRAL

GONE at last,
   That brave old hero of the Past!
His spirit has a second birth,
   An unknown, grander life;—
All of him that was earth
   Lies mute and cold,
   Like a wrinkled sheath and old
Thrown off for ever from the shimmering blade
That has good entrance made
   Upon some distant, glorious strife.

From another generation,
   A simpler age, to ours *Old Ironsides* came;
The morn and noontide of the nation
   Alike he knew, nor yet outlived his fame,—
   Oh, not outlived his fame!
The dauntless men whose service guards our shore
   Lengthen still their glory-roll
   With his name to lead the scroll,
As a flag-ship at her fore
   Carries the Union, with its azure and the stars,
Symbol of times that are no more
   And the old heroic wars.

He was the one
Whom Death had spared alone
   Of all the captains of that lusty age,

Who sought the foeman where he lay.
On sea or sheltering bay,
  Nor till the prize was theirs repressed their rage.
They are gone,—all gone:
    They rest with glory and the undying Powers;
    Only their name and fame and what they saved are ours!

It was fifty years ago,
    Upon the Gallic Sea,
    He bore the banner of the free,
And fought the fight whereof our children know.
    The deathful, desperate fight!—
    Under the fair moon's light
The frigate squared, and yawed to left and right.
    Every broadside swept to death a score!
Roundly played her guns and well, till their fiery ensigns fell,
    Neither foe replying more.

All in silence, when the night-breeze cleared the air,
    Old Ironsides rested there,
Locked in between the twain, and drenched with blood.
    Then homeward, like an eagle with her prey!
    Oh, it was a gallant fray,
    That fight in Biscay Bay!
Fearless the Captain stood, in his youthful hardihood;
    He was the boldest of them all,
    Our brave old Admiral!

And still our heroes bleed,
Taught by that golden deed.
    Whether of iron or of oak
The ships we marshal at our country's need,
    Still speak their cannon now as then they spoke;
Still floats our unstruck banner from the mast
    As in the stormy Past.

Lay him in the ground:
  Let him rest where the ancient river rolls;
Let him sleep beneath the shadow and the sound
  Of the bell whose proclamation, as it tolls,
Is of Freedom and the gift our fathers gave,
  Lay him gently down:
  The clamour of the town
Will not break the slumbers deep, the beautiful ripe sleep
  Of this lion of the wave,
  Will not trouble the old Admiral in his grave.

Earth to earth his dust is laid.
Methinks his stately shade
On the shadow of a great ship leaves the shore;
Over cloudless western seas
Seeks the far Hesperides,
  And the islands of the blest,
Where no turbulent billows roll,—
  Where is rest.
His ghost upon the shadowy quarter stands
Nearing the deathless lands.
  There all his martial mates, renewed and strong,
  Awaiting his coming long.
I see the happy Heroes rise
" With gratulation in their eyes;
  Welcome, old comrade," Lawrence cries,
" Ah, Stewart, tell us of the wars.
Who win the glory and the scars?
  How floats the skyey flag,—how many stars?
Still, speak they of Decatur's name,
Of Bainbridge and Perry's fame?
Of me, who earliest came?
  Make ready, all:
  Room for the Admiral.
Come, Stewart, tell us of the wars!"
                              —*Edmund Clarence Stedman.*

ON THE AMENDMENT TO THE CONSTITUTION

"RING OUT THE FALSE; RING IN THE TRUE."

RING out, ye Bells, a lusty peal!
　　Man names at last his brother free!
　God called him so at birth, but he
Awakes but now the truth to feel.

Ring out, clear Bells, o'er hill and lea,
　　Let Freedom vibrate on the air!
　From North to South the tidings bear,
The holy voice of Liberty.

Free as the bee 'mid summer's bloom,
　　Or happy bird that soars away,
　Free as the ocean's dashing spray
That fringes soft its robe of gloom.

Free to receive his labour's meed—
　　To call his wife and babes his own!
　Not others reap where he has sown,
And fatten on his daily need.

O years of hard unpitied toil,
　　Of sundered ties, and bloody sweat!
　Thank God! that Slavery's sun has set
For ever, on our native soil!

Then ring, ye Bells, a stirring peal!
　　Man calls at last his brother free—
　Heir of our glorious Liberty,
Her arms to bear, her power to feel.

DAVID GLASGOW FARRAGUT

IN this heroic mould were cast
   The mightiest captains of the sea,
Men who outrode the winter blast
   To bear the banner of the free.

Bred in the school of Nelson, Blake,
   Born of the brood of Coligny,
A lad, he sailed the coasts of Drake
   To bear the banner of the free;

A man, he made his potent choice
   And joined the goodly company
Of those whose lives and deeds and voice
   Were for the flag of liberty.

No sterner courage knows the world,
   No war more valorous the wave,
Than his, whose thunderbolt was hurled
   The starry ensign still to save.

He rests upon the shore, beside
   The surge that sighs for such as he,
And over him in newer pride
   Is spread the banner he kept free.
                 —Christopher Bannister.

AT THE FARRAGUT STATUE

TO live a hero, then to stand
   In bronze serene above the city's throng;
Hero at sea, and now on land
Revered by thousands as they rush along;

If these were all the gifts of fame—
To be a shade amid alert reality,
    And win a statue and a name—
How cold and cheerless immortality!

    But when the sun shines in the Square,
And multitudes are swarming in the street,
    Children are always gathered there,
Laughing and playing round the hero's feet.

    And in the crisis of the game—
With boyish grit and ardour it is played—
    You 'll hear some youngster call his name:
"The Admiral—he never was afraid!"

    And so the hero daily lives,
And boys grow braver as the Man they see!
    The inspiration that he gives
Still helps to make them loyal, strong, and free!
                                        —*Robert Bridges.*

GONE FORWARD

YES; "Let the tent be struck:" victorious morning
    Through every crevice flashes in a day
Magnificent beyond all earth's adorning:
    The night is over; wherefore should he stay?
    And wherefore should our voices choke to say,
        "The General has gone forward"?

Life's foughten field not once beheld surrender,
 But with superb endurance, present, past,
Our pure commander, lofty, simple, tender,
 Through good, through ill, held his high purpose fast,
 Wearing his armour spotless,—till at last,
  Death gave the final " Forward! "

All hearts grew sudden palsied: yet what said he
 Thus summoned?—" Let the tent be struck! "—For when
Did call of duty fail to find him ready
 Nobly to do his work in sight of men,
 For God's and for his country's sake—and then
  To watch, wait, or go forward?

We will not weep,—we dare not! such a story
 As his large life writes on the century's years
Should crowd our bosoms with a flush of glory
 That manhood's type, supremest that appears
 To-day, he shows the ages. Nay, no tears
  Because he has gone forward.

Gone forward?—whither? Where the marshalled legions,
 Christ's well-worn soldiers, from their conflicts cease,—
Where Faith's true Red-Cross Knights repose in regions
 Thick-studded with the calm, white tents of peace,—
 Thither, right joyful to accept release,
  The General has gone forward!
              —*Margaret Junkin Preston.*

CHICAGO

GAUNT in the midst of the prairie,
   She who was once so fair;
Charred and rent are her garments,
Heavy and dark like cerements;

294

Silent, but round her the air
Plaintively wails, "Miserere!"

Proud like a beautiful maiden,
    Art-like from forehead to feet,
Was she till pressed like a leman
Close to the breast of the demon,
    Lusting for one so sweet,
So were her shoulders laden.

Friends she had, rich in her treasures:
    Shall the old taunt be true,—
Fallen, they turn their cold faces,
Seeking new wealth-gilded places,
    Saying we never knew
Aught of her smiles or her pleasures?

Silent she stands on the prairies,
    Wrapped in her fire-scathed sheet;
Round her, thank God, is the Nation,
Weeping for her desolation,
    Pouring its gold at her feet,
Answering her "Miserere!"
                    —*John Boyle O'Reilly.*

"THE GOSPEL OF PEACE!"

AYE, let it rest! And give us peace.
    'T is but another blot
On Freedom's fustian flag, and gold
    Will gild the unclean spot.

Yes, fold the hands, and bear the wrong
    As Christians over-meek,
And wipe away the bloody stain,
    And turn the other cheek.

What boots the loss of freemen's blood
  Beside imperilled gold?
Is honour more than merchandise?
  And cannot pride be sold?

Let Cuba groan, let patriots fall;
  Americans may die;
Our flag may droop in foul disgrace,
  But "Peace!" be still our cry.

Aye, give us peace! And give us truth
  To nature, to resign
The counterfeit which Freedom wears
  Upon her banner fine.

Remove the Stars,—they light our shame;
  But keep the Stripes of gore
And craven White, to tell the wrong
  A prudent nation bore.
                    —*James Jeffrey Roche.*

AFTER THE COMANCHES

SADDLE! saddle! saddle!
  Mount, mount, and away!
Over the dim green prairie,
  Straight on the track of day;
Spare not spur for mercy,
  Hurry with shout and thong,
Fiery and tough is the mustang,
  The prairie is wide and long.

Saddle! saddle! saddle!
  Leap from the broken door,

Where the brute Comanche entered,
  And the white-foot treads no more!
The hut is burnt to ashes,
  There are dead men stark outside,
And only a long torn ringlet
  Left of the stolen bride.

Go like the east wind's howling,
  Ride with death behind,
Stay not for food or slumber,
  Till the thieving wolves ye find!
They came before the wedding,
  Swifter than prayer or priest;
The bride-men danced to bullets,
  The wild dogs ate the feast.

Look to rifle and powder,
  Buckle the knife-belt sure;
Loose the coil of the lasso,
  And make the loop secure;
Fold the flask in the poncho,
  Fill the pouch with maize,
And ride as if to-morrow
  Were the last of living days.

Saddle! saddle! saddle!
  Redden spur and thong,
Ride like the mad tornado,
  The track is lonely and long,
Spare not horse nor rider,
  Fly for the stolen bride!
Bring her home on the crupper,
  A scalp on either side.

CUBA

ISLE of a summer sea,
  Fragrant with Eden's flowers,
God meant thee to be free,
  And wills thee to be *ours!*

The blood of generous hearts
  Has freely drenched thy soil;
That blood but strength imparts,
  Which tyrants cannot foil!

Within thy fair retreat,
  'Mid victory and flame,
Thy sons shall yet repeat
  Huzzas in Freedom's name!

Yet, where his ashes rest,
  Whose eye revealed a world,
From towers and mountain crest,
  Our flag shall be unfurled!

In truth, it is but just,
  That Freedom's hand should hold,
Confided to her trust,
  The key to lands of gold!

—Harvey Rice.

LITTLE BIG HORN

BESIDE the lone river,
  That idly lay dreaming,
Flashed sudden the gleaming

Of sabre and gun
In the light of the sun
As over the hillside the soldiers came streaming.

One peal of the bugle
In stillness unbroken
That sounded a token
Of soul-stirring strife,
Savage war to the knife,
Then silence that seemed like defiance unspoken.

But out of an ambush
Came warriors riding,
Swift ponies bestriding,
Shook rattles and shells,
With a discord of yells,
That fired the hearts of their comrades in hiding.

Then fierce on the wigwams
The soldiers descended,
And madly were blended,
The red man and white
In a hand-to-hand fight,
With the Indian village assailed and defended.

And there through the passage
Of battle-torn spaces,
From dark lurking-places,
With blood-curdling cry
And their knives held on high,
Rushed Amazon women with wild, painted faces.

Then swung the keen sabres
And flashed the sure rifles

Their message that stifles
The shout in red throats,
While the reckless blue-coats
Laughed on 'mid the fray as men laugh over trifles.

Grim cavalry troopers
Unshorn and unshaven,
And never a craven
In ambuscade caught,
How like demons they fought
Round the knoll on the prairie that marked their last haven.

But the Sioux circled nearer,
The shrill war-whoop crying,
And death-hail was flying,
Yet still they fought on
Till the last shot was gone,
And all that remained were the dead and the dying.

A song for their death, and
No black plumes of sorrow,
This recompense borrow,
Like heroes they died
Man to man—side by side;
We lost them to-day, we shall meet them to-morrow.

And on the lone river,
Has faded the seeming
Of bright armour gleaming,
But there by the shore
With the ghosts of no-more
The shades of the dead through the ages lie dreaming.

—*Ernest McGaffey.*

CENTENNIAL HYMN

OUR fathers' God! from out whose hand
The centuries fall like grains of sand,
We meet to-day, united, free,
And loyal to our land and Thee,
To thank Thee for the era done,
And trust Thee for the opening one.

Here, where of old, by Thy design,
The fathers spake that word of Thine
Whose echo is the glad refrain
Of rended bolt and falling chain,
To grace our festal time, from all
The zones of earth our guests we call.

Be with us while the New World greets
The Old World thronging all its streets,
Unveiling all the triumphs won
By art or toil beneath the sun;
And unto common good ordain
This rivalship of hand and brain.

Thou, who hast here in concord furled
The war flags of a gathered world,
Beneath our Western skies fulfil
The Orient's mission of good-will,
And, freighted with love's Golden Fleece,
Send back its Argonauts of peace.

For art and labour met in truce,
For beauty made the bride of use,
We thank Thee; but, withal, we crave
The austere virtues strong to save,
The honour proof to place or gold,
The manhood never bought nor sold!

Oh make Thou us, through centuries long,
In peace secure, in justice strong;
Around our gift of freedom draw
The safeguards of thy righteous law:
And, cast in some diviner mould,
Let the new cycle shame the old!
                    —*John Greenleaf Whittier.*

YORKTOWN'S CENTENNIAL LYRIC

HARK! hark! down the century's long reaching slope
     To those transports of triumph, those raptures of hope,
The voices of main and of mountain combined
In glad resonance borne on the wings of the wind,
The bass of the drum and the trumpet that thrills
Through the multiplied echoes of jubilant hills.
And mark how the years melting upward like mist
Which the breath of some splendid enchantment has kissed,
Reveal on the ocean, reveal on the shore
The proud pageant of conquest that graced them of yore,
When blended for ever in love as in fame
See, the standard which stole from the starlight its flame,
And type of all chivalry, glory, romance,
The lilies, the luminous lilies of France.

Oh, stubborn the strife ere the conflict was won!
And the wild whirling war wrack half stifled the sun.
The thunders of cannon that boomed on the lea,
But reëchoed far thunders pealed up from the sea,
Where guarding his sea lists, a night on the waves,
Bold De Grasse kept at bay the bluff bull-dogs of Graves.
The day turned to darkness, the night changed to fire,
Still more fierce waxed the combat, more deadly the ire,
Undimmed by the gloom, in majestic advance,
Oh, behold where they ride o'er the red battle tide,
Those banners united in love as in fame,

From things occult our earth-turned eyes rebel;
  No sound of Destiny can reach our ears;
We have no time for dreaming—— Hark! a knell
  A knell at midnight! All the nation hears!

A second grievous throb! The dreamers wake—
  The merchant's soul forgets his goods and ships;
The weary workmen from their slumbers break;
  The women raise their eyes with quivering lips;

The miner rests upon his pick to hear;
  The printer's type stops midway from the case;
The solemn sound has reached the roysterer's ear,
  And brought the shame and sorrow to his face.

Again it booms! O Mystic Veil, upraise!
  —Behold, 't is lifted! On the darkness drawn,
A picture lined with light! The people's gaze,
  From sea to sea, beholds it till the dawn!

A death-bed scene—a sinking sufferer lies,
  Their chosen ruler, crowned with love and pride;
Around, his counsellors, with streaming eyes;
  His wife, heart-broken, kneeling by his side:

Death's shadow holds her—it will pass too soon;
  She weeps in silence—bitterest of tears;
He wanders softly—Nature's kindest boon;
  And as he murmurs, all the country hears:

For him the pain is past, the struggle ends;
  His cares and honours fade—his younger life
In peaceful Mentor comes, with dear old friends;
  His mother's arms take home his dear young wife.

He stands among the students, tall and strong,
  And teaches truths republican and grand;
He moves—ah, pitiful—he sweeps along
  O'er fields of carnage leading his command!

He speaks to crowded faces—round him surge
  Thousands and millions of excited men;
He hears them cheer—sees some vast light emerge—
  Is borne as on a tempest—then—ah, then,

The fancies fade, the fever's work is past;
  A deepened pang, then recollection's thrill;
He feels the faithful lips that kiss their last,
  His heart beats once in answer, and is still!

The curtain falls: but hushed, as if afraid,
  The people wait, tear-stained, with heaving breast;
'T will rise again, they know, when he is laid
  With Freedom, in the Capitol, at rest.
                              —*John Boyle O'Reilly.*

EMERSON

WHAT shall we say? In quietude,
      Within his home, in dreams unguessed,
He lies; the grief a nation would
      Evince must be repressed.

Nor meet is it the loud acclaim
      His countrymen would raise—that he
Has left the riches of his fame
      The whole world's legacy.

Then, prayerful, let us pause until
      We find, as grateful spirits can,

306

The way most worthy to fulfil
     The tribute due the man.

Think what were best in his regard
   Who voyaged life in such a cause:
Our simplest faith were best reward—
     Our silence, best applause.
                    —*James Whitcomb Riley.*

THE BROOKLYN BRIDGE

A GRANITE cliff on either shore:
     A highway poised in air;
Above, the wheels of traffic roar;
   Below, the fleets sail fair;—
And in and out, for evermore,
The surging tides of ocean pour,
And past the towers the white gulls soar,
   And winds the sea-clouds bear.

O peerless this majestic street,
   This road that leaps the brine!
Upon its heights twin cities meet,
   And throng its glad incline,—
To east, to west, with swiftest feet,
Though ice may crash and billows beat,
Though blinding fogs the wave may greet
   Or golden summer shine.

Sail up the Bay with morning beam,
   Or rocky Hellgate by,—
Its columns rise, its cables gleam,
   Great tents athwart the sky!
And lone it looms, august, supreme,
When, with the splendour of a dream,

Its blazing cressets gild the stream
  Till evening shadows fly.

By Nile stand proud the Pyramids,
  But they were for the dead;
The awful gloom that joy forbids,
  The mourners' silent tread.
The crypt, the coffin's stony lids,—
Sad as a soul the maze that thrids
Of dark Amenti, ere it rids
  Its way of judgement dread.

This glorious arch, these climbing towers,
  Are all for life and cheer!
Part of the New World's nobler dowers;
  Hint of millennial year
That comes apace, though evil lowers,—
When loftier aims and large powers
Will mould and deck this world of ours,
  And Heaven at length bring near!

Unmoved its cliffs shall crown the shore;
  Its arch the chasm dare;
Its network hang the blue before,
  As gossamer in air;
While in and out, for evermore,
The surging tides of ocean pour,
And past its towers the white gulls soar
  And winds the sea-clouds bear!
                              —*Edna Dean Proctor.*

VANQUISHED

NOT by the ball or brand
  Sped by a mortal hand,
Not by the lightning stroke

308

When fiery tempests broke,—
Not mid the ranks of war
Fell the great Conqueror.

Unmoved, undismayed,
In the crash and carnage of the cannonade,—
Eye that dimmed not, hand that failed not,
Brain that swerved not, heart that quailed not,
Steel nerve, iron form,—
The dauntless spirit that o'erruled the storm.

While the Hero peaceful slept
A foeman to his chamber crept,
Lightly to the slumberer came,
Touched his brow and breathed his name:
O'er the stricken form there passed
Suddenly an icy blast.

The Hero woke, rose undismayed,
Saluted Death, and sheathed his blade.

The Conqueror of a hundred fields
To a mightier Conqueror yields;
No mortal foeman's blow
Laid the great Soldier low:

Victor in his latest breath—
Vanquished but by Death.

—Francis Fisher Browne.

THE GRAY HORSE TROOP

ALL alone on the hillside—
Larry an' Barry an' me;
Nothin' to see but the sky an' the plain,
Nothin' to see but the drivin' rain,

Nothin' to see but the painted Sioux
Galloping, galloping: "Whoop—whuroo!
The divil in yellow is down in the mud!"
Sez Larry to Barry, "I 'm losin' blood."

"Cheers for the Grays!" yells Barry;
"Second Dragoons!" groans Larry;
Hurrah! hurrah! for Egan's Gray Troop!
Whoop! ye divils—ye 've got to whoop;
Cheer for the troopers who die: sez I—
"Cheer for the troop that never shall die!"

All alone on the hillside—
Larry an' Barry an' me;
Flat on our bellies, an' pourin' in lead—
Seven rounds left, an' the horses dead—
Barry a-cursin' at every breath;
Larry beside him, as white as death;
Indians galloping, galloping by,
Wheelin' and squealin' like hawks in the sky!

"Cheers for the Greys!" yells Barry;
"Second Dragoons!" groans Larry;
Hurrah! hurrah! for Egan's Gray Troop!
Whoop! ye divils—ye 've got to whoop;
Cheer for the troopers who die: sez I—
"Cheer for the troop that never shall die!"

All alone on the hillside—
Larry an' Barry an' me;
Two of us livin' and one of us dead—
Shot in the head, and God!—how he bled!
"Larry's done up," sez Barry to me;
"Divvy his cartridges! Quick! gimme three!"
While nearer an' nearer an' plainer in view,
Galloped an' galloped the murderin' Sioux.

"Cheers for the grays!" yells Barry;
"Cheer—" an' he falls on Larry.
Alas! alas! for Egan's Gray Troop!
The Red Sioux, hovering stoop to swoop;
Two out of three lay dead, while I
Cheered for the troop that never shall die.

All alone on the hillside—
Larry an' Barry an' me;
An' I fired an' yelled till I lost my head,
Cheerin' the livin', cheerin' the dead,
Swingin' my cap, I cheered until
I stumbled and fell. Then over the hill
There floated a trumpeter's silvery call,
An' Egan's Gray Troop galloped up, that's all.

Drink to the Grays,—an' Barry!
Second Dragoons,—an' Larry!
Here 's a bumper to Egan's Gray Troop!
Let the crape on the guidons droop;
Drink to the troopers who die, while I
Drink to the troop that never shall die!

—*Robert William Chambers.*

GERONIMO

BESIDE that tent and under guard
    In majesty alone he stands,
As some chained eagle, broken-winged,
With eyes that gleam like smouldering brands,—
A savage face, streaked o'er with paint,
And coal-black hair in unkempt mane,
Thin, cruel lips, set rigidly,—
A red Apache Tamerlane.

As restless as the desert winds,
Yet here he stands like carven stone,
His raven locks by breezes blown;
Silent, yet watchful as he waits
Robed in his strange, barbaric guise,
While here and there go searchingly
The cat-like wanderings of his eyes.

The eagle feather on his head
Is dull with many a bloody stain,
While darkly on his lowering brow
For ever rests the mark of Cain.
Have you but seen a tiger caged
And sullen through his barriers glare?
Mark well his human prototype,
The fierce Apache fettered there.

—*Ernest McGaffey.*

AN INTERNATIONAL EPISODE

WE were ordered to Samoa from the coast of Panama,
And for two long months we sailed the unequal sea,
Till we made the horseshoe harbour with its curving coral
bar,
Smelt the good green smell of grass and shrub and tree.
We had barely room for swinging with the tide—
There were many of us crowded in the bay:
Three Germans, and the English ship, beside
Our three—and from the *Trenton,* where she lay,
Through the sunset calms and after,
We could hear the shrill, sweet laughter
Of the children's voices on the shore at play.

We all knew a storm was coming, but, dear God! no man
could dream
Of the furious hell-horrors of that day:

Through the roar of winds and waters we could hear wild
    voices scream—
  See the rocking masts reel by us through the spray.
In the gale we drove and drifted helplessly,
  With our rudder gone, our engine-fires drowned,
And none might hope another hour to see;
  For all the air was desperate with the sound
Of the brave ships rent asunder—
Of the shrieking souls sucked under,
  'Neath the waves, where many a good man's grave was
    found.

About noon, upon our quarter, from the deeper gloom afar
  Came the English man-of-war *Calliope*:
"We have lost our anchors, comrades, and, though small
    the chances are,
  We must steer for safety and the open sea."
Then we climbed aloft to cheer her as she passed
  Through the tempest and the blackness and the foam:
"Now God speed you, though the shout should be our last,
  Through the channel where the maddened breakers comb,
Through the wild sea's hill and hollow,
On the path we cannot follow,
  To your women and your children and your home."

Oh! remember it, good brothers. We two people speak one
    tongue,
  And your native land was mother to our land;
But the head, perhaps, is hasty when the nation's heart is
    young,
  And we prate of things we do not understand.
But the day when we stood face to face with death
  (Upon whose face few men may look and tell),
As long as you could hear, or we had breath,

Four hundred voices cheered you out of hell.
By the will of that stern chorus,
By the motherland which bore us,
   Judge if we do not love each other well.
                                   —*Caroline King Duer.*

DANIEL PERITON'S RIDE

ALL day long the river flowed
   Down the winding mountain road,
Leaping and roaring in angry mood,
At stubborn rocks in its way that stood;
Sullen the gleam of its rippled crest,
Dark was the foam on its yellow breast;
The dripping banks on either side
But half-imprisoned the turgid tide.
By farm and village it quickly sped,—
The weeping skies bent low o'erhead,—
Foaming and rushing and tumbling down
Into the streets of pent Johnstown,
Down through the valley of Conemaugh,
Down from the dam of shale and straw,
To the granite bridge, where its waters pour,
Through the arches wide, with a dismal roar.

All day long the pitiful tide,
Babbled of death on the mountain-side;
And all day long with jest and sigh,
They who were doomed that day to die
Turned deafened ears to the warning roar
They had heard so oft and despised before.

Yet women trembled—the mother's eyes
Turned oft to the lowering, woful skies—
And shuddered to think what might befall
Should the flood burst over the earthen wall.

So all day long they went up and down,
Heedless of peril in doomed Johnstown.

And all day long in the chilly gloom
Of a thrifty merchant's counting-room,
O'er the ledger bent with anxious care
Old Periton's only son and heir.
A commonplace, plodding, industrious youth,
Counting debit and credit the highest truth,
And profit and loss a more honoured game
Than searching for laurels or fighting for fame.
He saw the dark tide as it swept by the door,
But heeded it not till his task was o'er;
Then saddled his horse,—a black-pointed bay,
High-stepping, high-blooded, grandson of Dismay;
Raw-boned and deep-chested,—his eyes full of fire;
The temper of Satan—Magog was his sire;
Arched fetlocks, strong quarters, low knees,
And lean, bony head—his dam gave him these;
The foal of a racer transformed to a cob
For the son of the merchant when out of a job.
"Now I'll see," said Dan Periton, mounting the bay,
"What danger there is of the dam giving way!"

A marvelous sight young Periton saw
When he rode up the valley of Conemaugh.
Seventy feet the water fell
With a roar like the angry ocean's swell!
Seventy feet from the crumbling crest
To the rock on which the foundations rest!
Seventy feet fell the ceaseless flow
Into the boiling gulf below!

Dan Periton's cheek grew pale with fear,
As the echoes fell on his startled ear,
And he thought of the weight of the pent-up tide,

That hung on the rifted mountain-side,
Held by that heap of stone and straw
O'er the swarming valley of Conemaugh!
The raw-boned bay with quivering ears
Displayed a brute's instinctive fears,
Snorted and pawed with flashing eye,
Seized on the curb, and turned to fly!

Dan Periton tightened his grip on the rein,
Sat close to the saddle, glanced backward again,
Touched the bay with the spur, then gave him his head,
And down the steep valley they clattering sped.
Then the horse showed his breeding—the close gripping
    knees
Felt the strong shoulders working with unflagging ease
As mile after mile, 'neath the high-blooded bay,
The steep mountain turnpike flew backward away,
While with outstretched neck he went galloping down
With the message of warning to periled Johnstown,
Past farm-house and village, while shrilly outrang,
O'er the river's deep roar and the hoof's iron clang,
His gallant young rider's premonitant shout,
"Fly! Fly to the hills! The waters are out!"

Past Mineral Point there came such a roar
As never had shaken those mountains before!
Dan urged the good horse then with word and caress:
'T would be his last race, what mattered distress?
A mile farther on and behind him he spied
The wreck-laden crest of the death-dealing tide!
Then he plied whip and spur and redoubled the shout,
"To the hills! To the hills! The waters are out!"
Thus horseman and flood-tide came racing it down
The cinder-paved streets of doomed Johnstown!

Daniel Periton knew that his doom was nigh,
Yet never once faltered his clarion cry;
The blood ran off from his good steed's side;
Over him hung the white crest of the tide;
His hair felt the touch of the eygre's breath;
The spray on his cheek was the cold kiss of death;
Beneath him the horse 'gan to tremble and droop—
He saw the pale rider who sat on the croup!
But clear over all rang his last warning shout,
"To the hills! To the hills! For the waters are out!"
Then the tide reared its head and leapt vengefully down
On the horse and his rider in fated Johnstown!

That horse was a hero, so poets still say,
That brought the good news of the treaty to Aix;
And the steed is immortal, which carried Revere
Through the echoing night with his message of fear;
And the one that bore Sheridan into the fray,
From Westchester town, "twenty miles away;"
But none of these merits a nobler lay
Than young Daniel Periton's raw-boned bay
That raced down the valley of Conemaugh,
With the tide that rushed through the dam of straw,
Roaring and rushing and tearing down
On the fated thousands in doomed Johnstown!
In the very track of the eygre's swoop,
With Dan in the saddle and Death on the croup,
The foam of his nostrils flew back on the wind,
And mixed with the foam of the billow behind.

A terrible vision the morrow saw
In the desolate Valley of Conemaugh!
The river had shrunk to its narrow bed
But its way was choked with the heaped-up dead.

'Gainst the granite bridge with its arches four
Lay the wreck of a city that delves no more;
And under it all, so the searchers say,
Lay the sprawling limbs of the gallant bay,
Stiff-cased in the drift of the Conemaugh.
A goodlier statue man never saw,—
Dan's foot on the stirrup, his hand on the rein!
So shall they live in white marble again;
And ages shall tell, as they gaze on the group,
Of the race that he ran while Death sat on the croup.

—Albion W. Tourgee.

THE LAST RESERVATION

SULLEN and dark, in the September day,
  On the bank of the river
They waited the boat that would bear them away
  From their poor homes for ever.

For progress strides on, and the order had gone
  To these wards of the nation.
"Give us more land and more room," was the cry, "and
    move on
  To the next reservation."

With her babe, she looked back at the home 'neath the trees
  From which they were driven,
Where the smoke of the last camp-fire, borne on the breeze,
  Rose slowly toward heaven.

Behind her, fair fields, and the forest and glade,
  The home of her nation;
Around her, the gleam of the bayonet and blade
  Of civilization.

Clasping close to her bosom the small dusky form,
  With tender caressing,
She bent down, on the cheek of her babe, soft and warm
  A mother's kiss pressing.

There's a splash in the river—the column moves on,
  Close-guarded and narrow,
With hardly more note of the two that are gone
  Than the fall of a sparrow.

Only an Indian! Wretched, obscure,
  To refinement a stranger,
And a babe, that was born, in a wigwam as poor
  And rude as a manger.

Moved on—to make room for the growth in the West
  Of a brave Christian nation,
Moved on—and, thank God, forever at rest
  In the last reservation.

—Walter Learned.

FROM "THE COLUMBIAN ODE"

COLUMBIA! on thy brow are dewy flowers
  Plucked from wide prairies and from mighty hills.
Lo! toward this day have led the steadfast hours.
  Now to thy hope the world its beaker fills.
The old earth hears a song of blessed themes,
And lifts her head from a deep couch of dreams.
Her queenly nations, elder-born of Time;
  Troop from high thrones to hear,
Clasp thy strong hands, tread with thee paths sublime,
  Lovingly bend the ear.

Spain, in her broidered robes of chivalry,
  Comes with slow foot and inward-brooding eyes.

Bow to her banner! 't was the first to rise
　　Out of the dark for thee.
And England, royal mother, whose right hand
　　Moulds nations, whose white feet the ocean tread,
Lays down her sword on thy belovéd strand
　　To bless thy wreathed head;
Hearing in thine her voice, bidding thy soul
Fulfil her dream, the foremost at the goal.
And France, who once thy fainting form upbore,
Brings beauty now where strength she brought of yore.
　　France, the swift-footed, who with thee
　　Gazed in the eyes of Liberty,
　　　　And loved the dark no more.

　　Around the peopled world
　　Bright banners are unfurled.
The long procession winds from shore to shore.
　　The Norseman sails
　　Through icy gales
To the green Vineland of his long-ago.
Russia rides down from realms of sun and snow.
　　Germany casts afar
　　Her iron robes of war,
And strikes her harp with thy triumphal song.
　　Italy opens wide her epic scroll,
In bright hues blazoned, with great deeds writ long,
　　And bids thee win the kingdom of the soul.
And the calm Orient, wise with many days,
　　From hoary Palestine to sweet Japan
　　　　Salutes thy conquering youth;
Bidding thee hush while all the nations praise,
　　Know, though the world endure but for a span,
　　　　Deathless is truth.
Lo! unto these the ever-living Past
Ushers a mighty pageant, bids arise

Dead centuries, freighted with visions vast,
  Blowing dim mists into the Future's eyes.
    Their song is all of thee,
    Daughter of mystery. . . .

—Harriet Monroe.

THE MAN WITH THE MUSKET

THEY are building, as Babel was built, to the sky,
  With clash and confusion of speech;
They are piling up monuments, massive and high,
  To lift a few names beyond reach;
And the passionate green-laurelled God of the Great
  In a whimsical riddle of stone,
Has chosen a few from the Field and the State
  To sit on the steps of His Throne.

But I—I will pass from this rage of renown,
  This ant-hill commotion and strife,
Pass by where the marbles and bronzes look down
  In their fast-frozen gestures of life,
On, out to the nameless who lie 'neath the gloom
  Of the pitying cypress and pine:
Your man is the Man of the Sword and the Plume,
  But the Man with the Musket is mine.

I knew him! By all that is noble I knew
  This commonplace hero I name!
I've camped with him, marched with him, fought with him,
    too,
  In the swirl of the fierce battle-flame!
Laughed with him, cried with him, taken a part
  Of his canteen and blanket, and known
That the throb of this chivalrous prairie-boy's heart
  Was an answering stroke of my own.

321

I knew him, I tell you! And, also, I knew
　　When he fell on the battle-swept ridge,
That the poor battered body which lay there in blue
　　Was only a plank in the bridge
Over which some should pass to a radiant fame
　　That shall shine while the high stars shall shine!
Your Hero is known by an echoing name,
　　But the Man with the Musket is mine.

In the cyclone of war, in the battle's eclipse,
　　Life shook out its lingering sands,
And he died with the names that he loved on his lips,
　　His musket still grasped in his hands;
Up close to the Flag my soldier went down
　　In the salient front of the line!
You may take for your hero the Man of Renown,
　　But the Man with the Musket is mine.

I knew him! All through, the good and the bad
　　Ran together and equally free;
But I judge as I trust Christ has judged the poor lad,
　　Since death made him noble to me;
For Freedom leaves sacred the simple good will
　　That poured out this blood, as if wine:
Every drop that he shed is a sacrament still—
　　Hers the Man with the Musket—and mine!

There is peace in the May-laden grace of the hours
　　That comes when the day's work is done,
And peace with the nameless who, under the flowers,
　　Lie asleep in the slant of the sun.
Beat the taps! Quench the lights! And silence all sound!
　　There is a rifle-pit strength in the grave.
They sleep well who sleep, be they crowned or uncrowned,
　　And death will be kind to the brave.

322

Old comrades of mine, by the fast-waning years
    That move to mortality's goal,
By my heart full of love and my eyes full of tears,
    I hold you all fast to my soul;
And I march with the May and its blossomy charms
    Which I tenderly lay on this sod,
And pray they may rest there, old comrades in arms,
    Like a kiss of forgiveness from God.

THE REAR GUARD

THE guns are hushed. On every field once flowing
    With war's red flood May's breath of peace is shed,
And spring's young grass and gracious flowers are growing
        Above the dead.

Ye gray old men whom we this day are greeting,
    Honour to you, honour and love and trust!
Brave to the brave. Your soldier hands are meeting
        Aross their dust.

Bravely they fought who charged when flags were flying
    In cannon's crash, in screech and scream of shell;
Bravely they fell, who lay alone and dying
        In battle's hell.

Honour to them! Far graves to-day are flinging
    Up through the soil peace-blooms to meet the sun,
And daisied heads to summer winds are singing
        Their long " well done."

Our vanguard, they. They went with hot blood flushing
    At battle's din, at joy of bugle's call.
They fell with smiles, the flood of young life gushing,
        Full brave the fall!

But braver ye who, when the war was ended,
  And bugle's call and wave of flag were done,
Could come back home, so long left undefended.
        Your cause unwon.

And twist the useless sword to hook of reaping
  Rebuild the homes, set back the empty chair
And brave a land where waste and want were keeping
        Guard everywhere.

All this you did, your courage strong upon you,
  And out of ashes, wreck, a new land rose:
Through years of war no braver battle won you,
        'Gainst fiercer foes.

And now to-day a prospered land is cheering
  And lifting up her voice in lusty pride
For you gray men, who fought and wrought, not fearing
        Battle's red tide.

Our rear guard, ye whose step is slowing, slowing,
  Whose ranks, earth-thinned, are filling otherwhere,
Who wore the gray—the gray, alas! still showing
        On bleaching hair.

For forty years you 've watched this land grow stronger,
  For forty years you 've been its bulwark, stay;
Tarry awhile; pause yet a little longer
        Upon the way.

And set our feet where there may be no turning,
  And set our faces straight on duty's track,
Where there may be for stray, strange gods no yearning
        Nor looking back.

And when for you the last tattoo has sounded,
  And on death's silent field you 've pitched your tent,
When, bowed through tears, the arc of life has rounded
      To full content,

We that are left will count it guerdon royal,
  Our heritage no years can take away,
That we were born of those, unflinching, loyal,
          Who wore the gray.
                              —*Irene Fowler Brown.*

THE KLONDIKE

NEVER mind the day we left, or the way the women clung
      to us;
All we need now is the last way they looked at us.
Never mind the twelve men there amid the cheering—
Twelve men or one man, 't will soon be all the same;
For this is what we know: we are five men together,
Five left o' twelve men to find the golden river.

Far we came to find it out, but the place was here for all
      of us;
Far, far we came, and here we have the last of us.
We that were the front men, we that would be early,
We that had the faith, and the triumph in our eyes:
We that had the wrong road, twelve men together,—
Singing when the devil sang to find the golden river.

Say the gleam was not for us, but never say we doubted it;
Say the wrong road was right before we followed it.
We that were the front men, fit for all forage,—
Say that while we dwindle we are front men still;
For this is what we know to-night: we 're starving here
          together—
Starving on the wrong road to find the golden river.

Wrong, we say, but wait a little: hear him in the corner
    there;
He knows more than we, and he 'll tell us if we listen there—
He that fought the snow-sleep less than all the others
Stays awhile yet, and he knows where he stays:
Foot and hand a frozen clout, brain a freezing feather,
Still he 's here to talk with us and to the golden river.

"Flow," he says, "and flow along, but you cannot flow
    away from us;
All the world's ice will never keep you far from us;
Every man that heeds your call takes the way that leads
    him—
The one way that 's his way, and lives his own life:
Starve or laugh, the game goes on, and on goes the river;
Gold or no, they go their way—twelve men together.

"Twelve," he says, "who sold their shame for a lure you
    call too fair for them—
You that laugh and flow to the same word that urges them:
Twelve who left the old town shining in the sunset,
Left the weary street and the small safe days:
Twelve who knew but one way out, wide the way or narrow:
Twelve who took the frozen chance and laid their lives on
    yellow.

"Flow by night and flow by day, nor ever once be seen by
    them;
Flow, freeze, and flow, till time shall hide the bones of them:
Laugh and wash their names away, leave them all forgotten,
Leave the old town to crumble where it sleeps;
Leave it there as they have left it, shining in the valley,—
Leave the town to crumble down and let the women marry.

"Twelve of us or five," he says, "we know the night is on
    us now:

Five while we last, and we may as well be thinking now:
Thinking each his own thought, knowing, when the light
     comes,
Five left or none left, the game will not be lost.
Crouch or sleep, we go the way, the last way together:
Five or none, the game goes on, and on goes the river.

"For after all that we have done and all that we have failed
     to do,
Life will be life and the world will have its work to do:
Every man who follows us will heed in his own fashion
The calling and the warning and the friends who do not
     know:
Each will hold an icy knife to punish his heart's lover,
And each will go the frozen way to find the golden river."

There you hear him, all he says, and the last we 'll ever get
     from him.
Now he wants to sleep, and that will be the best for him.
Let him have his own way—no, you needn't shake him—
Your own turn will come, so let the man sleep.
For this is what we know: we are stalled here together—
Hands and feet and hearts of us, to find the golden river.

And there 's a quicker way than sleep? . . . Never mind
     the looks of him:
All he needs now is a finger on the eyes of him.
You there on the left hand, reach a little over—
Shut the stars away, or he 'll see them all night:
He 'll see them all night and he 'll see them all to-morrow,
Crawling down the frozen sky, cold and hard and yellow.

Won't you move an inch or two—to keep the stars away
     from him?
—No, he won't move, and there 's no need of asking him.
Never mind the twelve men, never mind the women;

Three while we last, we'll let them all go;
And we'll hold our thoughts north while we starve her,
    together,
Looking each his own way to find the golden river.
                            —*Edwin Arlington Robinson.*

THE MEN OF THE "MAINE"

NOT in the dire, ensanguined front of war,
    Conquered or conqueror,
'Mid the dread battle-peal, did they go down
To the still under-seas, like fair Renown
To weave for them the hero martyr's crown.
They struck no blow
'Gainst an embattled foe;
With valiant-hearted Saxon hardihood
They stood not as the *Essex* sailors stood,
So sore bestead in that far Chilean Bay;
Yet no less faithful they,
These men who, in the passing of a breath,
Were hurtled upon death.

No warning the salt-scented sea-wind bore,
No presage whispered from the Cuban shore
Of the appalling fate
That in the tropic night-time lay in wait
To bear them whence they shall return no more.
Some lapsed from dreams of home and love's clear star
Into a realm where dreams eternal are;
And some into a world of wave and flame
Wherethrough they came
To living agony that no words can name.
Tears for them all,
And the low-tunéd dirge funereal!

Their place is now
With those who wear, green-set about the brow,

The deathless immortelles, —
The heroes torn and scarred
Whose blood made red the barren ocean dells,
Fighting with him the gallant *Ranger* bore,
Daring to do what none had dared before,
To wave the New World banner, freedom-starred,
At England's very door!
Yea, with such noble ones their names shall stand
As those who heard the dying Lawrence speak
His burning words upon the *Chesapeake,*
And grappled in the hopeless hand-to-hand;
With those who fell on Erie and Champlain
Beneath the pouring, pitiless battle-rain;
With such as these, our lost men of the *Maine!*

What though they faced no storm of iron hail
That freedom and the right might still prevail?
The path of duty it was theirs to tread
To death's dark vale through ways of travail led,
And they are ours—our dead!
If it be true that each loss holds a gain,
It must be ours through saddened eyes to see
From out this tragic holocaust of pain
The whole land bound in closer amity!

—*Clinton Scollard.*

THE FIGHTING RACE

READ out the names!" and Burke sat back,
   And Kelly drooped his head,
While Shea—they call him Scholar Jack—
   Went down the list of the dead.
Officers, seamen, gunners, marines,
   The crews of the gig and yawl,
The bearded man and the lad in his teens,
   Carpenters, coal passers—all.

329

Then, knocking the ashes from out his pipe,
  Said Burke in an off-hand way:
"We 're all in that dead man's list, by Cripe!
  Kelly and Burke and Shea."
"Well, here 's to the *Maine,* and I 'm sorry for Spain,"
  Said Kelly and Burke and Shea.

"Wherever there 's Kellys there 's trouble," said Burke.
  "Wherever fighting 's the game,
Or a spice of danger in grown man's work,"
  Said Kelly, "you 'll find my name."
"And do we fall short," said Burke, getting mad,
  "When it 's touch and go for life?"
Said Shea: "It 's thirty-odd years, bedad,
  Since I charged to drum and fife
Up Marye's Heights, and my old canteen
  Stopped a rebel ball on its way;
There were blossoms of blood on our sprigs of green—
  Kelly and Burke and Shea—
And the dead did n't brag." "Well, here 's to the flag!"
  Said Kelly and Burke and Shea.

"I wish 't was in Ireland, for there 's the place,"
  Said Burke, "that we 'd die by right,
In the cradle of our soldier race,
  After one good stand-up fight.
My grandfather fell on Vinegar Hill,
  And fighting was not his trade;
But his rusty pike 's in the cabin still,
  With Hessian blood on the blade."
"Aye, aye," said Kelly, "the pikes were great
  When the word was 'clear the way!'
We were thick on the roll in ninety-eight—
  Kelly and Burke and Shea."
"Well, here 's to the pike and the sword and the like!"
  Said Kelly and Burke and Shea.

And Shea, the scholar, with rising joy,
   Said: "We were at Ramillies;
We left our bones at Fontenoy
   And up in the Pyrenees;
Before Dunkirk, on Landen's plain,
   Cremona, Lille, and Ghent;
We 're all over Austria, France, and Spain,
   Wherever they pitched a tent.
We 've died for England from Waterloo
   To Egypt and Dargai;
And still there 's enough for a corps or crew,
   Kelly and Burke and Shea."
"Well, here 's to good honest fighting blood!"
   Said Kelly and Burke and Shea.

"Oh, the fighting races don't die out,
   If they seldom die in bed,
For love is first in their hearts, no doubt,"
   Said Burke; then Kelly said:
"When Michael, the Irish Archangel, stands,
   The angel with the sword,
And the battle-dead from a hundred lands
   Are ranged in one big horde,
Our line, that for Gabriel's trumpet waits,
   Will stretch three deep that day,
From Jehoshaphat to the Golden Gates—
   Kelly and Burke and Shea."
"Well, here 's thank God for the race and the sod!"
   Said Kelly and Burke and Shea.

                 —Joseph I. C. Clarke.

FOR CUBA

NO precedent, ye say,
   To point the glorious way
Towards helping one downtrod in blood and tears?

Brothers, 't is time there were!
We bare our swords for her,
And set a model for the coming years!

This act, to end her pain,
Without a hope of gain,
Its like on history's page where can ye read?
Humanity and God
Call us to paths untrod!
On, brothers, on! we follow not, but lead!
—*Robert Mowry Bell.*

ONE COUNTRY

AFTER all,
One country, brethren! We must rise or fall
With the Supreme Republic. We must be
The makers of her immortality,—
Her freedom, fame,
Her glory or her shame:
Liegemen to God and fathers of the free!

After all—
Hark! from the heights the clear, strong, clarion call
And the command imperious: " Stand forth,
Sons of the South and brothers of the North!
Stand forth and be
As one on soil and sea—
Your country's honour more than empire's worth! "

After all, ..
'T is Freedom wears the loveliest coronal;
Her brow is to the morning; in the sod
She breathes the breath of patriots; every clod

Answers her call
And rises like a wall
Against the foes of liberty and God!

—Frank Lebby Stanton.

THE CALL TO THE COLOURS

"ARE you ready, O Virginia,
　　Alabama, Tennessee,
People of the Southland, answer!
　For the land hath need of thee."
"Here!" from sandy Rio Grande,
　Where the Texan horsemen ride;
"Here!" the hunters of Kentucky
　Hail from Chatterawah's side;
Every toiler in the cotton,
　Every rugged mountaineer,
Velvet-voiced and iron-handed,
　Lifts his head to answer, "Here!"
Some remain who charged with Pickett,
　Some survive who followed Lee;
They shall lead their sons in battle
　For the flag, if need there be.

"Are you ready, California,
　Arizona, Idaho?
Come, oh, come unto the colours!
　Hear ye not the bugle blow?"
Falls a hush in San Francisco
　In the busy hives of trade;
In the vineyards of Sonoma
　Fall the pruning knife and spade;
In the mines of Colorado
　Pick and drill are thrown aside;
Idly in Seattle harbour
　Swing the merchants to the tide;

333

And a million mighty voices
  Throb responsive like a drum,
Rolling from the rough Sierras,
  "You have called us, and we come."

O'er Missouri sounds the challenge—
  O'er the great lakes and the plain;
"Are you ready, Minnesota?
  Are you ready, men of Maine?"
From the woods of Ontonagon,
  From the farms of Illinois,
From the looms of Massachusetts,
  "We are ready, man and boy."
Ax-men free, of Androscoggin,
  Clerks who trudge the cities' paves,
Gloucester men who drag their plunder
  From the sullen, hungry waves,
Big-boned Swede and large-limbed German,
  Celt and Saxon swell the call,
And the Adirondacks echo,
  "We are ready, one and all."

Truce to feud and peace to faction!
  All forgot is party zeal
When the war-ships clear for action,
  When the blue battalions wheel.
Europe boasts her standing armies,—
  Serfs who blindly fight by trade;
We have seven million soldiers,
  And a soul guides every blade.
Labourers with arm and mattock,
  Labourers with brain and pen,
Railroad prince and railroad brakeman
  Build our line of fighting men.
Flag of righteous wars! close mustered
  Gleam the bayonets, row on row,

Where thy stars are sternly clustered,
With their daggers towards the foe.
—Arthur Guiterman.

DEWEY AND HIS MEN

GLISTERING high in the midnight sky the starry rockets soar
To crown the height so soon to be uncrowned, Corregidor;
And moaning into the middle night resounds the answering shock
From Fraile's island battery within the living rock;
Like Farragut before him, so Dewey down the bay,
Past fort and mine, in single line, holds on toward Cavité.

When the earth was new a raven flew o'er the sea on a perilous quest,
By his broad black pinions buoyed up as he sought him a spot to rest;
So to-day from British China sweeps our Commodore 'mid the cheers
Of England's dauntless ships of steel, and into the night he steers,
With never a home but the furrowy foam and never a place for ease
Save the place he 'll win by the dint and din of his long, lean batteries.

A misty dawn on the May-Day shone, yet the enemy sees afar
On our ships-of-war great flags flung out as bright as the morning star;
Then the cannon of Spain crash over the main and their splendour flecks the ports
As the crackling thunder rolls along the frowning fleet and forts;

335

But the *Olympia* in her majesty leads up the broadening
bay
And behind her come gaunt ships and dumb toward crested
Cavité.

All pearl and rose the dawnlight glows, and ruddy and gray
the gloom
Of battle over their squadron sinks as we sweep like a vast
simoom;
When our broadsides flash and ring at last—in a hoarsen-
ing, staggering crush
On the arsenal and fleet in wrath our lurid lightnings rush.
Malate knows us, Cavité, Cañacoa crazed with hate;
But Corregidor shall speak no more, El Fraile fears his fate.

Montojo fights as fought the knights by the Cid Campeador;
He leaves his flagship all afire, the *Cuba* takes him o'er;
The *Don Antonio* roars and fumes, the *Austria* lights and
lifts;
From Sangley to Manila Mole the battle vapour drifts;
But the *Queen Christine* in one great blast dies as becomes
her name,
Her funeral shroud a pillar of cloud all filagreed with flame.

From peak to peak our quick flags speak, the rattling chorus
ends;
And cheer on cheer rolls over the sea at the word the signal
sends.
From Commodore to powder-boy, from bridge to stoker's
den,
No battle rips have found our ships, nor wounds nor death
our men.
We cheer and rest, we rest and cheer; and ever above the
tides
The flag that knows no conquering foes in newer glory rides.

When the reek of war is rolled afar by the breezes down
the bay
We turn our deadly guns again on the walls of Cavité.
The Spaniard dreamed of victory—his final hope is flown
As winged destruction up and down our batteries have
strown—
In horrid havoc, red and black, the storm throbs on amain
Till in the glare of carnage there fade all the flags of
Spain.

In old Madrid sad eyes are hid for an empire sore bestead:
Manila 's mad with misery, Havana sick with dread,
As the great bells toll each gallant soul Castile shall see no
more.
Toll Fraile's fort a thing for sport, toll lost Corregidor—
Spain's citadels are fluttering with banners blanched and
pale;
Her admiralty in agony lies shattered, steam and sail.

And the home we sought was cheaply bought, for no mother,
wife, nor maid
From Maine to Loma Point bewails the lad for whom she
prayed;
Now everywhere, from Florida to the blue Vancouver
Straits,
The flag we 've flown abroad is thrown, and a word of cheer
awaits.
The ships and men that never failed the nation from her
birth
Have done again all ships and men may do upon this earth.

Glistering high in the noontide sky the starry banners soar
To crown anew the height so soon uncrowned, Corregidor.
They bring the promise of the free to Philip's jewelled isles,
And hearts oppressed thrill hard with hope whene'er that
promise smiles;

For the spirit of *Old Ironsides* broods o'er that tropic day
And the wildfire lights as Dewey fights on the broad Manila
Bay.

—Wallace Rice.

A BALLAD OF MANILA BAY

YOUR threats how vain, Corregidor;
  Your rampired batteries, feared no more;
Your frowning guard at Manila gate,—
  When our Captain went before!

Lights out. Into the unknown gloom
From the windy, glimmering, wide sea-room,
Challenging fate in that dark strait
  We dared the hidden doom.

But the death in the deep awoke not then;
Mine and torpedo they spoke not then;
From the heights that loomed on our passing line
  The thunders broke not then.

Safe through the perilous dark we sped,
Quiet each ship as the quiet dead,
Till the guns of El Fraile roared—too late,
  And the steel prows forged ahead.

Mute each ship as the mute-mouth grave,
A ghost leviathan cleaving the wave;
But deep in its heart the great fires throb,
  The travailing engines rave,

The ponderous pistons urge like fate,
The red-throat furnaces roar elate,
And the sweating stokers stagger and swoon
  In a heat more fierce than hate.

338

So through the dark we stole our way
Past the grim warders and into the bay,
Past Kalibuyo, and past Salinas,—
    And came at the break of day

Where strong Cavité stood to oppose,—
Where, from a sheen of silver and rose,
A thronging of masts, a soaring of towers,
    The beautiful city arose.

How fine and fair! But the shining air
With a thousand shattering thunders there
Flapped and reeled. For the fighting foe—
    We had caught him in his lair.

Surprised, unready, his proud ships lay
Idly at anchor in Bakor Bay;—
Unready, surprised, but proudly bold,
    Which was ever the Spaniard's way.

Lit every vomiting, bursting hulk
With a crimson reek of hell.
Then soon on his pride the dread doom fell,
Red doom,—for the ruin of shot and shell

But to the brave though beaten, hail!
All hail to them that dare and fail!
To the dauntless boat that charged our fleet
    And sank in the iron hail!

    .   .   .   .   .

Manila Bay! Manila Bay!
How proud the song on our lips to-day!
A brave old song of the true and strong
    And the will that has its way;

Of the blood that told in the days of Drake
When the fight was good for the fighting's sake!
For the blood that fathered Farragut
    Is the blood that fathered Blake;

And the pride of the blood will not be undone
While war 's in the world and a fight to be won.
For the master now, as the master of old,
    Is "the man behind the gun."

The dominant blood that daunts the foe,
That laughs at odds, and leaps to the blow,—
It is Dewey's glory to-day, as Nelson's
    A hundred years ago!
                —*Charles George Douglas Roberts.*

"CUT THE CABLES!"

"CUT the cables!" the order read,
    And the men were there; there was no delay.
The ships hove to in Cienfuegos Bay,—
    The *Windom, Nashville, Marblehead,*—
Beautiful, grim, and alert were they,
    It was midway, past in the morning gray.
    "Cut the cables!" the order said—
Over the clouds of the dashing spray
The guns were trained and ready for play;
    Picked from the *Nashville,* Winslow led,—
Grim death waits ashore, they say;
"Lower the boats, godspeed, give way."
Did "our untried navy lads" obey?
    Away to their perilous work they sped.

Now, steady the keel, keep stroke the oar!
    They must go in close, they must find the wires;

Grim death is alert on that watching shore,
  That deadly shore of the " Hundred Fires."
In the lighthouse tower,—along the ledge,—
  In the block-house, waiting,—the guns are there;
On the lowland, too, in the tall, dry sedge;
  They are holding the word till the boats draw **near.**
One hundred feet from the water's edge,
  Dazzling clear is the sunlit air;
Quick, my men,—the moments are dear!
  Two hundred feet from the rifle-pit,
And our " untried " lads still show no **fear**—
  Whey they open now they 're sure to hit;
No question, even by sign, they ask,
In silence they bend to their dangerous task.

Quick now!—the shot from a smokeless gun
  Cuts close and spatters the glistening brine;
Now follows the roar of the battle begun,
But the boys were bent in the blazing sun
  Like peaceful fishermen, " wetting a line."
They searched the sea while a shrieking blast
  Swept shoreward, swift as the lightning flies,—
While the fan-like storm of the shells went past
  Like a death-wing cleaving the hissing skies.
Like a sheltering wing,—for the hurricane came
  From our own good guns, and the foe might tell
What wreck was wrought by their deadly aim;
  For the foe went down where the hurricane fell.
It shattered the block-house, levelled the tower,
  It ripped the face of the smoking hill,
It beat the battle back, hour by hour,
And then, for a little while, our guns were still.
For a little, but that was the fatal breath,—
  That moment's lull in the friendly crash,—
  For the long pit blazed with a vicious flash,
And eight fell,—two of them done to death.

Once more the screen of the screaming shot
    With its driving canopy covered the men,
While they dragged, and grappled, and, faltering not,
    Still dragged and searched, and grappled again,
And they stayed right there till the work was done,
The cables were found and severed, each one,
With an eighty-foot gap, and the " piece " hauled in,
And stowed in place,—then, under the din
Of that deafening storm, that had swept the air
For three long hours, they turned from shore.
(" Steady the keel " there; " stroke " the oar),
To the smoke-wreathed ships, and, under the guns,
They went up the side,—our " untried " ones.

Quiet, my brave boys; hats off, all!
    They are here, our " untried " boys in blue.
Steady the block, now, all hands haul!
    Slow on that line there!—look to that crew!
Six lads hurt!—and the colours there?
    Wrap two of them?—hold! Ease back the bow!
Slow, now, on the line!—slack down with care!
Steady!—they 're back on their own deck now!
The cables are cut, sir, eighty-foot spread,
Six boys hurt, and—two of them dead.
    Half-mast the colours! there 's work to do!
There are two red marks on the starboard gun,
There is some work that is not quite done,
    For our " untried " boys that are tried and true.
It was n't all play when they cut the wires,—
Well named is that bay of the " Hundred Fires."
                    —*Robert Burns Wilson.*

THE MEN OF THE "MERRIMAC"

HAIL to Hobson! hail to Hobson! hail to all the valiant
    set!

Clausen, Kelly, Deignan, Phillips, Murphy, Montagu,
    Charette;
Howso'er we laud and laurel we shall be their debtors yet!
Shame upon us, shame upon us, should the nation e'er for-
    get!

Though the tale be worn with telling, let the daring deed be
    sung!
Surely never brighter valour, since this wheeling world was
    young,
Thrilled men's souls to more than wonder, till praise leaped
    from every tongue!

Trapped at last the Spanish sea-fox in the hill-locked harbour
    lay;
Spake the Admiral from his flag-ship, rocking off the hidden
    bay,
"We must close yon open portal lest he slip by night
    away!"

"Volunteers!" the signal lifted; rippling through the fleet
    it ran;
Was there ever deadlier venture? was there ever bolder plan?
Yet the gallant sailors answered, answered well-nigh to a
    man!

Ere the dawn's first rose-flush kindled, swiftly sped the
    chosen eight
Toward the batteries grimly frowning o'er the harbour's nar-
    row gate;
Sooth, he holds his life but lightly who thus gives the dare
    to Fate!

They had passed the outer portal where the guns grinned,
    tier o'er tier,
When portentous Morro thundered, and Socapa echoed clear,
And Estrella joined a chorus pandemoniac to hear.

Heroes without hands to waver, heroes without hearts to
    quail,
There they sank the bulky collier 'mid the hurtling Spanish
    hail;
Long shall float our starry banner if such lads beneath it
    sail!

Hail to Hobson! hail to Hobson! hail to all the valiant set!
Clausen, Kelly, Deignan, Phillips, Murphy, Montagu,
    Charette!
Howso'er we laud and laurel we shall be their debtors yet!
Shame upon us, shame upon us, should the nation e'er forget.
                    —*Clinton Scollard.*

A RHYME OF THE ROUGH RIDERS

THE ways of fate they had trod were as wide
    As the sea from the shouting sea,
But when they had ranged them side by side,
Strenuous, eager, and ardent-eyed,
They were brothers in pluck, they were brothers in pride,
    As the veriest brethren be.

They heard no bugle-peal to thrill
    As they crouched in the tangled grass,
But the sound of bullets whirring shrill
From hidden hollow and shrouded hill;
And they fought as only the valiant will
    In the glades of Guasimas.

Aye, they fought, let their blood attest!—
    The blood of their comrades gone;
Fought their bravest and fought their best,
As when, like a wave, in their zealous zest
They swept and surged o'er the sanguine crest
    Of the heights of San Juan.

So here's to them all—a toast and a cheer!—
    From the greatest down to the least,
The heroes who fronted the deadliest fear,
Leader and lad, each volunteer,
The men whom the whole broad land holds dear
    From the western sea to the east!

               —*Clinton Scollard.*

THE CHARGE AT SANTIAGO

WITH shot and shell, like a loosened hell,
    Smiting them left and right,
They rise and fall on the sloping wall
  Of beetling bush and height.
They do not shrink at the awful brink
  Of the rifle's hurtling breath;
But onward press, as their ranks grow less,
  To the open arms of death.

Through a storm of lead, o'er maimed and dead,
  Onward and up they go,
Till hand to hand the unflinching band
  Grapple the stubborn foe.
O'er men that reel, 'mid glint of steel,
  Bellow or boom of gun,
They leap and shout over each redoubt,
  Till the final trench is won.

Oh, charge sublime! Over dust and grime
  Each hero hurls his name
In shot or shell, like a molten hell,
  To the topmost heights of fame!
And prone or stiff, under bush or cliff,
  Wounded or dead men lie,
While the tropic sun on a grand deed done
  Looks with his piercing eye!

—William Hamilton Hayne.

DEEDS OF VALOUR AT SANTIAGO

WHO cries that the days of daring are those that are
    faded far,
That never a light burns planet-bright to be hailed as the
    hero's star?
Let the deeds of the dead be laurelled, the brave of the
    elder years,
But a song, we say, for the men of to-day, who have proved
    themselves their peers!

High in the vault of the tropic sky is the garish eye of the
    sun,
And down with its crown of guns afrown looks the hill-top
    to be won;
There is the trench where the Spaniard lurks, his hold and
    his hiding-place,
And he who would cross the space between must meet death
    face to face.

The black mouths belch and thunder, and the shrapnel
    shrieks and flies;
Where are the fain and the fearless, the lads with the daunt-
    less eyes?

Will the moment find them wanting! Nay, but with valour
  stirred!
Like the leashéd hound on the coursing-ground they wait
  but the warning word.

"Charge!" and the line moves forward, moves with a
  shout and a swing,
While sharper far than the cactus-thorn is the spiteful
  bullets sting;
Now they are out in the open, and now they are breasting
  the slope,
While into the eyes of death they gaze as into the eyes of
  hope.

Never they wait nor waver, but on they clamber and on,
With "Up with the flag of the Stripes and Stars, and down
  with the flag of the Don!"
What should they bear through the shot-rent air but rout
  to the ranks of Spain,
For the blood that throbs in their hearts is the blood of the
  boys of Anthony Wayne!

See, they have taken the trenches! Where are the foemen?
  Gone!
And now "Old Glory" waves in the breeze from the heights
  of San Juan!
And so, while the dead are laurelled, the brave of the elder
  years,
A song, we say, for the men of to-day who have proved
  themselves their peers.

—Clinton Scollard.

WHEELER'S BRIGADE AT SANTIAGO

'NEATH the lances of the tropic sun
  The column is standing ready,

Awaiting the fateful command of one
    Whose word will ring out
      To an answering shout
   To prove it alert and steady.
And a stirring chorus all of them sung
   With singleness of endeavour,
Though some to the " Bonnie Blue Flag " had swung
   And some to " The Union For Ever."

The order came sharp through the desperate air
   And the long ranks rose to follow,
Till their dancing banners shone more fair
    Than the brightest ray
    Of the Cuban day
  On the hill and jungled hollow;
And to " Maryland " some in the days gone by
   Had fought through the combat's rumble,
And some for ' Freedom's Battle-Cry "
   Had seen the broad earth crumble.

Full many a widow weeps in the night
   Who had been a man's wife in the morning;
For the banners we loved we bore to the height
    Where the enemy stood
    As a hero should,
  His valour his country adorning;
But drops of pride with your tears of grief,
   Ye American women, mix ye!
For the North and South, with a Southron chief,
   Kept time to the tune of " Dixie."

                   —Wallace Rice.

SPAIN'S LAST ARMADA

THEY fling their flags upon the morn,
   Their safety 's held a thing for scorn,

As to the fray the Spaniards on the wings of war are borne;
 Their sullen smoke-clouds writhe and reel,
 And sullen are their ships of steel,
All ready, cannon, lanyards, from the fighting-tops to keel.

 They cast upon the golden air
 One glancing, helpless, hopeless prayer
To ask that swift and thorough be the victory falling there;
 Then giants with a cheer and sigh
 Burst forth to battle and to die
Beneath the walls of Morro on that morning in July.

 The *Teresa* heads the haughty train
 To bear the Admiral of Spain,
She rushes, hurtling, whitening, like the summer hurricane.
 El Morro glowers in his might;
 Socapa crimsons with the fight;
The *Oquendo's* blinding lightning blazes through her sombre
 night.

 In desperate and eager dash
 The *Vizcaya* hurls her vivid flash,
As wild upon the water her enormous batteries crash.
 Like spindrift scuds the fleet *Colon*,
 And, on her bubbling wake bestrown,
Lurch, hungry for the slaughter, *El Furor* and *El Pluton*.

 Round Santiago's armoured crest,
 Serene, in their gray valour dressed,
Our behemoths lie quiet, watching well from south and west.
 Their keen eyes spy the harbour-reek,
 The signals dance, the signals speak:
Then breaks the blasting riot as our broadsides storm and
 shriek.

There, poising on her eagle-wings,
The *Brooklyn* into battle swings;
The wide sea falls and wonders as the titan *Texas* springs;
The *Iowa* in monster-leaps
Goes bellowing above the deeps;
The *Indiana* thunders as her terror onward sweeps,

And, hovering near and hovering low
Until the moment strikes to go,
In gallantry the *Gloucester* swoops down on her double foe:
She volleys—*El Furor* falls lame;
Again—and *El Pluton* 's aflame,—
Hurrah! Leon has lost her; gone the twin destroyers' fame!

And louder yet and louder roar
The Oregon's artilleries o'er
The clangour and the booming all along the Cuban shore;
She 's swifting down her valkyr-path,
Her sword sharp for the aftermath,
With leven in her glooming, like Jehovah in His Wrath.

Great ensigns snap and shine in air
Above the furious onslaught where
Our sailors cheer the battle, danger but a thing to dare;
Our gunners speed, as oft they 've sped,
Their hail of shrilling, shattering lead,
Swift sure our rifles rattle: and the foeman's decks are red.

Like baying bloodhounds lope our ships,
Adrip with fire their cannon's lips;
We scourge the fleeing Spanish, whistling weals from scor-
pion-whips;
Till, livid in the ghastly glare,
They tremble on in drear despair,
And thoughts of victory vanish in the carnage they must bear.

Where Cuban blossoms gaily bloom,
Where Cuban breakers swirl and spume,
The *Teresa's* onset slackens in a scarlet spray of doom;
Near Nimanima's greening hill
The streaming flames cry down her will,
Her vast hull blows and blackens, prey to every mortal ill.

To Juan Gonzales' foaming strand
The *Oquendo* staggers 'neath our hand,
Her armaments all strangled and her hope a shower-
ing brand;
She strikes and grinds upon the reef
And, shuddering there in utter grief,
In misery and mangled, wastes away beside her chief.

The *Vizcaya* nevermore shall ride
From out Asseradero's tide,
With hate upon her forehead never shall she pass in pride;
Beneath our fearful battle-spell
She moaned and struggled, flared and fell,
To lie agleam and horrid while her piling fires swell.

Thence from the wreck of Spain alone
Tears on the terrified *Colon,*
In bitter anguish crying, like a storm-bird forth she's flown;
Her throbbing engines creak and thrum;
She sees abeam the *Brooklyn* come;
For life she's gasping, flying; for the combat is she dumb.

Till then the man behind the gun
Had wrought whatever must be done:
Here, now, beside our boilers is the fight fought out and won;

Where great machines pulse on and beat,
A-swelter in the humming heat
The Nation's nameless toilers make her mastery complete.

The Cape o' the Cross has cast a stone
Against the course of the *Colon,*
Despairing and inglorious, on the wind her white flag 's
thrown:
Spain's Last Armada, lost and wan,
Lies where Tarquino's stream purls on,
As round the world, victorious, looms the dreadnaught
Oregon.

The sparkling daybeams softly flow
To glint the twilight afterglow,
The Banner sinks in splendour that in battle ne'er was low,
The music of our country's hymn
Rings out like song of seraphim,
Fond memories and tender fill the evening fair and dim;

Our huge ships ride in majesty
Unchallenged o'er the summer sea,
Above them white stars cluster, mighty emblem of the free;
And all adown the long sea-lane
The fitful balefires wax and wane
To shed their lurid lustre on the empire that was Spain.
—*Wallace Rice.*

OUR FLEET AT SANTIAGO

THE heart leaps with the pride of their story,
Predestinate lords of the sea!
They are heirs of the flag and its glory,
They are sons of the soil it keeps free;

For their deeds the serene exaltation
  Of a cause that was stained with no shame,
For their dead the proud tears of a nation,
  Their fame shall endure with its fame.

The fervour, that, grim, unrelenting,
  The founders in homespun had fired,
With blood the free compact cementing,
  Was the flame that their souls had inspired.
They were sons of the dark tribulations,
  Of the perilous days of the birth
Of a nation sprung free among nations,
  A new hope to the children of earth!

They were nerved by the old deeds of daring,
  Every tale of Decatur they knew,
Every ship that, the bright banner bearing,
  Shot to keep it afloat in the blue;
They were spurred by the splendour undying
  Of Somers' fierce fling in the bay,
And the watchword that Lawrence died crying,
  And of Cushing's calm courage were they.

By the echo of guns at whose thunder
  Old monarchies crumbled and fell,
When the war-ships were shattered asunder
  And their pennants went down in the swell;
By the strength of the race that, unfearing,
  Faces death till the death of the last,
Or has sunk with the fierce Saxon cheering,
  Its colours still nailed to the mast—

So they fought—and the stern race immortal
  Of Cromwell and Hampton and Penn
Has thrown open another closed portal,
  Stricken chains from a new race of men.

353

So they fought, so they won, so above them
  Blazed the light of a consecrated aim;
Empty words! Who can tell how we love them,
  How we thrill with the joy of their fame!
                        —*Charles Edward Russell.*

BATTLE-SONG OF THE "OREGON"

THE billowy headlands swiftly fly
    The crested path I keep,
My ribboned smoke stains many a sky,
    My embers dye the deep;
A continent has hardly space—
    Mid-ocean little more,
Wherein to trace my eager race
    While clang the alarums of war.

I come, the war-ship Oregon,
    My wake a whitening world,
My cannon shotted, thundering on
    With battle-flags unfurled.
My land knows no successful foe—
    Behold, to sink or save,
From stoker's flame to gunner's aim
    The race that rules the wave!

A nation's prayers my bulwark are
    Though ne'er so wild the sea;
Flow time or tide, come storm or star,
    Throbs my machinery.
Lands Spain has lost for ever peer
    From every lengthening coast,
Till rings the cheer that proves me near
    The flag of Columbia's host.

Defiantly I have held my way
  From the vigorous shore where Drake
Dreamed a New Albion in the day
  He left New Spain a-quake;
His shining course retraced, I fight
  The self-same foe he fought,
All earth to light with signs of might
Which God our Captain wrought.

Made mad, from Santiago's mouth
  Spain's ships-of-battle dart:
My bulk comes broadening from the south,
  A hurricane at heart;
Its desperate armouries blaze and boom,
  Its ardent engines beat;
And fiery doom finds root and bloom
  Aboard of the Spanish fleet.

.   .   .   .   .

The hundredweight of the *Golden Hind*
  With me are ponderous tons,
The ordnance great her deck that lined
  Would feed my ravening guns;
Her spacious reach in months and years
  I 've shrunk to nights and days;
Yet in my ears are ringing cheers
  Sir Frank himself would raise;

For conquereth not mine engines' breath
  Nor sides steel-clad and strong,
Nor bulk, nor rifles red with death:
  To Spain, too, these belong;
What made that old Armada break
  This newer victory won:

Jehovah spake by the sons of Drake
    At each incessant gun.

I come, the war-ship Oregon,
    My wake a whitening world,
My cannon shotted, thundering on
    With battle-flags unfurled.
My land knows no successful foe—
    Behold, to sink or save,
From stoker's flame to gunner's aim
    The race that rules the wave!

                              —*Wallace Rice.*

THE "BROOKLYN" AT SANTIAGO

'TWIXT clouded heights Spain hurls to doom
    Ships staunch and brave,
Majestic, forth they flash and boom
    Upon the wave.

El Morro raises eyes of hate
    Far out to sea,
And speeds Cervera to his fate
    With cannonry.

The *Brooklyn* o'er the deep espies
    His fame-wreathed side;
She sets her banners on the skies
    In fearful pride.

On, to the harbour's mouth of fire,
    Fierce for the fray,
She darts, an eagle from his eyre,
    Upon her prey.

She meets the brave *Teresa* there—
    Sigh, sigh for Spain!—
And beats her clanging armour bare
    With glittering rain.

The bold *Vizcaya's* lightnings glance
    Into the throng
Where loud the bannered *Brooklyn* chants
    Her awful song.

Down swoops, in one tremendous curve,
    Our Commodore;
His broadsides roll, the foemen swerve
    Toward the shore.

In one great round his *Brooklyn* turns
    And, girdling there
This side and that with glory, burns
   Spain to despair.

Frightful in onslaught, fraught with fate,
    Her missiles hiss;
The Spaniard sees, when all too late,
    A Nemesis.

The *Oquendo's* diapason swells;
    Then, torn and lame,
Her port-holes turn to yawning wells,
    Geysers of flame.

Yet fierce and fiercer breaks and cries
    Our rifles' dread:
The doomed *Teresa* shudders—lies
    Stark with her dead.

How true the *Brooklyn's* battery speaks
    Eulate knows,
And as the *Vizcaya* staggers, shrieks
    Her horrent woes.

Sideward she plunges; nevermore
    Shall Biscay feel
Her heart throb for the ship that wore
    Her name in steel.

The *Oquendo's* ports a moment shone,
    As gloomed her knell;
She trembles, bursts—the ship is gone
    Headlong to hell.

The fleet *Colon* in lonely flight—
    Spain's hope, Spain's fear!
Sees, and it lends her wings of fright
    Schley's pennant near.

The fleet *Colon* scuds on alone—
    God, how she runs!—
And ever hears behind her moan
    The *Brooklyn's* guns.

Our ruthless cannon o'er the flood
    Roar and draw nigh;
Spain's ensign, stained with gold and blood,
    Falls from on high.

The world she gave the World has passed—
    Gone with her power—
Dead, 'neath the *Brooklyn's* thunder-blast
    In one great hour.

The bannered *Brooklyn!* gallant crew,
  And gallant Schley!
Proud is the flag his sailors flew
  Along the sky.

Proud is his country: for each star
  Our Union wears,
The fighting *Brooklyn* shows a scar—
  So much he dares.

God save us war upon the seas;
  But, if it slip,
Send such a chief, with men like these
  On such a ship!

—*Wallace Rice.*

ANGEL OF PEACE

ANGEL of Peace, thou hast wandered too long!
  Spread thy white wings to the sunshine of love!
Come while our voices are blended in song,—
  Fly to our ark like the storm-beaten dove!
Fly to our ark on the wings of dove,—
  Speed o'er the far-sounding billows of song,
Crowned with thine olive-leaf garland of love,—
  Angel of Peace, thou hast waited too long.

Brothers we meet, on this altar of thine
  Mingling the gifts we have gathered for thee,
Sweet with the odours of myrtle and pine,
  Breeze of the prairie and breath of the sea,—
Meadow and mountain and forest and sea!
  Sweet is the fragrance of myrtle and pine,
Sweeter the incense we offer to thee,
  Brothers once more round this altar of thine!

Angels of Bethlehem, answer the strain!
Hark! a new birthstone is filling the sky!—
Loud as the stormwind that tumbles the main
Bid the full breath of the organ reply,—
Let the loud tempest of voices reply,—
Roll its long surge like the earthshaking main!
Swell the vast song till it mounts to the sky!
Angels of Bethlehem, echo the strain!

THE FIFTEENTH OF FEBRUARY

IS it not well, my brethren? They whose sleep
Beneath the nodding palm
Where the strong currents of the trade win sweep,
Is measureless and calm,
If from those loyal lips, now one year dumb,
One word across the heaving seas might come
What other word
Than this should hail the morning? Might they know
That where the tides where grim Cabanas flow
The mirrored beauties of their banner glow,
What other cheer be heard?

Is it not well—the surer, stronger sight
And for that pain and shame
The sense of all things slowly set aright
Unto a destined aim?
That gazing where beyond our utmost dreams
The way new broken through the darkness gleams,
Fresh wreaths we bring,
And heeding all that these with life have bought,
What wondrous things the circling months have wrought,
For these held dear in all a nation's thought
Pro patria mori sing.

Is it not well? *Pro patria mori!* Yea,
    For her dear sake no less
Than those that on some hard-fought glorious day
    Fall in the strife and stress.
Though not as Anglo-Saxons love to go,
Stern-set, hard-gripped, with answering blow for blow—
    Not thus they died—
Yet not without such sacrifice might be
Full wrought the perfect work of Liberty,
Nor we, the children of her first-born, see
    Her sunlit wings spread wide.

Is it not well? Lo! where the shade was cast
    Of outworn kingly sway
To gloom the future with a blighted past,
    That curse is swept away;
And now above the fading dark arise
New constellations in the glittering skies;
    And in our ears,
That heard but now the universal groan,
The prison shot and tortured prisoner's moan,
The chorus of a people freed is blown
    From verge of coming years.

Is it not well that far beyond, below,
    The market's empty strife
We have made sure what tides of feeling flow
    To make the people's life?
How deeply shrined the sacred flag has place
In all the toiling million-hearted race,
    And at her need
The youthful giant of the nation wakes,
Within his hand a disused weapon takes,
Lays down for her his ready life, or shakes
    The world with deathless deed.

Is it not well—the hope, as if new born,
　　The first of glimmering light,
The slender herald of the promised morn
　　　Athwart the ancient night?
That comes with healing for her wounded breast
Of that old East that is the radiant West
　　　Of times to be;
While in her prostrate place as loaded long
With chains of might and blinded hate and wrong,
She trembles at the first heard morning song
　　　From across the morning sea?

Is it not well, my brethren? There is made
　　　One song through all the land;
Before one light old doubts and shadows fade,
　　　With old lines drawn in sand.
The past lies dead. New sight, a broader view,
For the Republic sees a purpose new
　　　Of boundless scope.
While like a sun that burns with clearer flame
Sweeps rising through the sky her spotless fame,
And lights a land that knows one love, one aim,
　　　One flag, one faith, one hope.
　　　　　　　　　—Charles Edward Russell.

REBELS

SHOOT down the rebels—men who dare
　　　To claim their native land!
Why should the white invader spare
　　　A dusky heathen band?

You bought them from the Spanish King,
　　　You bought the men he stole;
You bought perchance a ghastlier thing—
　　　The Duke of Alva's soul!

" Freedom ! " you cry, and train your gun
  On men who would be freed,
And in the name of Washington
  Achieve a Weyler's deed.

Boast of the benefits you spread,
  The faith of Christ you hold;
Then seize the very soil you tread
  And fill your arms with gold.

Go, prostitute your mother-tongue,
  And give the rebel " name "
To those who to their country clung,
  Preferring death to shame.

And call him " loyal," him who brags
  Of countrymen betrayed—
The patriot of the money-bags,
  The loyalist of trade.

Oh, for the good old Roman days
  Of robbers bold and true,
Who scorned to oil with pious phrase
  The deeds they dared to do—

The days before degenerate thieves
  Devised the coward lie
Of blessings that the enslaved receives
  Whose rights their arms deny !

I hate the oppressor's iron rod,
  I hate his murderous ships,
But most of all I hate, O God,
  The lie upon his lips !

Nay, if they shall demand recruits
    To curse Manila Bay,
Be men; refuse to act like brutes
    And massacre and slay.

Or if you will persist to fight
    With all a soldier's pride,
Why, then, be rebels for the right
    By Aguinaldo's side!

                              —*Ernest Crosby.*

THE BALLAD OF PACO TOWN

IN Paco town and in Paco tower,
    At the height of the tropic noonday hour,
Some Tagal riflemen, half a score,
Watched the length of the highway o'er,
And when to the front the troopers spurred,
Whiz-z! whiz-z! how the Mausers whirred!

From the opposite walls, through crevice and crack,
Volley on volley went ringing back
Where a band of regulars tried to drive
The stinging rebels out of their hive;
"Wait till our cannon come, and then,"
Cried a captain, striding among his men,
"We'll scatter that bothersome buzz and drone
With a merry little tune of our own!"

The sweltering breezes seemed to swoon,
And down the *calle* the thickening flames
Licked the roofs in the tropic noon.
Then through the crackle and glare and heat,
And the smoke and the answering acclaims
Of the rifles, far up the village street
Was heard the clatter of horses' feet,

And a band of signal-men swung in sight,
And a band of signalmen swung in sight,
Hasting back from the ebbing fight
That had swept away to the left and right.

" Ride ! " yelled the regulars, all aghast,
And over the heads of the signal-men,
As they whirled in desperate gallop past,
The bullets a vicious music made,
Like the whistle and whine of the midnight blast
On the weltering wastes of the ocean when
The breast of the deep is scourged and flayed.

It chanced in the line of the fiercest fire
A rebel bullet had clipped the wire
That led, from the front and the fighting, down
To those that stayed in Manila town;
This gap arrested the watchful eye
Of one of the signal-men galloping by,
And straightway, out of the plunge and press,
He reined his horse with a swift caress
And a word in the ear of the rushing steed;
Then back with never a halt nor heed
Of the swarming bullets he rode, his goal
The parted wire and the slender pole
That stood where the deadly tower looked down
On the rack and ruin of Paco town.

Out of his saddle he sprang as gay
As a schoolboy taking a holiday;
Wire in hand up the pole he went
With never a glance at the tower, intent
Only on that which he saw appear
As the line of his duty plain and clear.
To the very crest he climbed and there
While the bullets buzzed in the scorching air,

Clipped his clothing, and scored and stung
The slender pole-top to which he clung,
Made the wire that was severed sound,
Slipped in his careless way to the ground,
Sprang to the back of his horse, and then
Was off, this bravest of signal-men.

Cheers for the hero! While such as he,
Heedless alike of wounds and scars,
Fight for the dear old Stripes and Stars,
Down through the years to us shall be
Ever and ever the victory.

—*Clinton Scollard.*

THE DEED OF LIEUTENANT MILES

WHEN you speak of dauntless deeds
　　When you tell of stirring scenes,
Tell this story of the isles
Where the endless summer smiles,—
Tell of young Lieutenant Miles
　　In the far-off Philippines!

'T was the Santa Ana fight!—
　　All along the Tagal line
From the thickets dense and dire
Gushed the fountains of their fire;
You could mark their rifles' ire,
　　You could hear their bullets whine.

Little wonder there was pause!
　　Some were wounded, some were dead;
" Call Lieutenant Miles!" He came,
In his eyes a fearless flame.
" Yonder blockhouse is our aim!"
　　The battalion leader said.

" You must take it—how you will;
    You must break this damnèd spell ! "
" Volunteers ! " cried Miles. 'T was vain,
For that narrow tropic lane
'Twixt the bamboo and the cane
Was a very lane of hell.

There were five stood forth at last;
    God above, but they were men !
" Come ! " exultantly he saith !—
Did they falter? Not a breath !
Down the path of hurtling death
    The Lieutenant led them then.

Two have fallen—now a third !
    Forward dashed the other three;
In the onrush of that race
Ne'er a swerve of stay of pace.
And the Tagals—dare they face
    Such a desperate company?

Panic gripped them by the throat,—
    Every Tagal rifleman;
And as though they seemed to see
In those charging foemen three
An avenging destiny,
    Fierce and fast and far they ran.

So a salvo for the six !
    So a round of ringing cheers !
Heroes of the distant isles
Where the endless summer smiles,—
Gallant young Lieutenant Miles
    And his valiant volnnteers !

                              —*Clinton Scollard.*

COLONEL LISCUM OF THE NINTH

COLONEL LISCUM of the Ninth, yours the same brave
     blood that won,
Ere the pearly break of dawn, bastioned old Fort Carillon;
Son of that staunch fighting line of the boys of Bennington!

Colonel Liscum of the Ninth, yours the valour without fleck,
Such as theirs who stormed thy heights, rock-enthroned
     Chapultepec!
You knew Bull Run's gory dew, Cedar Mountain's roar and
     wreck!

Colonel Liscum of the Ninth, when the whizzing Mausers
     bore
From the hill of San Juan such a sanguinary store,
On that cruel Cuban slope, you and yours were to the fore!

Colonel Liscum of the Ninth, take a Nation's sad farewells!
You have journeyed to the bourne where the valiant Law-
     ton dwells;
Yours the soldier's battle-crown; yours the hero's im-
     mortelles!

Colonel Liscum of the Ninth, long your dying words shall
     ring—
"Don't retreat, boys!"—in our ears as the years go hasten-
     ing.
Ah, the pity of it all, th' irremediable sting!
                    —Clinton Scollard.

BENJAMIN HARRISON

FULL on his forehead fell the expiring light
    Of old wreathed altars where his fathers died,
While at his back the dull devouring night
    Poured the advancing tide.

He would the ancient light relume, would fain
    The dear old faith keep still without a blot,
The flag he fought for scathless of a stain,
    The shield without a spot.

He sided with the weak and ceaseless strove
    With failing hands against the tyrannous strong;
Here was no place for him where unarmed Love
    Is strangled by old Wrong.

Here was no place for him where Force and Greed
    Upon the sacred fillets lay their hands
Red from the spoil of stricken souls that bleed
    And wrecks of ruined lands.

He has won peace at last—the peace that knows
    In dreamless tides no hint of hate or tears,
And falls where once his dauntless voice arose
    The silence of the years.

And men walk by and gaze, and wondering ask,
    Now that the white clear-visioned soul is fled,
Where is the hand to seize the torch and task
    New fallen from the dead?

Was all in vain? Is any word of worth,
    Though winged with truth and shot home to the mark,
If all the answer is this silent earth
    And lost voice in the dark?

But lost is never living word or deed.
　　As toward great waves unseen the ripple flows,
As hour by hour, unguessed, the fervent seed
　　Up to the sunlight grows,

The true man's word, though sown in fallow soil
　　And fruitless lying many a day and night,
In its own way beyond the sower's toil,
　　Bursts into deathless light.

—Charles Edward Russell.

BUFFALO

A TRANSIENT city, marvellously fair,
　　Humane, harmonious, yet nobly free,
She built for pure delight and memory.
　At her command by lake and garden rare,
Pylon and tower majestic rose in air,
　　And sculptured forms of grace and symmetry.
　　Then came a thought of God, and, reverently,—
"Let there be Light!" she said, and Light was there.

O miracle of splendour! Who could know
　　That Crime, insatiate, egoist and blind,
　　Destructive, causeless, caring but to smite,
Would in its dull Cimmerian gropings find
　　A sudden way to fill those courts with woe,
　　And swallow up that radiance in night?

—Florence Earle Coates.

FAITHFUL UNTO DEATH

H IS work is done, his toil is o'er;
　　A martyr for our land he fell—
　　The land he loved, that loved him well;
Honour his name for evermore!

Let all the world its tribute pay,
   For glorious shall be his renown;
   Though duty's was his only crown,
Yet duty's path is glory's way.

For he was great without pretense;
   A man of whom none whispered shame,
   A man who knew nor guile nor blame;
Good in his every influence.

On battlefield, in council hall,
   Long years with sterling service rife
   He gave us, and at last his life—
Still unafraid at duty's call.

Let the last solemn pageant move,
   The nation's grief to consecrate
   To him struck down by maniac hate
Amid a grateful nation's love;

And though the thought its solace gives,
   Beside the martyr's grave to-day
   We feel 't is almost hard to say:
" God reigns and the republic lives! "
            —*Richard Handfield Titherington.*

HYMN OF THE WEST

O THOU, whose glorious orbs on high
   Engird the earth with splendour round,
From out thy secret place draw nigh
   The courts and temples of this ground;
      Eternal Light,
      Fill with thy might
These domes that in thy purpose grew,
And lift a nation's head anew!

Illumine Thou each pathway here,
 To show the marvels God hath wrought!
Since first thy people's chief and seer
 Looked up with that prophetic thought,
   Bade time unroll
   The fateful scroll,
 And empire unto Freedom gave
 From cloudland height to tropic wave.

Poured through the gateways of the North
 Thy mighty rivers join their tide,
And, on the wings of morn sent forth,
 Their mists the far-off peaks divide.
   By Thee unsealed
   The mountains yield
 Ores that the wealth of Ophir shame,
 And gems wrought of seven-hued flame.

Lo, through what years the soil hath lain
 At thine own time to give increase—
The greater and the lesser grain,
 The ripening boll, the myriad fleece!
   Thy creatures graze
   Appointed ways;
 League after league across the land
 The ceaseless herds obey thy hand.

Thou, whose high archways shine most clear
 Above the plenteous western plain,
Thine ancient tribes from round the sphere
 To breathe its quickening air are fain:
   And smiles the sun
   To see made one
 Their brood throughout Earth's greenest space,
 Land of the new and lordlier race!
                    —*Edmund Clarence Stedman.*

PAUL JONES

ONCE more the favouring breezes blow
  In briny piping gales—
Housed in a warship as of old
  Once more the hero sails.
With bended head and lifted cap
  They raise him from his grave,
And place him where he loved to rest—
  Upon the white-topped wave.

The night comes down upon the deep,
  The warship calmly rides,
And proudly on the quarter-deck
  The sailor's spirit strides.
" These turrets and these iron plates
  Seem more than strange to me—
For walls of oak were fort enough
  When I was on the sea!
These throbbing engines, and the lack
  Of sail to dare the blast—
All strange and new—but what care I?
  My pennon crowns the mast!
That flag first danced above a ship
  I sailed amid the foam—
And now floats high above the craft
  That bears me back to home! "

The mist grows thicker, and the night
  Is black with heavier clouds—
A crew of ghosts glides down the deck,
  Or clambers up the shrouds.
A phantom shape, a phantom ship,
  Looms grimly through the shade—
And George's cross above the peak
  Gleams spectrally displayed!

The rusty cannon flash and flame,
   And through the haunted night,
Rings out the old defiance—" I
   Have just begun to fight ! "
With grisly yard-arms lashed they strive—
   Smoke-palled each reeling wreck—
The ghostly hero leads his tars
   Upon the wan-lit deck !
A deadly struggle in the murk—
   The stars flash up in pride,
And through the reek the George's cross
   Goes fluttering o'er the side !
The smoke-clouds pass—the parting night
   Gives way before the dawn—
The ship of steel swings on her way—
   The phantom crew is gone !

Once more the favouring breezes blow
   In briny piping gales—
Housed in a warship as of old
   Once more the hero sails.
With bended head and lifted cap
   They wait upon the shore—
To greet him from his final cruise—
   He voyages no more !
               —*William Arthur Phelon.*

SAN FRANCISCO

WHO now dare longer trust thy mother hand?
   So like thee thou hast not another child;
The favourite flower of all thy western sand,
  She looked up, Nature, in thy face and smiled,
Trustful of thee, all-happy in thy care.
  She was thine own, not to be lured away
Down joyless paths of men. Happy as fair,

Held to thy heart—that was she yesterday.
To-day the sea is sobbing her sad name;
  She cannot answer—she that loved thee best,
That clung to thee till Hell's own shock and flame
  Wrenched her, swept her, from thy forgetting breast.
Day's darling, playmate of thy wind and sun—
Mother, what hast thou done, what hast thou done!

—John Vance Cheney.

A SONG OF PANAMA

"CHUFF! chuff! chuff!" An' a mountain bluff
    Is moved by the shovel's song;
"Chuff! chuff! chuff!" Oh, the grade is rough
    A-liftin' the landscape along!

We are ants upon a mountain, but we 're leavin' of our dent,
An' our teeth-marks bitin' scenery they will show the way we
        went;
We 're a liftin' half creation, an' we 're changin' it around,
Just to suit our playful purpose when we 're diggin' in the
        ground.

"Chuff! chuff! chuff!" Oh, the grade is rough,
    An' the way to the sea is long;
"Chuff! chuff! chuff!" an' the engines puff
    In tune to the shovel's song!

We 're shiftin' miles like inches, and we grab a forest here
Just to switch it over yonder so 's to leave an angle clear;
We 're a-pushin' leagues o' swamps aside so 's we can hurry
        by—
An' if we had to do it we could probably switch the sky!

"Chuff! chuff! chuff!" Oh, it 's hard enough
    When you 're changin' a job gone wrong;
"Chuff! chuff! chuff!" and there 's no rebuff
    To the shovel a-singin' its song!

You hear it in the mornin' an' you hear it late at night—
It 's your battery keepin' action with support o' dynamite;
Oh, you gets it for your dinner, an' the scenery skips along
In a movin' panorama to the chargin' shovel's song!

"Chuff! chuff! chuff!" an' it grabs the scruff
  Of a hill and boosts it along;
"Chuff! chuff! chuff!" Oh, the grade is rough,
  But it gives to the shovel's song!

This is a fight that 's fightin', an' the battle 's to the death;
There ain't no stoppin' here to rest or even catch your breath;
You ain't no noble hero, an' you leave no gallant name—
You 're fightin' Nature's army, an' it ain't no easy game!

"Chuff! chuff! chuff!" Oh, the grade is rough,
  An' the way to the end is long,
"Chuff! chuff! chuff!" an' the engines puff
  As we lift the landscape along!

—Alfred Damon Runyon.

GROVER CLEVELAND

BRING cypress, rosemary, and rue
For him who kept his rudder true;
Who held to right the people's will,
And for whose foes we love him still.

A man of Plutarch's marble mould,
Of virtues strong and manifold,
Who spurned the incense of the hour,
And made the nation's weal his dower.

His sturdy, rugged sense of right
Put selfish purpose out of sight;
Slowly he thought, but long and well,
With temper inperturbable.

Bring cypress, rosemary and rue
For him who kept his rudder true;
Who went at dawn to that high star
Where Washington and Lincoln are.

—*Joel Benton.*

LINCOLN

YON red orb, in fame's azure hung,
  Is Alexander's; flushed and young,
 The sword of Macedon
In world-wars long agone.

Beyond it, poised where no clouds are,
Flashes, alone, the cold keen star
 Of Cæsar, where it clomb
High over seven-hilled Rome;

Shine, next, as naked greatness can,
The rival lights of Charlemagne
 And that fair Saxon king
Who knew no wicked thing.

Brave stars, against the darkness bold,
Shine for the mighty men of old,
 Who, as the strength was given,
Leapt into memory's heaven.

But he that never thought to climb,
Our crownless king of later time,
 Who walked the humble way,
Coming, as comes the day;

He that, for kings and princes all,
Would once more read the mystic wall,—

Spell out, there, what was meant
Whereso the Finger went;

He that, over the anvil lowered,
Would beat the ploughshare from the sword,
Lest peace from man depart—
Yea, hope out of his heart;—

Earth held to him. The rough-hewn form,
Looming through that unnatural storm,
Hinted the rude, mixed mould
Era chaos loosed her hold;

A lone, wind-beaten hill-top tree,
His that pathetic majesty;
Forlorn even in his mirth,
His roots deep in the earth.

Earth's is he yet. When from the hill
The warm gold flows, and hollows fill,
The sunlight shines his fame,
The winds blaze Lincoln's name.

Aye, Earth's he is; not hers alone,
Blood of our blood, bone of our bone,
Love folded him to rest
Upon a people's breast.

—*John Vance Cheney.*

THE MAN LINCOLN

NOT as the great who grow more great
    Until they are from us apart—
He walks with us in man's estate;
    We know his was a brother heart.

The marvelling years may render dim
  The humanness of other men,
To-day we are akin to him
  As they who knew him best were then.

Wars have been won by mail-clad hands,
  Realms have been ruled by sword-hedged kings,
But he above these others stands
  As one who loved the common things;
The common faith of man was his,
  The common faith in man he had—
For this to-day his grave face is
  A face half joyous and half sad.

A man of earth! Of earthy stuff,
  As honest as the faithful soil,
Gnarled as the friendly tree, and rough
  As hillsides that have known his toil;
Of earthy stuff—let it be told,
  For earth-born men rise and reveal
A courage fair as beaten gold
  And the enduring strength of steel.

So now he dominates our thought,
  This humble great man holds us thus
Because of all he dreamed and wrought,
  Because he is akin to us.
He held his patient trust in truth
  While God was working out His plan,
And they that were his foes, forsooth,
  Come to pay tribute to the man.

Not as the great who grow more great
  Until they have a mystic fame—
No stroke of fortune nor of fate
  Gave Lincoln his undying name.

A common man, earth-bred, earth-born,
One of the breed who work and wait—.
His was a soul above all scorn,
His was a heart above all hate.
—*Wilbur Dick Nesbit.*

THE ULTIMATE NORTH

NOW doth the North her inmost secret yield;
Now is there nothing more beyond; we know
The Thulè Ultima. The final woe
Of the vast frozen zone, though triple-steeled
With cold and storm, lays off the decent shield
Granted it an eternity ago
Among great gales, and silence, ice, and snow,
As though pale Hela's horrors stalked afield.

No more the lure of the North's hidden things
Tempts man to pay the last and awful price;
For secret was there none. Long wanderings
Have proved again what trifles may entice
Mankind; if but denied, the spirit springs
Even at a fleck of palæocrystic ice.

Yet has the frosty deed full excellence.
It is no barren thing to set a goal
High and afar, and strive with iron soul,
Throwing aside despair as vain pretence,
Facing the terrors of the elements,
Discarding failure, till, beside the Pole
One's name is set, as on the eternal scroll
Of those who win from Fate's own dissidence.

Praise to the victor! Yet let laurels rest
As well upon the still undaunted brows

Of those who sought and won not from the rime
The final triumph; they are not unblest,
  Though to a single mortal Fate allows
  This binding of Valhall and Nifleheim.
                                    —*Wallace Rice.*

FOUR CENTURIES: HUDSON AND FULTON

MDCIX

INTO March weather amid the gales,
  In Sixteen Hundred and Nine,
Bold Henry Hudson spreads his sails,
  Defying the storms of the line,
As forth for the golden land he goes
Into the sunset's purple and rose;
And what cares he for the wind that blows,
  Or the billows that stir the brine?

Comes September, and along the shore
  Where the broad Atlantic swells
The splendour of autumn brightens o'er
  The woods with its sunset spells;
And up the mighty river he rides
As his ship to the ultimate East he guides,
And gayly he sings, as the *Half-Moon* glides,
  For the hope that in him wells;

Up the river, and past the strand
  That rives the stream in twain,
Steadily, smoothly, on through the land,
  Till he turns to the sea again;
And little he thinks that the stony isle
That he sees and passes with half a smile
Shall ever be worth a sailor's while
  Who is seeking the sunset main.

A hundred years! and the river's mouth
   And the shore that Hudson knew,
From the rocks of Maine far to the south
   Are filled with a doughty crew,
Who have driven the savage with sword and flame
Back to the forests from which he came;
And the ancient East is an empty name
   To those whose world is New.

Good Queen Anne, she cares not much
   As she sits on the English throne
For the land that Hudson gave to the Dutch—
   Though it is England's now, alone;
And its folk are fighting, tooth and nail,
Cannon and musket, ship and sail,
To conquer the French on shore and trail,
   And leave their hope a-groan.

And where there were grim old forest trees
   With a wigwam's smoke between,
Are houses and pleasant boweries,
   With spire and fort and green:
Ladies go gayly in silken stuff,
And gentlemen haughty in wig and ruff,
For those were cheerful days enough,
     When good Queen Anne was queen.

A hundred years! and the placid stream
   Where Hudson's broad bows slip
Has heard the puffing of snowy steam
   And the blast from an iron lip:
Where once the Indian turned to view
The white man pass in his great canoe,

382

The white man stares, for the engines' hue
    And the wheels of the sailless ship.

There, from the isle that the old *Half-Moon*
    Sailed by that September morn,
Steams the wonderful *Clermont,* Fulton's boon,
    On the self-same waters borne.
No more at the mercy of wind and tide
Shall the ships of man in terror ride;
They laugh at the gale with a new-born pride,
    And whistle the winds to scorn.

Only less marvellous rises the town
    On the isle that Hudson saw;
The British flag has come tattered down
    In the clutch of the eagle's claw:
How it laughs at princes and at kings,
At potentates and their maunderings,
And boasts of other, better things
    In Liberty and Law.

MCMIX

A hundred years! and its haughty crest
    The proud old city rears,
For a Nation bends at its high behest
    That knows no doubts or fears.
Here is built on its island home
Mart and palace and temple dome,
And fleets and navies hither roam
    Where once the *Half-Moon* steers.

Now the *Clermont,* once so marvellous,
    Is a pygmy, shrunk and thin,
While a myriad children glorious
    Acknowledge themselves akin;
And a thousand myriad souls there are

383

Who have come from near and come from far
To dwell under Freedom's guiding star,
  A better fate to win.

The gold that Hudson sought is here,
  Surpassing the envied East,
But it is not drawn from a vassal's fear
  For a monarch's thoughtless feast:
The steam that Fulton chained is slave,
All powerful to raise and save
Where Liberty's sunlit banners wave
  O'er the greatest and the least.

—Oliver Marble.

OUR TWENTY-SIX PRESIDENTS IN RHYME

FIRST is a name the world reveres,
  He led through years of hopes and fears,—
Our Washington, of wondrous fame.

Then Adams came, of humbler name.
He first Vice-President had been,
And 'mid war's din had helped to win
In kings' courts place for nations new.
His heart was true, when friends were few.

Four years he steered the ship of state
Through danger great, for France so late
Our country's friend had foe become.
" The warships come ! " men said, while some
As sentinels upon the land
From him so grand await command,—
From Washington, the army's chief.
Whose service brief (as seemed to grief)
Had end amid this vexing strife,—
Had end with life while tears of wife

And nation followed to his rest
The one called best.   He stood life's test.
Mark this of Adams: First was he
To dwell where we by wise decree
Built our new nation's capital,—
That pride of all; may it never fall!

Two terms you know, had Washington.
Adams but one; his service done
Plain Thomas Jefferson held sway,
This we may say he had his way,
In adding to our nation great,
A realm where state is piled on state:—
What was to France, land of romance,
He bought, thus showed prophetic glance.

Eight years had passed; and war-cloud dark,
With lightning's spark for all to mark,
Hung over our Atlantic seas.
The realm to please, her fears to ease,
James Madison his duty found.
Soon came war's sound and deadly wound.

Monroe next ruled; our land was blest.
Great grew the West; as honored guest
Came Lafayette the land to see
He helped to free,—for you and me!

Another Adams next held sway,
Then one grown gray in war's fierce way:
The sturdy Jackson whose command
Smote treason's hand in erring land.

Van Buren next was nation's guide,
Then one who died while yet untried

In his great office, Harrison.
Soon set his sun, his duty done.

Then Tyler served; next, James K. Polk,
When war awoke with deadly stroke.

Next dying in his well-won fame,
Brave Taylor came, of honoured name.

Then Fillmore served: next Franklin Pierce.
Alas for Pierce! When strife was fierce
He ruled; and then Buchanan came.
Next, greatest name and purest fame
Since Washington our Lincoln earned.
Right he had learned and wrong he spurned.
By fearful deed,—the nation's woe,—
Crime laid him low. Next, Johnson know.

Then came the unboasting soldier Grant,
So free from cant and silly rant.

Next Hayes the exalted office filled.
Then voters willed (who soon were thrilled
Once more with tale of crime's wild thrust)
To give the trust to Garfield just.

Then Arthur President became.
This roll of fame next bears the name
Of Cleveland. Then in filial pride
Called to preside as nation's guide
We find a younger Harrison.

Twice Cleveland won; his service done
McKinley took the helm of state
When, dark and great, war's cloud and fate
Broke peace with Spain. With grief deep-felt
McKinley passed. Then Roosevelt

Was long our chief and steered our craft
Full well, till William Howard Taft
Took up the helm. And now 't is time
To end our rhyme.

—*John Nelson Davidson.*

THE LONG FIGHT

DREAMS! but no dream is this, I know.
  One cause through all the centuries! Lo!
The chariot wheels go dripping blood as when
    The chain-bound captives made them slow,
    And gleaming spears, ranged row on row,
Flashed the imperial blight on souls of men.
    Naught changes but the face and form.
Not often now, with sword to sharp sword set
And face to face opposed as sun to storm,
Man and his carnificial foe are met
In tense-drawn joy of open conflict. Yet
Not since the first dead tyrant lay along
The battle stays between the weak and strong,
            Between the Truth and Wrong.

Because one thing has weaker grown,
    Because the shadow of the throne
Dwells now less darkly in the wide world's breast,
    Because less plain his might is known,
    Or that his sceptre is not shown,
Think ye old Force is numb and laid to rest?
    Listen! For this have heroes striven?
This clank of unseen chain, as to his wheel
The fettered slave goes daily, lashed and driven,
This sound of hammered hearts like bits of steel,
This silent sentence wherefrom toilers feel

The long slow shadow creeping like a blight,
Suppress, as some great starless darkness might,
The sovereign soul of light?

One cause! For this in dimmer years
One man put by all doubts and fears,
Drew sword and smote till in the southern sun,
Washed and made bright with many tears,
Proud and flung far amid its peers,
His flag flamed on a land made free and one.
So rose Italia! But the strife
That from her heart drove forth the vulture's beak
Knew never pause with her returning life!
Men in these years of darkness turn to seek
A newer Garibaldi for the weak,
Whose sword ringed round with light that has not waned
Leaves not the perfect Freedom still ungained,
The goal half way attained.

For this the blood of saints was shed,
The long roll of the deathless dead
For this has light and lustre like the sea.
From altar fires of old years fled
The future's portals glimmer red
With promise of the Freedom yet to be,
For by the first bright glorious stain
Of Persian blood on Grecian sword, and by
The breast that gathered spears as golden grain,
The earliest light of morn in Concord's sky,
And those brave souls that by Colenso lie,
By all the deeds and daring of the past,
Reversed, pressed on, she goes, or slow or fast,
To triumph at the last.

She knows all dark of bitter days,
She knows all thorns of stony ways;

Of old her lighted fires, before her eyes,
    Lost one by one their sanguine rays,
    And from the temples to her praise
She saw the citadels of Force arise.
    Defeat! She hath drunk deep thereof
And known each smart of it and all the pain,
And wept for other sons that for her love
The voiceless darkness dared like these in vain.
But steadfast through all chance of loss and gain,
From wasted blood heroic and old tears,
Democracy, this arch of coming years,
                This perfect span, she rears.
                    —*Charles Edward Russell.*

AD PATRIAM

To deities of gauds and gold,
        Land of our Fathers, do not bow!
But unto those beloved of old
        Bend thou the brow!

Austere they were of front and form;
        Rigid as iron in their aim;
Yet in them pulsed a blood as warm
        And pure as flame;—

Honour, whose foster-child is Truth;
        Unselfishness, in place and plan;
Justice, with melting heart of ruth;
        And Faith in man.

Give these our worship; then no fears
        Of future foes need fright thy soul;
Triumphant thou shalt mount the years
        Toward thy high goal!
                    —*Clinton Scollard.*

FROM "THE COLUMBIAN ODE"

COLUMBIA! Men beheld thee rise
　　A goddess from the misty sea.
Lady of joy, sent from the skies,
　　The nations worshipped thee.
Thy brows were flushed with dawn's first light
By foamy waves with stars bedight
　　Thy blue robe floated free.

Now let the sun ride high o'erhead,
　　Driving the day from shore to shore.
His burning tread we do not dread,
　　For thou art evermore
Lady of love whose smile shall bless,
Whose brave deeds win to tenderness,
　　Whose tears the lost restore.

Lady of hope thou art. We wait
　　With courage thy serene command.
Through unknown seas, toward undreamed fate,
　　We ask thy guiding hand.
On! though sails quiver in the gale!—
Thou at the helm, we cannot fail.
　　On to God's time-veiled strand!

Lady of beauty! thou shalt win
　　Glory and power and length of days.
The sun and moon shall be thy kin,
　　The stars shall sing thy praise.
All hail! we bring thee vows most sweet
To strew before thy wingéd feet.
　　Now onward be thy ways!

—Harriet Monroe.

NOTES

Page 3. On July 4, 1826, the fiftieth anniversary of the signing of the Declaration of Independence, John Adams, who had been a member of the committee that drafted it, died at Quincy, Massachusetts, and Thomas Jefferson, who wrote it, died at Monticello, his country seat in Virginia. Five years later, July 4, 1831, as if to accentuate the importance of the day, James Monroe died in New York City. History has few coincidences so remarkable.

Page 5. On September 16, 1830, Doctor Holmes wrote these stirring verses upon the announcement by the Navy Department that the *Constitution* was to be dismantled and sold. As a result the gallant old ship was retained in the service, and still survives.

Page 6. Marie Jean Paul Roch Yves Gilbert Motier, Marquis de Lafayette, died at Paris on May 20, 1834. His services to the cause of the American Revolution will never be forgotten. The sonnet is the work of the gifted wife of President James Madison.

Page 6. Benjamin R. Milam, one of the picturesque and heroic figures in the Texan War of Independence, led the charge against the beleagured town of Bejar on December 1, 1835, forcing the surrender of General Cos and 1500 Mexicans, a force outnumbering that of the besiegers. Milam perished in his bravery during the attack.

Page 7. Colonel William Travis and 183 Texans perished to a man in defence of the Alamo, the fortress commanding the town of San Antonio, Texas, on March 6, 1836, after a siege of eleven days conducted by General Santa Ana with 2000 Mexicans.

Page 13. This famous hymn was written for the dedication of the battle monument at Concord, Massachusetts, on July 4, 1837.

Page 10. General Sam Houston and 783 Texans utterly

overthrew Santa Ana and 2000 Mexicans at San Jacinto, Texas, on April 21, 1836, and exacted a just vengeance for the slaughter of Colonel Fannin and his 400 men at Goliad on March 27, who had surrendered on the assurance that their lives should be spared.

Page 12. The freedom and independence of Texas was acknowledged as a result of the battle of San Jacinto, and the treaty to that effect formally ratified on May 14, 1836.

Page 13. General William Henry Harrison died at Washington on April 4, 1841, just one month after his inauguration as the ninth President of the United States. The victor at the battles of the Tippecanoe and the Thames, he was the son of Benjamin Harrison, signer of the Declaration of Independence and revolutionary governor of Virginia, and grandfather of Benjamin Harrison, twenty-third President of the United States.

Page 15. This was written in 1844 for a meeting in Faneuil Hall, Boston, to protest against the annexation of Texas and the aggressions and evils of chattel slavery.

Page 16. Texas having been admitted to the Union on December 29, 1845, Mexico regarded it as an act of war and sent an army which attacked Fort Brown, built by General Zachary Taylor opposite Matamoras in pursuance of his instructions to occupy Texas. May 8, 1846, Taylor and 2100 men moving to the relief of the fort confronted a Mexican force of 6000 men at Palo Alto and forced them to retreat after an artillery duel, following it by the battle of Resaca de la Palma the next day, in which Arista, the Mexican commander, was badly defeated.

Page 18. On September 24, 1846, after three days' fighting, General Taylor stormed and took the city of Monterey, Mexico, with his 6500 Americans, defeating 10,000 Mexicans under Ampudia.

Page 19. Santa Ana with 15,000 men demanded that Taylor and his 5000 Americans surrender. This was on February 22, 1847. Taylor having refused with some harshness, Santa Ana promptly attacked, fighting through that and the next day. He was beaten, with a loss of 2000 men, the American loss being 746.

Page 24. Colonel Alexander Doniphan, commanding the First Missouri Volunteers, after a few weeks' drill, left Fort Leavenworth, Kansas, on June 26, 1846, marching to Santa Fe, New Mexico, in the Army of the West under General Stephen Kearny. They entered the city on August 6, the Mexicans fleeing at their approach, and New Mexico became a part of the United States. Kearny left to conquer California on September 25, after ordering Doniphan to report to General Wool at Chihuahua. Doniphan brought the Navajo Indians under control, leaving Santa Fe on October 26, and began his march for the invasion of Mexico, on December 19, after concentrating his small force at Valverde, crossing the Jornado del Muerto, or Journey of Death, to confront General Ponce de Leon and 1300 men at Brazito on Christmas Day. De Leon was defeated with a loss of seventy killed and 150 wounded after half an hour's fighting, the Americans having eight men wounded and none killed. Proceeding, on February 28, 1847, he found himself opposed at the pass of Sacramento, eighteen miles from Chihuahua, by Major-General José Heredia and 4200 men behind a line of field-works made up of twenty-eight strong redoubts and entrenchments. Doniphan had 1164 men, all Misssouri volunteers. The ensuing battle lasted three hours and a half, the Mexican army being wholly overthrown and disorganised, so that it never appeared thereafter, with a loss of 300 killed and 500 wounded, the American loss being one killed and eleven wounded. Chihuahua was occupied the next day. The approach of Doniphan prevented Heredia's marching to reinforce Santa Ana at Buena Vista.

Page 27. General Winfield Scott landed at Vera Cruz, Mexico, on March 9, 1847, with 12,000 regulars. He beat off Santa Ana at Cerro Gordo on April 18, and arrived before the City of Mexico on August 20. Molino del Rey, the King's Mill, was carried by storm on September 8, General Worth leading 4000 Americans against an equal number of Mexicans behind strong fortifications. The loss on both sides was heavy.

Page 29. Chapultepec still stood between the Americans and the capital. This was carried on September 13, 1847, by two storming parties after a severe hand-to-hand conflict. The day following, Scott marched into the City of Mexico at the head of his victorious army.

Page 30. Meanwhile General Kearny had brought all California under the American flag, and Mexico was anxious for peace. The treaty of Guadalupe-Hidalgo was signed February 2, 1848, by which New Mexico, comprising Arizona, and California were ceded to the United States, which paid $15,000,000 therefor, assuming in addition $3,000,000 of Mexican debts.

Page 33. Though the volunteer forces played a conspicuous and gallant part in the defeat of the Mexicans, the war is unique in our history in having been under the control of the regulars.

Page 38. This beautiful elegy was written for the dedication of the monument at Louisville erected to commemorate the Kentucky volunteers who fell at the battle of Buena Vista.

Page 41. Gold was discovered in El Dorado county, California, on January 24, 1848, and this and the following year saw an enormous influx of treasure-seekers.

Page 43. General Zachary Taylor, twelfth President of the United States, died at Washington on July 9, 1850, having taken his seat as chief magistrate on March 4, 1849.

Page 45. California was admitted to the Union as a State on September 9, 1850.

Page 46. The Yosemite Valley, in Mariposa Valley, California, was discovered on February 20, 1851.

Page 47. Colonel William L. Crittenden of Kentucky and fifty others were killed at Havana on August 16, 1851, having been captured by the Spanish while taking part in a filibustering expedition led by Narciso Lopez from New Orleans earlier in the month.

Page 49. Daniel Webster died at Marshfield, Massachusetts, on October 24, 1852.

Page 49. On May 30, 1854, Congress passed the Kansas-Nebraska bill, leaving the question of slavery within that territory to be decided by its inhabitants; and the struggle for the slavery and abolition causes began forthwith.

Page 50. This "incident of Strain's Expedition" commemorates the sufferings of the party headed by Lieutenant Isaac G. Strain in 1854 during a survey of the Isthmus of Darien, the company exhibiting the greatest heroism.

Page 52. General John Charles Frémont was the first candidate of the newly formed Republican party for the Presidency in 1856, and his progress to his political goal is likened to the hardships he endured as a pathfinder in the western wilderness.

Page 53. The contest between the slavery and abolition forces in Kansas reached such a height that on September 14, 1856, 2500 Missourians attacked the free-soilers in Lawrence and were beaten off.

Page 53. This notable Arctic explorer, who commanded the second Grinnell expedition in search of Sir John Franklin's party in 1853-55, having been a member of the previous one of 1850-51, died at Havana on February 16, 1857.

Page 57. This ode was written to advance the cause of the abolition of slavery, and was sung for the first time at a breakfast in the town hall at Concord, Massachusetts, on July 4, 1857.

Page 58. This stirring international episode was brought about through an unwarranted attack made upon British forces on their way to Pekin on June 25, 1859, for the ratification of a treaty which specified the day following. Tattnall had no authority except his own for his interference, but without it the British force of 1100 men would have been captured or slain; eighty-nine were killed and 345 wounded, as it was.

Page 61. John Brown, lately of Ossawatomie, Kansas, where he had been a leader among the free-soil guerillas, surprised and took the United States arsenal at Harper's Ferry, Virginia, on the night of October 16, 1859, intending a demonstration against the slave power which would lead the slaves to open revolt.

Page 67. Brown was taken, with his small force, by federal troops the day following his capture, sentenced to be hanged, and executed, with his men, on December 2, 1859.

Page 68. On December 20, 1860, following the election of Abraham Lincoln to be President of the United States, South Carolina passed an ordinance of secession.

Page 70. Written for the encouragement of the anti-slavery forces after the Republican victory in the presidential campaign of 1860.

Pages 71-73. Kansas was admitted to the Union on January 29, 1861, as a free State.

Page 75. Fort Sumter in the harbour of Charleston, South Carolina, after refusing to surrender to the secession forces, was bombarded on April 12-13, 1861, the first engagement of the Civil War.

Page 76. The bombardment of Fort Sumter and the consequent firing on the flag caused a tremendous excitement through the North.

Pages 77-79. The war spirit of the South is reflected in these stanzas.

Pages 80-82. The North took up arms immediately, and the long conflict began.

Page 84. This, perhaps the most notable production of the Civil War in song, was written after a visit to the encamped forces around Washington in 1861.

Page 85. Virginia was long in deciding whether to cast

in her lot with the Confederacy, and the passing of the ordinance of secession by the State on April 17, 1861, was hailed with joy throughout the South.

Page 86. The Sixth Massachusetts was attacked by a mob in the streets of Baltimore while on its way to the defence of Washington, on April 19, 1861. Several were killed on both sides, and many wounded.

Page 87. This was written in April, 1861, when there was still hope that Maryland would join the Confederacy. The prompt occupation of Baltimore and Annapolis by federal troops prevented.

Page 90. This, though by no means the best, was the most popular of the war songs of the South.

Page 91. In April, 1861, the United States Sanitary Commission was founded in Washington for the relief of the suffering soldiers.

Pages 92-94. This was written originally as a comic song for negro minstrels, but its vigorous tune and the inspiring words provided by Albert Pike elevated it to the dignity of a war song which has been particularly dear to the South for many years.

Page 95. Colonel Ephraim Elmer Ellsworth, commanding the Eleventh New York, was shot and killed at Alexandria, Virginia, on May 24, 1861, by the proprietor of an hotel from which he had just lowered a confederate flag.

Page 96. Stephen Arnold Douglas died in Chicago on June 3, 1861. Defeated by Lincoln in the presidential contest of 1860, he held Lincoln's hat while he was being inaugurated, waited upon him with assurances of support for the Union, and generously expended what of life and strength remained in rallying his great following to the union cause.

Page 98. The first battle of Manassas was fought at Bull Run, twenty-five miles southwest of Washington, on July 21, 1861. The Federals were defeated and put to rout with heavy loss.

Page 99. On August 31, 1861, without authorisation by

law or by his superior officers, General Frémont, commanding in Saint Louis, issued a proclamation declaring his intention to emancipate the slaves of those in insurrection against the authority of the United States. The proclamation was withdrawn.

Page 100. The battle of Ball's Bluff, fought thirty-three miles northwest of Washington on October 21, 1861, resulted in a victory for the Confederates.

Page 100. An incident of the blockade of the North Carolina coast in 1861.

Page 101. The phrase, "All quiet along the Potomac," had become a reproach because of the eagerness of the people to see the great army organised by McClellan advance upon the enemy.

Page 103. General Felix Kirk Zollicoffer, a confederate congressman and commander, was killed at the battle of Mill Springs, Kentucky, on January 19, 1862.

Page 104. The federal gunboat *Essex* led the attack on Fort Henry, Kentucky, on February 2, 1862, and was severely punished. Brittan, though a lieutenant, was only seventeen.

Page 107. The confederate ironclad *Virginia,* formerly the *Merrimac,* attacked the federal squadron lying at Newport News on March 8, 1862, and practically destroyed it. The *Cumberland* was rammed and sunk.

Page 108. On March 9, 1862, when the *Virginia* came forth to renew her work of destruction, she found the "Yankee cheese-box on a raft," Captain John Ericsson's *Monitor,* which drove her back to her station after an epoch-marking duel.

Page 111. Burnside assaulted Newberne, North Carolina, on the Neuse River, on March 14, 1862, and carried it with heavy loss on both sides. But for Kady Brownell's resourcefulness, the loss would have been greater.

Page 112. Albert Sidney Johnston, one of the greatest of the confederate commanders, was killed at the battle of Shiloh, Hardin county, Tennessee, on April 6, 1862.

Page 116. Pierre Gustave Toutant Beauregard succeeded to the command of the confederate army on April 6, 1862, upon the death of Johnston.

Page 117. Slavery was abolished in the District of Columbia, and the slave owners compensated by act of Congress approved by President Lincoln on April 16, 1862.

Page 120. David Glasgow Farragut, the admiral commanding, attacked the strong fortifications of the Confederates below New Orleans, silenced them after a bombardment of five days, and on April 18, 1862, passed the forts and forced the surrender of the armed vessels in front of the city.

Page 130. General Benjamin F. Butler occupied New Orleans. His soldiers being subjected to repeated insults by the confederate women of the city, he ordered that they be treated as if common women of the town if the offence was repeated. The order brought opprobrium upon him, but it stopped the offences.

Page 131. General Philip Kearny rallied the federal troops when retreating from a confederate attack in force on May 31, 1862, at the battle of Seven Pines or Fair Oaks, near Richmond, Virginia, and did much toward winning the victory for McClellan.

Page 133. General Turner Ashby, one of the most brilliant of the confederate generals of cavalry, was killed in a skirmish just before the battle of Cross Keys, Virginia, on June 6, 1862.

Page 134. At Malvern Hill, Virginia, the federal forces under McClellan defeated Lee on July 1, 1862, in the last of the Seven Days' Battles.

Page 135. President Lincoln issued a call for 300,000 more soldiers on July 2, 1862, after McClellan's failure to take Richmond. This song, immensely popular on the federal side, was written by a banker and author of New York City.

Page 136. The federal forces under Pope were beaten by

Jackson and Longstreet at the second battle of Manassas, Virginia, on August 30, 1862.

Page 137. General Philip Kearny was killed while on a reconnoissance near Chantilly, Virginia, on September 1, 1862, in the fighting following the second battle of Manassas.

Page 138. Admitting that this famous incident has not been correctly reported in some of its details, the poet Whittier states that it is in strict conformity to information obtained from trustworthy sources. Friends of Jackson indignantly deny that he ordered his men to fire on a woman in such circumstances. The march through Fredericksburg, Virginia, took place on September 6, 1862.

Page 141. The battle of Antietam, or Sharpsburg, Virginia, was fought between McClellan and Lee on September 17, 1862. Lee retreated across the Potomac the next day, but the battle was indecisive.

Page 143. Rosecrans defeated Van Dorn and Price at Corinth, Mississippi, on October 3-4, 1862, with heavy losses.

Page 147. Burnside was badly beaten by Lee at Fredericksburg, Virginia, on December 13, 1862, suffering a loss of 15,000 men and being relieved of command soon after.

Page 150. This episode was a part of the battle of Murfreesboro, Tennessee, where Rosecrans and Bragg fought desperately for four days, December 29-31, 1862. The hero of the incident was nursed back to life by the author, a physician.

Pages 152-155. The preliminary proclamation of emancipation was issued by President Lincoln on September 22, 1862, promising freedom to the slaves of all those who were in rebellion against the United States on the first day of the ensuing year. Accordingly, Lincoln's final proclamation freeing the slaves was issued on January 1, 1863.

Page 158. General John S. Mosby made a daring cavalry attack upon the union lines on March 16, 1863, after Hooker, who succeeded Burnside, had gone into winter quarters.

Page 159. Not a large but a fiercely fought battle took

place at Kelly's Ford, Virginia, on March 17, 1863, between General W. W. Averill, who attacked, and General Fitzhugh Lee, who repulsed him with heavy loss. Unfortunately for the Confederacy, General John Pelham was among the slain.

Page 161. Admiral Dupont was wholly unsuccessful in his attempt to take Fort Sumter on April 7, 1863, retiring with one ship sunk and others seriously injured.

Page 163. On the night of April 16, 1863, Admiral Porter successfully ran the batteries before Vicksburg, Mississippi, preparing the way for Grant's siege of the place. The poet was an eye-witness of the event.

Page 166. General Joseph Hooker, moving to attack Lee near Fredericksburg, carried his army across the Rappahannock successfully, completing the movement on April 30, 1863.

Page 167. The battle of Chancellorsville, a confederate victory, began with a serious repulse on the afternoon of May 2, 1863, when the Eighth Pennsylvania Cavalry under Major Keenan charged Stonewall Jackson's men and held them in check until the artillery could open. The regiment was almost annihilated.

Page 170. Jackson had almost destroyed the right wing of Hooker's army when held back by Keenan's charge. His movements contrast favourably with those of any commander in history, both for celerity and understanding.

Page 171. Most unfortunately for the South, Jackson going to the front to see why his men were being held back just after Keenan went into the battle, was mistaken for a federal officer by his own men on his return, and shot. He died on May 10, 1863.

Page 172. The North began recruiting coloured regiments, two of which, the First and Second Louisiana, distinguished themselves in General Banks's assault on Port Hudson, Louisiana, May 27, 1863. The fortress did not fall into federal hands until its surrender on July 8.

Page 174. The first intimation Hooker had of the series of

movements which led to the battle of Gettysburg came on June 17, 1863, when the appearance of confederate cavalry at Ashby's Gap, Virginia, was the signal for a gallant and successful charge by General Hugh Judson Kilpatrick.

Page 176. Though the name of the heroine of this pleasant and chivalrous episode is not known, the story is vouched for by Colonel William R. Aylett. Greencastle is in Franklin county, Pennsylvania, not far from the Maryland line. The date is June 25, 1863.

Pages 178-179. The battle of Gettysburg, Pennsylvania, was fought on July 1-3, 1863. It was the most decisive engagement of the Civil War. Meade having defeated Lee and forced his retreat to Virginia, the Confederacy never again was able to take the offensive. The total federal loss, killed, wounded, and missing, was 23,186, the confederate 31,621. Between 70,000 and 80,000 men were engaged on each side.

Pages 182-183. Incidents of the siege of Vicksburg, Mississippi, which lasted from its investment by Grant on May 18, 1863, until Pemberton, starved out, surrendered it on July 3, the federal troops marching in the next day.

Page 185. An outbreak against the conscription for the Union armies broke out in New York City on July 13, 1863, marked by several hundred deaths and the destruction of much property. It was finally suppressed by local and federal authorities on July 16.

Page 186. Fort Wagner, South Carolina, was stormed without success by the federal soldiers, among them the Fifty-Fourth Massachusetts, the first regiment of coloured men to be recruited from a free State.

Page 187. These touching lines were written in memory of Colonel Robert Gould Shaw, commander of the Fifty-Fourth Massachusetts, who died at the head of his men in the assault on Fort Wagner, on July 18, 1863.

Page 190. Lincoln's address at the dedication of the

national cemetery at Gettysburg on November 19, 1863, has become and will remain one of the great documents in American history, as well as a classic. The poem is an extract from " The Gettysburg Ode."

Page 191. On November 24, 1863, General Hooker was ordered by Grant to take the confederate intrenchments at the foot of Lookout Mountain, Tennessee. The enthusiasm of the union men was such that they did not stop, but drove the enemy up the steep slope of the mountain and occupied it.

Page 194. The next day, November 25, 1863, Grant viewed the operations from the top of Orchard Knob, and saw Bragg driven by Thomas, Sherman, and Sheridan. The federal victory led directly to Grant's appointment to the head of the armies three months later.

Page 196. Ulric Dahlgren, son of the admiral, fell while attempting the release of the union prisoners at Richmond and Belle Isle on the night of March 2, 1864. He was still a cripple from a wound when killed.

Page 198. This battle was fought in the wilderness of Virginia, south of the Rapidan River on May 5-6, 1864, between Grant and Lee. The union loss was the heavier. Grant had about 100,000 soldiers to Lee's 65,000.

Page 200. General James Ewell Brown Stuart, a confederate officer of the highest distinction, was mortally wounded at the battle of Yellow Tavern, near Richmond, on May 12, 1864.

Page 203. General Leonidas Polk, a bishop of the Protestant Episcopal Church before entering the confederate service, was killed at the battle of Pine Mountain, Georgia, on June 14, 1864.

Page 204. The *Kearsarge* met and sunk the confederate cruiser *Alabama* off the harbour of Cherbourg, France, on Sunday, June 19, 1864, putting an end to most serious depredations upon the commerce of the North.

Pages 205-207. General James Birdseye McPherson was

killed on July 22, 1864, in the desperate fighting around Atlanta, Georgia, before Sherman reduced the city. Logan's famous charge has been commemorated in an equestrian statue in Grant Park, Chicago.

Pages 208-225. Admiral Farragut came in front of Mobile early in August, 1864, and on the 5th attacked the forts in Mobile Bay after disabling the confederate ram *Tennessee*. Brownell, the poet, was with Farragut on the flag-ship *Hartford* throughout the engagement.

Page 227. The battle of Cedar Creek, in the Shenandoah Valley, Virginia, after Early had surprised the Federals under Wright and driven them into confusion from the field, was saved by the arrival of Sheridan, who was on his way from Washington to rejoin his command. It was fought on October 19, 1864.

Page 229. The confederate ram *Albemarle,* after menacing the federal blockading fleet along the Carolina coast for months, was destroyed on the night of October 27, 1864, by Lieutenant William B. Cushing, in Plymouth Harbour, North Carolina. Approaching the ship in a small boat with his thirteen men, he successfully exploded a torpedo under the ram and escaped by plunging in the water.

Pages 232-234. On November 16, 1864, having captured and destroyed Atlanta, Georgia, General William Tecumseh Sherman began his march to the sea, leaving a path of desolation through the State forty miles in width.

Page 236. On December 22 Sherman completed his march of 250 miles, and occupied Savannah, Georgia, which the Confederates had abandoned.

Page 238. The thirteenth amendment to the federal constitution by which chattel slavery was for ever abolished in the United States was submitted to the States for ratification on January 31, 1865. The two-thirds necessary were obtained on December 18, 1865, as officially announced.

Page 240. Halting at Savannah, Georgia, to recuperate

his men, Sherman took up his march on January 15, 1865, for the invasion of South Carolina. Charleston was occupied without resistance on February 18.

Pages 242-243. At Appomattox Court-House, Virginia, General Robert E. Lee surrendered the war-worn but still warlike remnant of the Army of Northern Virginia to General Grant on April 9, 1865. It practically ended the Civil War.

Pages 245-255. President Abraham Lincoln was assassinated on the night of April 18, 1865, in Washington by John Wilkes Booth, and died the next day. The grief felt by the nation was profound, and the passage of the funeral train across the country to Springfield, Illinois, where the body rests, marks the most heartbroken episode in our national history.

Page 256. General Joseph Eccleston Johnston surrendered to Sherman at Durham Station, North Carolina, on April 26, 1865, and General Edmund Kirby Smith on May 26. Peace ensued.

Page 259. The armies of Grant and Sherman, 200,000 strong, were reviewed by President Andrew Johnson at Washington on May 24, 1865.

Page 261. This ode, the most noteworthy of the literary productions called forth by the Civil War, was delivered at the 230th anniversary of the founding of Harvard College, at Cambridge, Massachusetts, on July 21, 1865.

Page 274. The first Atlantic cable, connecting Ireland and Newfoundland, was completed on July 29, 1866. Its construction was almost wholly due to the enterprise and persistence of Cyrus West Field.

Page 276. The rise to power of the newly emancipated negroes in the South, and the suffering inflicted upon the whites through northern men who misused the power obtained by the negro vote, led to the formation of secret societies to awe the coloured population. Of these, the so-called Ku-Klux-Klan was the most notable and effective, however outside the pale of the law.

Page 277. The rancour and hatred of civil strife was healed in no small part by the institution of the pious custom of Memorial Day, on which the graves of both confederate and federal soldiers were strewn with flowers. Early in 1867 the women of Columbus, Mississippi, paid this kindly tribute to the dead of both armies, and Mr. Coogler's lines were written of the day in Columbia, South Carolina.

Page 279. The aid extended to the stricken South during a yellow fever epidemic in 1867 by the North brought forth this tribute from Father Ryan.

Page 281. Alaska was purchased by the United States from Russia under a treaty finally ratified by the senate on June 20, 1867.

Page 281. The last spike completing the transcontinental railway from Omaha, Nebraska, to San Francisco, California, was driven on May 10, 1869.

Page 283. Jay Gould and his associates drove the price of gold up far beyond its real value in American currency on September 24, 1869. One of the severest panics in American history followed, causing the day to be named Black Friday.

Page 287. William Henry Seward retired from his position as secretary of state in 1869, and travelled extensively in the West. He reached San Francisco, California, on October 4, of that year, and was greeted with much enthusiasm.

Page 288. Charles Stewart, rear admiral on the retired list, died at Bordentown, New Jersey, on November 6, 1869, the last to survive of the heroes of the earlier navy. Stewart won distinction of no common kind in the naval war with France, in the war with Tripoli, and more particularly as commander of the *Constitution* on her last great cruise.

Page 291. On February 25, 1869, Congress submitted the fifteenth amendment to the federal constitution to the several States, which provided for manhood suffrage for all citizens of the United States, regardless of race, colour, or previous condition of servitude. The number of States necessary for its taking effect was secured on March 30, 1870.

Page 292. David Glasgow Farragut, the naval hero of the Civil War, died in Portsmouth, New Hampshire, on August 14, 1870. His statue, one of the most notable of Saint-Gaudens' works, stands in Madison Square, New York City.

Page 293. Written to commemorate the death of General Robert Edward Lee, the hero of the Confederacy, at Lexington, Virginia, on October 12, 1870.

Page 294. A great part of Chicago, Illinois, including its central business district with property valued at nearly $200,-000,000, was destroyed by fire on October 8-10, 1871. Many hundreds were killed, and 2100 acres denuded.

Page 295. The *Virginius,* an American vessel bound for Cuba in aid of the insurgents there, was captured on the high seas by a Spanish gunboat, taken to Santiago de Cuba, and her captain with fifty of his officers and crew, nearly all Americans, shot on November 4, 1873. The country was for immediate war, but an indemnity was accepted and the incident declared closed in spite of popular indignation.

Page 296. The entry of prospectors into the newly discovered gold region on the Sioux reservation in the Black Hills, in South Dakota and Wyoming, and the slaughter of bison drove many Indian tribes to the war-path in 1874, and the massacre of whites assumed large proportions.

Page 298. Cuba was granted a number of reforms and promised many more which were not granted upon the possibility of foreign intervention being shown to the Spanish government, the insurgents being treated with marked inhumanity throughout the long insurrection.

Page 298. General George Armstrong Custer with his entire command was killed on June 25, 1876, on the Little Big Horn River, Montana, by Sitting Bull, Rain-in-the-Face, and other Sioux chieftains.

Page 301. Sung at the World's Centennial Exposition at Philadelphia, on the celebration of the Nation's one hundredth birthday, July 4, 1876.

Page 302. Written and read at the celebration of the hundredth anniversary on October 19, 1881, of the surrender of Cornwallis to Washington and Lafayette at Yorktown, Virginia.

Page 304. James Abram Garfield, twentieth President of the United States, was shot and mortally wounded by Charles Guiteau, a disappointed office-seeker, at Washington on July 2, 1881. Garfield died at Elberon, New Jersey, on September 19, 1881. These lines were written upon the reception of the news of death, late at night.

Page 306, Ralph Waldo Emerson, the celebrated essayist and poet, died at Concord, Massachusetts, on April 27, 1882.

Page 307. The Brooklyn Bridge across the East River, connecting the boroughs of Manhattan and Brooklyn in New York City, was completed in 1884, the work of John Augustus Roebling, and his son, Washington Augustus Roebling.

Page 308. These fine lines were written upon the death of General Ulysses Simpson Grant on July 23, 1885, at Mount McGregor, New York.

Page 309. An episode of the Sioux uprising in 1886.

Page 311. Geronimo, the last notable war-chief of the Apaches, left his reservation for murder and rapine in 1886, and was captured by General Nelson A. Miles after a long chase.

Page 312. The Samoan Islands were struck by a hurricane on March 15, 1889, and three American war-ships wrecked. One of these, the flag-ship *Trenton,* had its crew stand by to cheer the British cruiser *Calliope,* which won its way to the open sea and was saved by its more powerful engines, just before the American vessel went down.

Page 314. Johnstown, Conemaugh, and several smaller settlements in western Pennsylvania were overwhelmed by a great body of water, the contents of a reservoir above them, on May 31, 1889,

Page 318. An episode of the opening of territory known as Oklahoma to white settlement in 1889, the Sioux being moved farther on. Sitting Bull was killed at this time, having offered resistance.

Page 319. Read on the four hundredth anniversary of the discovery of America by Columbus, October 22, 1892, at the formal dedication of the World's Columbian Exposition at Chicago.

Pages 321-323. These two poems represent admirably the feeling of the American people toward the veterans of the Civil War, on the Northern and Southern sides, respectively, being written a long generation after its close.

Page 325. Gold was discovered in 1897 in the Klondike region in the Northwestern Territory of British America, near the point where the Klondike River has its confluence with the Yukon. As in the case with California, a great army of explorers entered the country in that and succeeding years.

Page 328. The people of the United States had been following the cruelties of Spain toward the Cuban insurgents with growing horror. This was raised to indignation when the battleship *Maine* was destroyed by a submarine explosion while lying in the harbour of Havana on the night of February 15, 1898. Two officers and 264 men were killed. It made war with Spain almost certain, the popular belief being that it was done by Spanish officers.

Pages 329-332. Such patriotic poems as these did much toward bringing the American people to a sense of the duty they owed the oppressed patriots of Cuba.

Page 332. Congress passed a resolution on April 19, 1898, declaring that the people of Cuba were and of right ought to be free and independent. A formal declaration of war followed on April 22.

Pages 335-337. Dewey's victory was hailed with delight throughout the United States, and he became a popular hero forthwith.

Page 340. While Dewey was operating in the Orient, the Atlantic Squadron went in search of Spanish battleships and cruisers, while such incidents as this at Cienfuegos on May 11, 1898, were numerous about the island of Cuba.

Page 342. On June 3, 1898, Lieutenant Richmond Pearson Hobson entered the narrow entrance to the harbour of Santiago de Cuba with seven volunteers and there sunk the collier *Merrimac* with the expectation of keeping the Spanish warships in port. The idea originated with acting Rear Admiral Sampson.

Page 344. The First Volunteer United States Cavalry, better known as the " Rough Riders," was composed of western cowboys, eastern college athletes, and others, under the command of Colonel Leonard Wood and Lieutenant-Colonel Theodore Roosevelt.

Pages 344-347. On July 1, 1898, General Joseph Wheeler with dismounted cavalry charged the Spanish forces entrenched on the hills about Santiago, and a general advance of the American forces followed. The Spaniards were everywhere beaten back.

Pages 348-352. On Sunday, July 3, 1898, the American squadron blockading Santiago met the emerging ships of Spain and utterly destroyed them. Rear Admiral Winfield Scott Schley was the senior officer present, Admiral Sampson, who had gone to Siboney to confer with the army officers besieging the town, not arriving on the scene of action for more than an hour after the last Spanish ship had surrendered.

Page 354. The *Oregon,* first-class battleship, left Puget Sound, in the region Sir Francis Drake had named New Albion in 1578, on March 6, under command of Captain Charles E. Clark. Rounding Cape Horn, she joined the

American squadron before Santiago on May 25, 1898, and took a part in the fight of July 3, only less prominent than that of the *Brooklyn*.

Page 356. The *Brooklyn* was Rear Admiral Schley's flagship, and as such took the lead in the fighting on July 3, 1898, and in the pursuit of the Spanish ships of war.

Page 359. Spain seeing no hope in prosecuting the war after the destruction of her ships and the loss of the Philippines and Porto Rico, made overtures for peace. A protocol was signed on August 12, 1898, by which hostilities ceased, and the treaty of Paris was concluded on December 10, 1898.

Page 360. This noble poem was written on the first anniversary of the sinking of the *Maine,* and sums up in an admirable manner the effect of the war with Spain upon the feeling of the United States at that time.

Page 362. The Philippine Archipelago being purchased under the treaty of Paris for $20,000,000, and the members of the government of the Philippine Republic being denied participation in the negotiations leading to the treaty, a series of misunderstandings arose between the American officials and the Filipinos, leading at last to open war. This poem represents the point of view of those who believe, with Lincoln, that no man is fit to govern another without that other's consent.

Pages 364-366. These two ballads celebrate events in a battle near Santa Ana, on the island of Luzon, in which the Filipinos were put to rout.

Page 368. An outbreak in China in the summer of 1900 led to the shutting up in their legations of all the diplomatic representatives at Pekin. The nations of Europe combined with the United States in marching to their relief. In the fighting at Tien-Tsin, on the march to the capital, Colonel Liscum was mortally wounded.

Page 369. Benjamin Harrison, twenty-third President of the United States, died at Indianapolis, Indiana, on March 14, 1901

Page 369. The Pan-American Exposition was opened at Buffalo, New York, in May, 1901.

Page 370. On September 5, 1901, known as President's Day at the Buffalo Exposition, William McKinley, twenty-fourth President of the United States, was shot by an assassin whose motive remains unexplained. The President lived until September 14.

Page 371. This is the official hymn written for the Exposition held at Saint Louis, Missouri, to commemorate the one hundredth anniversary of the purchase of Louisiana from the first Napoleon by President Jefferson, and was sung on the opening day.

Page 373. The body of John Paul Jones was exhumed from the cemetery in Paris, France, by the efforts of Ambassador Fitz-John Porter, and brought to the United States on the *Brooklyn,* arriving at Annapolis, Maryland, on July 24, 1905. Final ceremonies were held at the United States Naval Academy there on April 24, 1906, the anniversary of the fight between the *Ranger* and the *Drake.*

Page 374. The city of San Francisco, California, was overwhelmed by an earthquake, followed by a fire even more destructive, on April 18, 1906.

Page 375. Work on the canal at Panama, to connect the Atlantic and Pacific Oceans, was begun during the autumn of 1906.

Page 376. Grover Cleveland, twenty-second President of the United States, died at Princeton, New Jersey, on June 24, 1908.

Pages 377-378. The one hundredth anniversary of the birth of Abraham Lincoln, on February 12, 1809, was celebrated elaborately throughout the United States, bringing into being many finely conceived poems, of which these two examples are given.

Page 380. Robert Edwin Peary, a civil engineer in the American navy, discovered the North Pole on April 6, 1910.

Page 381. A great naval review and civic and military

procession was held in New York City on September 25, 1910, and a week was given up to the celebration of the discovery of the Hudson River by Henry Hudson in September, 1609. The demonstration also included the celebration of the beginning of steam navigation with Robert Fulton's *Clermont,* which made its initial and successful voyage from New York to Albany on August 11, 1807, 102 years and a month before.

Pages 387-390. An extraordinary awakening of the spirit of righteousness in the American people, leading to many acts of the state and federal legislatures for the better securing of justice to all, has characterised recent years, forming a public opinion which has given new hope to every lover of his country.

INDEX OF FIRST LINES

415

416

INDEX OF TITLES

423

426

427

428

430

432

434

INDEX OF AUTHORS

436